Luminos is the Open Access monograph publishing program
from UC Press. Luminos provides a framework for preserving and
reinvigorating monograph publishing for the future and increases
the reach and visibility of important scholarly work. Titles published
in the UC Press Luminos model are published with the same high
standards for selection, peer review, production, and marketing as
those in our traditional program. www.luminosoa.org

The publisher and the University of California Press Foundation
gratefully acknowledge the generous support of the
Barbara S. Isgur Endowment Fund in Public Affairs.

Banished Men

Banished Men

How Migrants Endure the Violence of Deportation

———

Abigail Andrews

And the students of the Mexican Migration Field Research Program

UNIVERSITY OF CALIFORNIA PRESS

University of California Press
Oakland, California

Suggested citation: Andrews, A. *Banished Men: How Migrants Endure the Violence of Deportation*. Oakland: University of California Press, 2023. DOI: https://doi.org/10.1525/luminos.161

Cataloging-in-Publication Data is on file at the Library of Congress.

ISBN 978-0-520-39597-8 (pbk. : alk. paper)
ISBN 978-0-520-39598-5 (ebook)

Manufactured in the United States of America

32 31 30 29 28 27 26 25 24 23
10 9 8 7 6 5 4 3 2 1

For all the parents who've been torn from their children
and
For my students, who give me hope

CONTENTS

PREFACE

I began to work with deported men in Tijuana shortly after I moved to San Diego in 2014. I was already a scholar of gender, state violence, and immigration. But when I wrote my first book on Oaxacan villages and their migrants in Southern California, the research occurred "somewhere else." At the time, I was a graduate student at Berkeley. Following an old anthropological tradition, I flew in to "the field." At the end of the project, I left. For my second book, I wanted to work in the same place I lived and loved—the place I thought of as home.

I had just been hired as an assistant professor at the University of California-San Diego (UCSD). With the new job, I could no longer travel so simply. In 2016, I had my first child. By the time I started designing this research, I was pregnant again. I craved roots. So, I decided to work in Tijuana, a 25-minute drive from my door. Tijuana epitomized both the violence and vibrance of the relationship between Mexico and the United States. I met many migrants there who felt stranded, even as my own U.S. passport let me cross freely over the border. Still, I hoped that staying nearby would help me show up for the long term, instead of parachuting in and out of the field. I also believed that working locally would facilitate ties with advocacy organizations that could hold me accountable and help me act on my findings. In *Undocumented Politics*, I had written about the militarization of the U.S.-Mexico border and the hostility of this region toward migrants. Now, it was time to do something.

As a professor at UCSD, I also got to know extraordinary students from Mexican and Central American immigrant families. They could have been, quite literally, the children of migrants whose stories I told in my earlier book. Many of their parents had moved from Mexico to the U.S. in the 1990s, undocumented. Some of the students had crossed the border as children themselves. I wanted to collaborate with such students to understand what our country was doing to immigrant families—and then fight together to change it.

In 2017, I became director of UCSD's Mexican Migration Field Research Program (MMFRP), which let me bring teaching and research together. The MMFRP is a yearlong sequence of four courses that enrolls 30 undergraduate and 5 to 10 graduate students a year. Spanish-speaking students apply in the summer and spend the year learning about migration and doing original research. Founded by immigration scholar Wayne Cornelius, the MMFRP had been around for more than a decade when I came along. Each year, Dr. Cornelius took students to Mexican sending communities to do surveys. They produced a vast body of coauthored research on Mexico-U.S. migration.[1] Incidentally, I participated in the program as a graduate student from 2010 to 2011 and used some of the data we gathered in my first book.

I was thrilled to take over the program, but I also wanted to change it. First, I moved the work "home" to the San Diego-Tijuana border. The border is an acute site of violence and contestation around migration that I felt deserved our attention. Many of my students had grown up here and felt deeply tied to the region. By working near UCSD, we could also show up more consistently than in the past. Second, I began to collaborate with immigration advocates, as partners in the design, implementation, and dissemination of MMFRP research. My team and I worked closely with shelter staff in Tijuana to frame our questions, recruit participants, and evaluate our results.[2] While aid workers were too overwhelmed to play an extensive role, they taught us to move slowly and listen deeply to those on the ground.

Donald Trump's election set the stage for this work. When Trump took office, my students and I talked often about the deportations rending their families and home communities. I wanted our research to shed light on this violence. I also wanted MMFRP to position students from immigrant families as experts. I hoped we could build from their experience, empathy, and fluidity between two languages and cultures. I saw the students as bridges from the powerful (but white-dominated) world of U.S. scholarly research to the lives of their immigrant families.

Between 2018 and 2020, 31 students from the MMFRP interviewed deported men (and a few women) in Tijuana, contributing to the 186 interviews that make up this book. Their names are: Breanny Andrade, Samantha Canseco, Nanitzia Comparán Cuadras, Rubi de Lira, Jasmin Divas Villeda, Pamela Elguezabal, Yaneth Escobosa, Nathally Fernández, Jena Fierro-Hirales, Stephanie Flores, Marisa García Pérez, David Husson, Fátima Khayar Cámara, Ana López Ricoy, Cintia Martínez, Janet Miranda Hernández, Kayleigh Mitchell, Maomi Mojica, Maria Morales, Miriam Nuñez, Frieda Orbach, Zeltzin Pérez Reyes, Itzel Rodríguez, Adrian Rodríguez Valdez, Zianía Ruiz-Marina, Niccolo Sabia, Camila Sánchez, Paulina Santiago-Rodríguez, Karla Trujillo Rogel, Ivette Vargas, and Faviola Zamudio-Díaz. Each did roughly four interviews, earning course credit for their work. In summer 2019, I also hired four students from the Tijuana team to interview men in Oaxaca and Mexico City. Undergraduates Samantha Canseco and Camila Hernández Cruz[3] led the interviews in Oaxaca, where their parents were from, and PhD students Fátima Khayar Cámara and Ana López Ricoy did the same in Mexico City, the place both called home.

From early on, the students were my teachers. Colleagues sometimes ask how I can trust undergraduates to interview "real" respondents. To be sure, students had to learn to secure informed consent, draw out people's stories, and listen like scholars. Still, their passion and empathy made the research richer and deeper. I do not know how the process would have gone with students from other backgrounds. But there is a certain veneration that comes from hearing a migrant tell of their suffering, especially if that person's history closely aligns with one's own. In my experience, the more control I handed over to students, the more they asked questions and came to insights I had not noticed myself.

Working outside a traditional classroom was also inspiring. Most students in the MMFRP had attended underfunded high schools in Southern California. Few were accustomed to academia's "hidden curriculum," and several struggled with grades.[4] Yet, in migrant shelters, in courtyards filled with men just torn from their lives, these students shined. I watched them connect, laugh, and really *hear* the words from deported men's mouths. They built a range of relationships that I could not have created alone. They brought out stories that I, as a privileged, white PhD, might never have heard. In response, many participants shared generously of their lives.

The students did more than interviews. They also shifted the focus of the work, pushing me to *feel* before I could analyze the lives of deported men. For many students, talking with deportees triggered grief. Interviewees often remarked that students were just like their children. In turn, students frequently saw their fathers or brothers in men we met in Tijuana. Rubi de Lira, a student who joined the program in 2019, spent her childhood fearing that ICE would deport her dad. For her, it hurt too much to write about men like him. Instead, she wrote a report about what it felt like for students from mixed-status families to do research on immigration.

In one example, Rubi described volunteering to staff the phones at a soup kitchen in Tijuana.[5] During her shift, two deportees used the free phone to call family in the U.S. The first one spoke with his mother. The second tried three times to reach his daughter in California, failed, and left with tears streaming down his face. Rubi wrote:

I handed [the man] the phone saying he only had five minutes, and maybe two minutes in, he started crying and apologizing for not having called [his mother] sooner, but he had been in an accident and wasn't physically able to. Coming from a *machista* culture and seeing a grown man crying to his mother sent a chill down my spine and left me sort of paralyzed, unable to process what had just happened. The man kept apologizing for not having been there for his mom's surgery, but how could he have even changed that? He was deported, with no way to see her. Later, a man came in to call his daughter and after a few calls, he said, "It's fine. She doesn't want to talk to me anyway." Again, it hit me hard, and my eyes got watery. . . . I could see my own father in their place, and it broke my heart.

Driven by students like Rubi, our team came to focus on the *emotional* impacts of U.S. removal.

For such painful work, students needed comprehensive support. Our interviews drew out stories of beatings, psychological torture, and violence against migrants in the United States. Many of my 20- and 21-year-old students had family members surviving the same abuse. If I wanted these students involved, I could not leave trauma to the psychologists, as many professors (and social scientists) are wont to do. I scoured books, therapy resources, and other work on vicarious trauma.[6] I built a curriculum to train students in trauma-informed interviewing, secondary trauma, and self-care. Today, I do not allow students to do fieldwork until they have been through this training, a process of learning to protect oneself and to heal.

Students also showed me the need for greater community care. Though I am an "expert" on Mexico-U.S. migration, I am a white U.S. citizen. Immigrant students often understood deportation viscerally on a level that I might not. But I learned that if I showed up to listen and practice compassion (literally, feel things together), I could help them connect with each other and realize they were not alone. We started each class with space to debrief and talk about our emotions. We named our trauma and that of respondents. And we had long conversations about violence, state mistreatment, and what we, as scholars, could do.

This process sparked guilt and critique. Most students who participated in the program thought of themselves as marginalized in the United States. In Tijuana, they were in a position of relative privilege, often for the first time. In contrast to deported migrants, students were U.S. citizens or residents, fluent English speakers, and soon-to-be college graduates. This positioning triggered conflicted feelings. Some students worried that our study exploited deported men. Others rejected research entirely, as an enterprise premised on violent relations, such as the ones between the U.S. and Mexico. They also questioned the power I held in our work. After all, I controlled their grades and, in the case of the four paid research assistants, their wages. We started talking about these dynamics in class, discussing and voting on things like whether to pay respondents, how to hand over control to the people we interviewed, and whether to continue doing research at all. Ultimately, their critiques inspired me to eliminate grades in the program and give respondents near total control of the interviews. Today, students grade themselves, using prompts for reflection. In short, the students reframed the program itself.

Latinx students at UCSD, a flagship campus, seemed to embody the myth of successful young immigrant "DREAMers." They were the crème de la crème of their high schools. Despite the burdens they carried, they had "made it" into the University of California. Many said they felt intense obligations to honor their parents' struggles by "getting ahead."[7] Of course, they were human: amid the hard work, some got tired and overwhelmed or flaked out. Still, it was easy to see them with reverence, as if they confirmed the American Dream.

The public often frames deported men as just the reverse: vilified even as high-achieving students are venerated.[8] Echoing stereotypes, some men we met had gang signs on their knuckles or teardrops tattooed under their eyes, to mark the people they'd killed. In person, their appearances resembled the pictures that politicians use to shout about threats of criminal migrants and gangs.[9] Many had been in prison.

Yet, my "excellent" immigrant students were not so distant from these deportees. Sometimes, quite literally, we interviewed brothers and other relatives of students at UCSD. The divisions between them seemed almost a matter of chance: the people who appear in these pages had the (bad) luck to be born in Mexico or to come out a boy.

It is not a coincidence that nearly all my students were women and nearly all the people we spoke to were men. U.S. police and carceral institutions beat Latino boys down (in every sense) from the time they reach adolescence. When we spoke to such men, they often insisted that the only thing standing between them and students like mine were accidents of birth, of gender, or of how the state and their neighborhoods saw them. As one young man put it, "I am a DREAMer, too."[10]

This point came home with "Ever," whose story runs through the text. Ever's sister Camila, a UCSD undergraduate, worked on this project for more than two years. Their parents left Oaxaca, Mexico for Los Angeles when Ever was only a toddler. Camila was born in LA, a few years after they crossed. By the time Ever turned 13 years old, he had a criminal record. Shortly before Camila enrolled at UCSD, he got locked up and taken away.

Dehumanizing state treatment hits both "sides" of immigrant families. On the surface, Latinx students like mine appear to be thriving. Yet around them looms the U.S. carceral state. At 19 or 20 years old, they, too, were fighting to keep their families together—even to keep them alive. Though students who participated in this project were all U.S. citizens or legal permanent residents, about half had undocumented parents and nearly a quarter had a parent or sibling who'd been deported. Sometimes, ICE deported their loved ones while students were in the program. Occasionally, I would get a call from a student saying their uncle or cousin had been arrested. Soon, we were racing around in the night to figure out where ICE had detained them and where along the U.S.-Mexico border they might be let out. As we did, I felt the sting of my students' longing to keep their loved ones from harm.

One might say the U.S. is failing these students. We are also failing their brothers. Despite the resilience, drive, and intelligence of both the most successful *and* the most criminalized Mexican immigrants, the United States systematically locks up young men and throws them out to the wolves (or cartels, to be more concrete). From a policy standpoint, this practice is deeply shortsighted. My students remember. They are smart and determined. They are highly educated. Most are U.S. citizens, and they will never forget the feeling of having their fathers or brothers ripped from their homes.

Meanwhile, deportation does *not* make men disappear, as some in the U.S. might hope. My students and I often heard their stories just minutes from San Diego, within sight of its iron gates. We learned that men almost always keep fighting—sometimes formally, for the right to get back to their families, and sometimes informally, for a place to call home. Their siblings, spouses, and children in the U.S. continue to struggle as well. In some cases, they start that fight by telling their stories.

The goal of this book is to elevate deportees' voices. As a scholar, a border-dweller, and a mother, I designed and oversaw the research, and I wrote the words. But the book is also the work of my students, whose passion and empathy ripple throughout its pages. In honoring men like their brothers and fathers, my students have told their own stories as well. I have tried to highlight their contributions throughout and to recognize how true understanding comes from the labor of many minds—and the love of many, traumatized hearts. As students insistently showed me, the men we banish are, in fact, our brothers.

Above all, I am honored that the men (and women) in this book were willing to share their stories with me and the team of students who helped do the research. Thank you for taking the leap to trust us and give us a part of yourselves. This book is for you.

Second, I feel an incredible debt to the students who brought their hearts and souls to this project: Breanny Andrade, Samantha Canseco, Nanitzia Comparán Cuadras, Rubi de Lira, Jasmin Divas Villeda, Pamela Elguezabal, Yaneth Escobosa, Nathally Fernández, Jena Fierro-Hirales, Stephanie Flores, Marisa García Pérez, David Husson, Fátima Khayar Cámara, Ana López Ricoy, Cintia Martínez, Janet Miranda Hernández, Kayleigh Mitchell, Maomi Mojica, Maria Morales, Miriam Nuñez, Frieda Orbach, Zeltzin Pérez Reyes, Itzel Rodríguez, Adrian Rodríguez Valdez, Zianía Ruiz-Marina, Niccolo Sabia, Camila Sánchez, Paulina Santiago-Rodríguez, Karla Trujillo Rogel, Ivette Vargas, and Faviola Zamudio-Díaz. In particular, Ana López Ricoy and Fátima Khayar Cámara guided the work for its first three years, bringing brilliance and sensitivity to all of our conversations. Camila Hernández Cruz and Samantha Canseco also did critical interviews in Oaxaca in summer 2019. Later, Ally Orrick, Nathally Fernández, Samantha Fakhimi, and Inaaya Hassan helped analyze data with care and initiative. This was truly a team effort, and I learned so much from you. The work is richer for your engagement.

Third, none of this would have happened without the NGOs that guided us through the chaotic world of deportation, hosted us, helped frame our questions, and made us feel at home. These include, in Tijuana, the Casa del Migrante, Puente TJ United, Madre Assunta, Desayunador Padre Salesiano, Espacio Migrante, Ejército de Salvación, Templo Embajadores de Jesús, and the YMCA Tijuana.

Father Pat Murphy, Gilberto Martínez, Jose Carlos Yee Quintero, and Valeria Ruiz Griego were especially generous with their time, jokes, and insights. In Mexico City, we got important support from Deportados Unidos en la Lucha, ODA, and New Comienzos. Special thanks to Maggie Laredo and Jill Anderson for taking in Ana for several months. In Oaxaca, Florence Weinberg and Nancy García offered key orientation.

Fourth, I am grateful to the many colleagues who read drafts and gave feedback. This book might not have taken flight had it not been for the brilliant Jennifer Carlson, who offered encouragement, camaraderie, and deeply considered suggestions on every chapter. I also sincerely enjoyed my monthly meetings and chapter swaps with book buddies and fellow pandemic parents, Rebecca Galemba and David Trouille. Thank you to Rebecca for bringing us together. On Zoom, Stephanie Canizales proved a stalwart weekly writing companion, keeping my spirits up.

Several others also played shorter-term roles. Thanks to Katrina Burgess and the Tufts Institute for Migration and Human Security crew for welcoming me into their 2017 workshop on migration in Tijuana; you got this all started! Abi Thornton and Fátima Khayar Cámara, who both attended that workshop and did ethnography at the Casa del Migrante between 2017 and 2019, were also key intellectual partners. Thanks also to Rafael Alarcón Acosta and Laura Velasco Ortiz at El Colegio de la Frontera Norte for early advice. In Mexico City, Robert Irwin and the team from Humanizing Deportation convened a fantastic and formative conference in 2019. Meanwhile, Fidan Elçioglu, Lauren Duquette-Rury, Vanesa Ribas, Joe Wiltberger, Juan Pablo Pardo-Guerra, and the participants in the UCSD migration workshop gave me important feedback on an early proposal, helping to guide the book. Outside UCSD, the Gender and Power Workshop anchored me in feminist theory and offered crucial direction (with special thanks to Marie Berry, Susila Gurusami, Lynne Haney, Zakiya Luna, Jordanna Matlon, Rhacel Parreñas, Smitha Radhakrishnan, Raka Ray, Poulami Roychowdhury, Leslie Salzinger, Nazanin Shahrokni, and Cinzia Solari). Before submission, Letta Page tackled the whole manuscript with her signature fine-toothed comb. Then, reviewers Jennifer Randles and Nancy Plankey-Videla offered attentive, thoughtful, and quick analyses of the book. Finally, I am thankful to Naomi Schneider for her enthusiasm about the project, to her assistants Aline Dolinh and LeKeisha Hughes for answering questions, to Julie Van Pelt for production support, and to Irina du Quenoy for her careful copyediting.

Fifth, of course, research costs money. This project was funded by a 2018 UCSD Academic Senate Grant, a 2019 UCSD Social Sciences Divisional Research Grant, and a 2019 American Sociological Association Fund for the Advancement of the Discipline Grant, with student involvement supported by the UC-Mexico Initiative (now Alianza UC-MX), a UCSD Changemaker Faculty Fellowship, and staff support from the UCSD Center for U.S.-Mexican Studies and Center for Comparative

Immigration Studies. I am especially grateful to Melissa Floca, Ana Minvielle, David Fitzgerald, Claire Adida, and Kristen Walker for helping me secure and manage this funding. I also appreciate the UCSD Library for providing a grant to make this book Open Access.

Finally, my friends and family have kept my feet on the ground, through the roller coaster of parenting young kids amid COVID-19, Trump, and all the trauma that comes with work at the border. Danielle Raudenbush, Vanesa Ribas, and Amy Lerner gave me a core space of care and camaraderie at UCSD. Ariana Thompson-Lastad, Mary Doyno, and Maria Alejandra Perez offered empathic weekly support. In addition, Isaac Martin, Mirle Rabinowitz Bussell, Leslie Lewis, Keith Pezzoli, Fonna Forman, Teddy Cruz, Cat Lettieri, and Carolyn Sandoval, among others, helped me think about how to weave teaching, research, and social justice in our complex world at the border.

On the home front, I am grateful to Fidan Elçioglu and Ashley Simonsen for keeping me thinking and laughing through so many years. I couldn't have finished this book without immense patience and extra support from Ben Sanoff, Jane Andrews, Bob Harrington, and Lara Dumont. Mom, thank you for moving to San Diego to help us and for giving me roots, that I might have wings. Ben, thank you for being a steady optimist and loving me through it all. Finally, to Adrian and Amalia, who showed me how deeply a mother can love—and thus, what deported parents have lost. As toddlers, you saw the wall at the U.S.-Mexico border and simply asked "Why?" Trust your instincts. Your generation can (and must) build a better world.

Introduction

Ángel Morales had been locked up for almost two years the day U.S. Immigration and Customs Enforcement (ICE) pulled him out of detention and loaded him into a van for the Mexican border. He'd lived in California since he was 4. At the time of his arrest, he was a 23-year-old community college student fluent in English. According to the police, Ángel hit an officer during an immigration protest. Ángel said the charges were false. In jail, he hired a lawyer. He tried to fight deportation, but none of it took. Instead, Ángel spent 18 months in prison and 6 in immigration detention before the U.S. removed him.

Behind bars, Ángel felt he was losing his soul. Every day, guards woke the men at three in the morning to bring someone to court, flooding the cells with fluorescent lights. Ángel often saw people beaten by guards or gangs. If inmates did not sign their own deportation orders, ICE could hold them for years, even if they had committed no crimes. When Ana, a PhD student, interviewed Ángel a few years later, he told her quietly, "It was horrible. How did I survive? I have asked myself that. I don't know. I guess by the grace of God." He added, "They break you. They don't let you sleep. So, you're numb . . . You actually don't know what's going on till you just accept any offer [to leave the country], just for the sake of 'leave me alone.' So, they break you. They break you psychologically."

The day ICE set Ángel "free" (into Mexico), agents chained his hands in a box and cuffed his feet so tight he could hardly walk. When Ángel asked for his stuff, they barked that if he wanted it, he could go back to jail. Ángel got in the van.

When he got out, he was on a bridge to Tijuana. Each step felt like the longest one of his life. He remembered watching his world fall behind him, as if in a dream. When Ángel faltered, guards pushed him through the door, into Mexico.

Though Ángel tried to "return" to his birthplace in Guadalajara, he hadn't been there in 20 years, and his closest relative left was a great aunt he hardly knew. People on the street made fun of Ángel's "American" Spanish. In this place the U.S. said was his home, they insisted that he was a stranger. Ángel's head spun. He worried, "Are they gonna think I'm the worst person in the world? Are they gonna be afraid of me because I'm a 'criminal'? Are they gonna think that I maybe committed something really horrible? . . . If that [incarceration] happened to me in the U.S., is the same thing gonna happen to me here in Mexico?" Ángel felt deeply alone—out of place in the only place he had left.

Mentally, Ángel also felt trapped in that prison in Bakersfield, California. He constantly watched his back. He struggled to trust other people. For months, he grappled with deep depression. He explained: "You're so used to being stuck inside four walls that you feel like you have to be inside to be protected . . . It's two different shocks: the shock of being inside four walls and then the shock of you being free, but you don't recognize anything . . . Your whole identity—*you*—get lost, like, 'Okay, who am I now? What am I supposed to do?' You get so clouded you cannot think clearly." After prison, Ángel could barely function, let alone in a country he hardly knew. He grasped for a sense of himself.

Ángel was not alone. Most of the men we interviewed struggled with alienation. Some had been ripped from their homes in the night by armed teams from ICE. Fathers could not say goodbye to their children. Husbands and college-aged sons were locked up for years, for no crime. After deportation, they struggled to (re)build social connections and reclaim their very humanity. Some died by suicide. Others ended up killed.

But Ángel got lucky. A few months after ICE removed him, he started browsing the web. He discovered organizations in Mexico City that trained deportees for jobs and helped get them back on their feet. He moved to the capital and found work in programming. He joined an NGO that championed deportees' bilingual, bicultural skills. There, he helped create a *new* kind of home.

BANISHED MEN

This is a book about men we banish. From 2009 to 2020, the U.S. government deported more than five million people. Almost half were Mexican. Three-quarters had lived in the U.S. for more than a year and many for more than a decade. Importantly, nearly 95 percent of the people removed from inside the U.S. were men.[1] Men like Ángel, who had lived 21 of his 25 years in the United States.

Deportation is nothing new. But starting in the early 2000s, new laws wove detention and incarceration into the act of removal. Even though less than half the people the U.S. deports have been convicted of crimes (other than crossing the border), nearly all spend a few months detained. Another 40 percent are removed after sentences in U.S. prisons or jails. I refer to this combination of detention, incarceration, removal, and border militarization as *carceral deportation*.[2]

Deportation itself is not *supposed* to be punishment. However, the federal government now bans deportees from returning to the United States for 3, 5, 10, or 20 years once they are removed. If migrants attempt to rejoin their loved ones north of the border, the U.S. can send them to prison. Still, many try. At the border, they often get stopped by U.S. Customs and Border Patrol (CBP), leading to cycles of detention, incarceration, and further expulsion.

Carceral deportation targets Latino men. To legitimate caging and exile, U.S. politicians, cops, and judges invoke masculine and racialized tropes of "illegal" Latino "criminals" and "rapists."[3] This language has consequences. Though roughly half of unauthorized immigrants in the United States are female, U.S. police and ICE detain, imprison, and deport men at more than nine times the rate of women. Likewise, though migrants from Mexico, Guatemala, El Salvador, and Honduras make up about two thirds of the undocumented, they represent up to 95 percent of all deportees.[4] To understand this gendered and racialized system, this book takes an in-depth look at Mexican migrant men.

What becomes of men the U.S. locks up and casts off as criminals? How does living through U.S. detention and prison shape their emotions, relationships, and choices about where to live and how to claim rights and resources? How does it sway their faith in their own humanity?

To answer these questions, I worked with 31 bilingual students from the University of California, San Diego (UCSD) to interview 171 deported men and 15 deported women. Most of the team did interviews in Tijuana, near our homes at the U.S.-Mexico border. I also hired four paid research assistants to help me interview people in the major sending state of Oaxaca and the capital, Mexico City. All but two of the students were of Mexican or Central American origin. Half were children of undocumented parents, and almost a quarter had had a parent or sibling deported, sometimes during our research. A quarter were immigrants themselves. The students' experiences of U.S. enforcement set the tone for the research, orienting us toward the emotions, perspectives, and love of immigrant men.

We found that carceral deportation makes men feel banished not only from the United States but also from belonging at all. Detention, incarceration, and removal beat people down both physically and psychologically. Despite key variations, men repeatedly said they felt treated like cockroaches, pigs, and dogs. U.S. carceral institutions also weakened men's social ties. Locked up and kicked out, they lost their places as workers, fathers, brothers, and sons. Many also lost a sense of themselves.

This feeling of human banishment extends across borders as well. Men carry the trauma of U.S. imprisonment with them to Mexico. Though fewer than two in five deportees have been convicted of a crime, Mexicans often shun them as felons or assume they are members of gangs.[5] Most of those from small towns find it hard to go back. Instead, they land in big cities or at the border—"elsewheres" that are neither "home" nor "away."[6] There, they linger in limbo, unsure whether to risk a return to the United States. Many endure kidnapping, robbery, arrest, extortion, police assaults, and cartel recruitment. As deported men struggle to (re)claim their lives and loves, they look less like returning migrants than like the stateless: stripped of pride and a place to call home.

BACKGROUND: THE RISE
OF CARCERAL DEPORTATION

The United States has scapegoated Mexican migrants and forcibly removed them for almost two centuries.[7] But today, removal comes hand in hand with time behind bars.

Starting in the late 1980s and 1990s, U.S. policies merged immigration and criminal law, in what scholars call "crimmigration."[8] In 1986, the U.S. Immigration Reform and Control Act (IRCA) required the government to expel noncitizens convicted of "deportable" crimes. In answer—and to help relieve overcrowding—immigration officials began to check inmates' legal status in prisons and jails.[9] At the time, however, only a few, violent crimes were considered grounds for removal.

Then, in 1996, Congress passed the Anti-Terrorism and Effective Death Penalty Act (AEDPA) and the Illegal Immigration Reform and Control Act (IIRIRA), which radically increased deportations, via prisons and jails. These laws added numerous minor crimes as grounds for removal, including identity fraud, drug possession, shoplifting, turnstile jumping, and disorderly conduct—even if those crimes had happened well in the past.[10] They also mandated that anyone convicted of such crimes be detained and deported. They made illegal entry a misdemeanor and reentry a felony, punishable by prison.[11] For the first time, IIRIRA enabled the U.S. to deport lawful permanent residents. In addition, IIRIRA reduced judges' power to cancel deportation orders, enabling the government to remove immigrants with little to no due process.[12]

In the 2000s, more funding, technology, and programs entwined incarceration and deportation. From 2004 to 2008, Congress increased ICE funds nearly thirtyfold, to $180 million. In 2006, ICE merged past jail-check programs into the Criminal Alien Program (CAP), expanding ICE presence in prisons.[13] In 2008, the Obama administration introduced the Secure Communities Program, enabling law enforcement to fingerprint people as they were booked into jail and check them against ICE databases (*before* a trial or any conviction). By 2013, Secure Communities was active in every jurisdiction in the United States. When Obama suspended the program, ICE folded its operations into CAP, keeping it going in practice.

Secure Communities and Section 287(g) of IIRIRA, which trained police to collaborate with ICE, empowered local law enforcement to find and turn over undocumented immigrants. In turn, every police encounter became a chance to check papers. These programs also actively targeted migrants *outside* of prisons and jails. Under 287(g), for instance, police could question individuals suspected of violating immigration laws (until 2012) and execute ICE warrants. While some cities have resisted these practices, police in many parts of the country now routinely submit people's fingerprints to ICE on point of arrest. Even if immigrants have legal residency, minor violations (or no violations), or have already served their sentences, they are subject to deportation.[14]

Finally, stricter punishments sent deportees to prison if they tried to return. Historically, the U.S. treated crossing the border as an administrative offense, which it mostly ignored.[15] IIRIRA made entry punishable. Starting in the 1990s, the U.S. also fortified urban parts of the U.S.-Mexico border, pushing migrants to remote zones in the desert where they were easier to police and more vulnerable to death.[16] In 2011, CBP announced that it would more systematically charge migrants caught with unauthorized entry and reentry, under the Consequence Delivery System.[17] Today, if the U.S. apprehends someone returning after a deportation, it can send them to prison for 2 years, or up to 20 if they have a record, including traffic violations or multiple deportations.[18] By 2015, about 9.1 percent of all federal prisoners (17,000 people) were locked up for crossing the border, now the most common federal crime.[19]

These policies radically increased the number of deportations. Prior to the mid-1990s, the U.S. deported less than 50,000 people a year, 94 percent of whom had just crossed the border.[20] Today, the United States deports 287,000 to 432,000 people a year, roughly half from inside the country.[21] They are contractors, chefs, small business owners, and members of deep communities. Many were brought over the border as kids. Some are lawful permanent residents. More than a third have children under 18; three-quarters of their children are U.S. citizens.[22]

These men are rarely criminals. In general, immigrants are less likely than U.S. citizens to commit crimes or be incarcerated.[23] Yet, programs like 287(g) and Secure Communities encourage police to stop and arrest people for offenses like driving without a license.[24] While white Americans often look at such infractions as minor misdeeds, for immigrants, a traffic stop can set in motion arrest and then deportation.[25] Even the immigrants ICE finds *inside* prisons and jails tend to be there for minor violations or have not (yet) been convicted of crimes. From 2010 to 2013, for instance, 55.4 percent of people removed under the Criminal Alien Program had been convicted of nonviolent, nonserious offenses, and 27.5 percent had no convictions at all (in short, they were hardly criminals).[26] As of 2019, only 35 to 40 percent of people detained by ICE had a criminal record.[27] Of those, roughly 31 percent had immigration offenses, 15 percent traffic violations, and 15 percent drug offenses.[28] Very few had been convicted of serious crimes.

As deportations ballooned, the U.S. rapidly expanded immigration detention, too.[29] From 2001 to 2018, ICE doubled the number of people detained. It now locks up over 400,000 people a year, sometimes holding more than 50,000 at a time (with most there for weeks or months). Even those who give up their right to a hearing and agree to removal can expect to stay locked up at least a few weeks. As of 2021, those who refuse to sign off on their own deportations wait more than 4.5 years for their case to come before a judge.[30] Immigrants deported from prison may also be sent to detention after their sentences, sometimes for years.

If crimmigration is the legal framework merging prison, detention, and deportation, banishment is the lived experience: the physical and emotional harms wrought by getting locked up and then being sent off to Mexico.

A THEORY OF BANISHMENT

Carceral deportation has fundamentally changed the Mexico-U.S. immigration system. From the 1940s to early 2000s, U.S. immigration control echoed South African apartheid.[31] Apartheid refers to the laws and legally sanctioned violence that imposed racial segregation in South Africa for most of the twentieth century. South African apartheid was also a migrant labor system. It made Black migrant workers exploitable by marking them racial "others" (considered less deserving) and by separating families. While South Africa let Black men enter white cities to work, it relegated Black women to Bantustans (Black homelands). Thus, apartheid deflected the costs of raising children to cheap rural areas where women could grow food to supplement men's meager earnings.[32] South Africa also used apartheid laws to manage surplus labor, expelling Black men during downturns and admitting them when needs for workers increased.[33] Some scholars argue that this system also deflected resistance out of white cities and into the Black periphery.[34]

Similarly, starting in the 1940s, the U.S. let Mexican men enter the country to work, recruiting them as temporary labor on farms and in other low-wage jobs, both formally and informally. As in South Africa, U.S. laws labeled these men racially inferior to whites, less deserving of living wages, and more deserving of deportation.[35] Meanwhile, U.S. enforcement excluded Mexican women as "breeders," and many stayed in sending villages, where they could farm and raise families cheaply.[36] The U.S. also used deportation to regulate surplus labor and threaten migrant workers who protested against low wages.[37]

Today, U.S. immigration control still uses racial "othering," gendered ideologies, and family separation. Yet, if apartheid aimed to *exploit* migrant men, carceral deportation strives to *erase* them.

The effect of carceral deportation is banishment. At the most general level, banishment means spatial exclusion imposed by law.[38] Theorist Ananya Roy, who studies urban removals in the United States, describes a more specific process of *racial* banishment. By forcing people of color to move and marking their presence illegal, she argues, U.S. laws and policing extend the logic of mass incarceration beyond the prison. When the government moves people out of public spaces and makes their return illegal, it turns their very presence into a crime. As Roy puts it, "Banishment is not the movement of racialized bodies from one place to another or what we might call displacement. It is expulsion from everywhere."[39]

Thus, banishment is a form of "social death." Sociologist Orlando Patterson introduced the term "social death" to describe how slavery stripped Black people of full humanity and cast them out of society.[40] Others have used the phrase to show how racial segregation, imprisonment, and government violence more broadly mark some people undeserving or subhuman, normalizing their social exclusion and even physical death.[41] The concept is similar to philosopher Giorgio Agamben's theory of "bare life."[42] Agamben argues that when government officials suspend individuals' legal rights, they reduce those people to mere survival, expelling them from the social and political fabric. In short, banishment attacks men's humanity, marking them outside society as a whole.

Banishment is distinct from apartheid in five key ways: (1) it is carceral; (2) it targets men; (3) it leaves men in limbo, funneling them to urban peripheries; and (4) it undermines agency. Nevertheless, in some cases (5) it can spark new modes of refusal.

Banishment is carceral.   Today, policing, detention, incarceration, deportation, and border militarization work in tandem.[43] Deportation is entwined both concretely and ideologically with mass incarceration: the system that locks up, expels, and murders Black and Latino Americans in disproportionate numbers, especially men.[44] Detention—itself de facto imprisonment—is part of almost all removals today. The logic of prisons also extends outside penal institutions and across the U.S.-Mexico border.[45] After removal, deportees carry both trauma from U.S. prisons and stigma as criminals, enabling Mexican cartels and state authorities to assault and mistreat them as well.

To understand deportation, scholars must study the psychic and interpersonal impacts of being locked up. Expansive research shows that even for U.S. citizens, imprisonment degrades mental health, erodes intimate relationships, cuts social ties, and imposes stigmas that make it hard to establish a life after prison or jail.[46] For migrants, the consequences of prison are compounded by forced relocation, often to unknown places, from which they cannot visit their U.S.-based families.

Banishment targets men.[47]   The U.S. has long used gendered tropes to justify barring immigrants. In the second half of the twentieth century, under the system that resembled apartheid, the U.S. marked immigrant *women* as looming "public charges" and "breeders" of "anchor babies,"[48] reinforcing their confinement to Mexico. Under carceral deportation, U.S. leaders invoke *masculine* Latino threats (Trump's "bad hombres") to legitimate restrictions, walls, detention, and deportation.[49] Today, the U.S. apprehends men far more often than women and gives them fewer reprieves.[50] Though men are only half of undocumented migrants, they represent 9.5 in 10 deportees. Every year, the U.S. rips up to 100,000 fathers from their U.S.-born children. Yet, the U.S. public and media tend to tolerate men's removal, raising loud outcries only when separation comes to hit immigrant mothers.[51]

To understand the effects of this gendered violence, I focus on men. This is not just a study of "their" masculinity. Rather, I am concerned with what happens to men when *states* use gendered practices to erase them.

U.S. assaults on Black and Brown men are part of a global pattern. Today, amid jobless growth, poor and working-class men all over the world face mass unemployment.[52] Few can attain neoliberal ideals of breadwinning masculinity.[53] Yet, government policies still prize paid labor and punish those who cannot find work. As a result, men struggle to find their places in politics and even in families.[54] In turn, governments now mark poor and racialized men as "terrorists" and "criminal threats," increasingly locking them up. In the process, they rob men of citizenship, jobs, homes, and manhood.

What does it *feel* like for men to be crushed by the state? To answer this question, scholars of gender must flip their usual frameworks. Often, studies focus on how hegemonic ideas about masculinity legitimate, reinforce, and build consent to men's domination.[55] Meanwhile, feminist scholarship on the state tends to highlight its patriarchal character and control over women.[56] Vast research looks at *women's* agency and resistance and their emotions.[57] Yet studies say less about how states control marginalized *men* or how men resist, let alone how they feel.

Emergent research has started to fill these gaps. For instance, sociologist Lynne Haney reveals how prisons and state-imposed debt work in tandem to undermine men's ability to parent, hold down jobs, and make sense of themselves and their place in the nation.[58] Jennifer Randles adds that government programs for poor men of color, combined with the threat of incarceration, paradoxically prevent fathers from being there for their children.[59] This book, too, looks at how U.S. policies undermine families, target men, and leave them scrambling for ways to reestablish their masculinity.

Banishment leaves men in limbo, funneling them to urban peripheries.   Apartheid systems relied on a symbiosis between Bantustan and metropole, reproduction and production, home and away. This binary logic still dominates a lot of scholarly thinking on Mexico-U.S. migration.[60] For instance, studies of migrant transnationalism and return focus on people's relationships with their hometowns.[61] Yet, few deported men go back to live in their places of birth.[62] Rural migrant-sending states are often economically stagnant.[63] Deportees face stigma there, too.[64] Many have trouble finding work or building social connections in rural areas. Few can truly "go home." Instead, they tend to see deportation as *exile.*[65]

Immigration scholars have also written about how migrants channel money, political influence, and social ideas across borders, known as remittances.[66] Yet, theories of the U.S. carceral state tend to stop at the border, taking for granted that mass incarceration is part of an internal state monopoly on legitimate violence.[67] Under banishment, the impacts of this system also cross borders in the suffering and alienation of deportees. Deported men "remit" psychological degradation from U.S. policing, prisons, and ICE detention.

Traumatized, alone, unable to go "home," and hesitant to risk a return to the United States, deportees land in limbo: "betwixt and between" emotionally as they search for a home.[68] This feeling of limbo echoes the emotional experiences of many undocumented people in the United States.[69] Men's uncertainty also shapes the *places* they go. Many deportees land in dense urban neighborhoods at the border, in Mexico City, or in state capitals.[70] Cities and border zones tend to feel closer to life in the United States. Some men also wait indefinitely at the border for chances to cross back north.

Deportees are vulnerable in such spaces. Border zones like Tijuana are emerging economic powerhouses, political flashpoints, and staging grounds for traffickers to the United States.[71] As scholars like Shaylih Muehlmann and Jeremy Slack reveal, cartels and transnational gangs permeate border institutions up to the highest levels, and cartels often recruit or kidnap repatriated migrants.[72] Mexican police also extort, abuse, and arbitrarily arrest returnees, echoing the treatment meted out by their counterparts in the U.S.[73] Both sets of organizations target deportees based on their isolation and their connections to the United States.

In other cities—especially Mexico City—deportees also live on urban peripheries and endure crime. Yet, Mexico's long history of centralized governance has funneled resources to Mexico City, concentrating political and economic activity—as well as civil society—in the capital.[74] Moving there can mitigate deportees' limbo. Men's carceral histories also "sort" them into different receiving sites, as I detail throughout the book. The interplay between U.S. removal and Mexican urban space then shapes their chances to act.

Banishment undermines agency.   Some scholars argue that South African apartheid shunted protests to the hinterlands, offering a "geographic fix" for resistance to exploitation.[75] By contrast, carceral deportation undermines men's agency altogether. Most researchers agree that deportation inhibits migrants' ability to speak for their rights.[76] Upon removal to unfamiliar places, deportees endure social isolation, familial chaos, stigma, and state violence.[77] Facing high rates of mental illness, homelessness, and drug abuse, many struggle to maintain their baseline well-being, let alone organize or protest.[78] Banished from personhood, they find it hard to reclaim it. Yet, migrants do not *always* succumb to erasure.

Banishment can *spark new forms of refusal.*   If migrants resisted apartheid by protesting back in their homelands, men and women transcend the limbo of deportation by finding new terms on which to exist as multinational humans. Again, Ananya Roy is eloquent: "The antonym of racial banishment is [not] . . . integration. It is a radical imagination."[79] Deportees' reimagining goes beyond the goal of "reintegration," described by some scholars of return migration. Rather, deported individuals reclaim humanity by reconfiguring deportation as an asset and themselves as multifaceted, multinational women and men.

Some of these new modes of action buck "legitimate" outlets for politics. So doing, they echo a broader pattern. Today, most grassroots movements arise outside formal democratic institutions—as demonstrated in research on India and the Middle East.[80] Similarly, sociologist Jordanna Matlon shows, men excluded by racial capitalism may use "apolitical" tools like consumption to show their worth.[81] In other cases—including some described in this book—men reject a violent state order or reclaim masculinity by defying the law—reinforcing the stereotypes for which they have been so maligned. For instance, they participate in organized crime, (re)cross the U.S. border, or challenge the imaginary order forged by a wall. (Ironically, their displays of violence can sometimes echo the practices of the white supremacist U.S. state). In examining these forms of action, scholars must reflect on our own role in dismissing Latino men's anger as illegitimate, violent, or risky. Deportees' resistance may not arrive on our terms.

METHODS: FINDING THE ERASED

How do you "find" a set of people the U.S. has tried to erase? How do you convince them to tell you their stories and build enough trust to share their emotions, when society has dismissed them as criminals? And how do you do all of this as a team of 29 undergraduates, two PhD students, and one untenured professor?

Multisited Team Research

Between January 2018 and March 2020, the Mexican Migration Field Research Program (MMFRP) team interviewed 171 deported men and 15 deported women. For context, we also interviewed 47 Mexican civil servants and nonprofit staff, 8 of whom had been deported themselves.[82] I conducted 30 interviews, paid RAs conducted 20–50 each, and the remaining students conducted 4–5 each, for course credit. All the researchers were bilingual. Since all the students graduated and/or got jobs before the writing began, I wrote the findings. But the whole team helped uncover—and share—this story with rigor and care.

Tijuana was an exemplary place to start our study of banishment. It is consistently the largest single repatriation site, receiving between 18 to 30 percent of Mexican deportees.[83] It is also a chokepoint, as deportees gear up to reenter the United States, move elsewhere in Mexico, or figure out what comes next.[84] To understand this landscape, in 2017 PhD student Fátima Khayar Cámara and I interviewed more than 25 Tijuana shelter directors and NGO leaders, honing our focus and helping us meet deportees. We also interviewed 13 deported men at the Casa del Migrante, the city's most prominent shelter.[85]

In fall 2018, I took over the MMFRP, which allowed me to integrate my courses into the project. Students applied to MMFRP in the summer.[86] In fall, I taught a course on immigration and trained the team in interview methods and ethics. In winter, during an eight-unit (double) class, we traveled to Tijuana. For a week, we lived in the Casa del Migrante, in an area reserved for volunteers. During the day, students spread out to volunteer and conduct interviews in six different shelters.

For six more weeks, we returned every Friday.[87] Students did an average of 4–5 interviews each, which made up the core of their coursework. In spring, I guided the students through a preliminary analysis of the results. I repeated this whole process twice, once in 2019 and again in 2020.

After our first set of interviews in Tijuana, I wondered if the impacts of carceral deportation were different in other parts of Mexico. Was there a distinction between those who stayed at the border, moved to Mexico City, or returned to live near their hometowns? How were men shaped by the places in which they settled? I wanted to understand how people like Ángel thought about where they might live.

So, I added new sites in Mexico City, a major urban metropolis, and Oaxaca, a paradigmatic sending state. Mexico City was the nexus of national politics and a site of innovative deportee organizing. Oaxaca was the third top state of origin of deportees, after Guerrero and Michoacán.[88] I was also familiar with Oaxaca, having lived there on and off since 2004.

I hired four students from the Tijuana team to do 79 interviews at these sites, using the same questionnaire as the earlier stages of research. Ana López Ricoy and Fátima Khayar Cámara, PhD students from Mexico City, conducted the bulk of interviews there, with Fátima reaching out to NGO stakeholders and Ana to deported men. Camila Hernández Cruz and Samantha Canseco, children of immigrants from Oaxaca, helmed efforts there.[89] I spent three weeks in each place, overseeing and participating in recruitment and interviews.

Tijuana, Oaxaca, and Mexico City are not commensurable cases. Nor do they stand for every possible context in Mexico. As a border city, Tijuana had more social services and was less overwhelmed by organized crime than the eastern end of the U.S.-Mexico border. Likewise, Oaxaca was less touched by cartel violence than other sending regions like Michoacán and Guerrero. If anything, our interviews may understate Mexican state abuse, cartel recruitment, and other destabilizing elements of return. We also cannot account for deportees who make it back into the United States. The team filled this gap by interviewing people at the border who hailed from 23 Mexican states (some in cartel-heavy areas), had been deported to varying parts of the border, and/or planned to return to the United States. Taken together, the data shed light on how places can interact in an archipelago of deportation.

Getting to Know Deportees

At each site, local organizations helped us build trust. In Tijuana, we worked in six migrant shelters. Each housed 40–160 migrants at once, almost all of them deportees. Several provided meals to additional migrants as well. Given security risks at the border, shelters offered our team a controlled space for volunteering and research.[90] Working in shelters was also a strategic way to meet deportees. At the border, Grupo Beta, the "hospitality" wing of Mexico's National Institute of Migration, transports migrants directly from the border to shelters, so most deportees stay in a shelter at least a night after being removed.[91] This approach also had drawbacks, which I consider below.

In each of the Tijuana shelters, the students and I presented our study in public spaces, where guests had to wait until dormitories opened at night. We invited every deportee who was over 18, born in Mexico, and had lived in the U.S. for more than a year to join our study.[92] We also mingled and got to know people–often across several visits—before requesting an interview.

In Oaxaca and Mexico City, there were few such shelters. Instead, RAs and I met with every migrant-serving organization we could find and asked for referrals. We also asked family and friends, stood outside large employers, and posted ads on social media, radio, and the streets.[93] Ana used her experience working in a Mexico City call center to recruit employees. She also volunteered at Otros Dreams en Acción (ODA), an NGO in Mexico City, where she met activists and deported men. Samantha's and Camila's families in Oaxaca also introduced us to several people.[94]

Each site's character shaped who we met. In Oaxaca, where deportation was stigmatized and NGOs sparse, we struggled to find respondents. In Mexico City, deportee advocacy organizations and employers directed us to people working for change. In Tijuana, all our interviews came through the shelters, which exposed us to more recent, poor, isolated, and vulnerable deportees.[95] Students readily noticed how shelters themselves engaged in containment, surveillance, and deterrence from remigration.[96] Tijuana's Casa del Migrante reminded some of a halfway house or a prison (minus the bars). Shelters also filtered out people who appeared drunk, on drugs, or involved in smuggling. A deportee could easily be wary of this kind of site. In early 2020, I planned to address this selection effect by adding more interviews in other spaces around Tijuana. COVID made this impossible.[97] Instead, I note the potential bias here in the text.

The Process of Gathering Stories

This book is built on data from interviews. Interviews allowed men (and women) to frame their stories themselves and to tell us about their feelings, life trajectories, and responses to state erasure.[98] In these conversations, we also learned details about spaces otherwise closed to us scholars, including border enforcement, detention, U.S. prisons, and intimate family relationships.

We did interviews in coffee shops and unused offices in shelters. We talked in each respondent's language of choice, for roughly an hour. I suggested content and supervised student work. We asked about people's family relationships, political attitudes and activism, emotional lives, and plans. Always, we spoke of deportation, detention, and prison. But I also trained students to let respondents tell their *own* stories and steer conversations to topics they felt were important and away from traumatic events.[99]

Students were an incredible asset. Many had grown up in the same California neighborhoods where respondents had lived, and several had siblings or parents who'd been deported. Most of the students were also women, and I noticed that men seemed to enjoy confiding in them, treating interviews like an intimate, confessional space.

Content varied with the interests, personalities, and connection between researchers and respondents. Many students drew out stories that I, as a white U.S. citizen, might not have heard. Interviews did not cover all topics in equal depth. Instead of insisting on uniformity, I tried to let students and interviewees take the lead. In turn, they drew attention to the emotional degradation of carceral deportation—the story we tell in this book.

Deportees' narratives of their lives are necessarily partial. As Deborah Boehm points out, their stories are hard to verify.[100] Recent deportees rarely have legal documents, and the information they do have can be incomplete or incorrect (as in Ángel's wrongful conviction). People disappear, lose their papers, avoid sharing unflattering information, and present personas inflected by the context of interviews (just imagine 31 compassionate young people, most of them women, interviewing vulnerable men a bit older than they). Some men refused to name their past crimes. Others exaggerated such violations. At times, students and I felt respondents had withheld part of a story: the pieces did not add up. Other times, stories changed. A mishap is telling: on a few occasions, two students accidentally interviewed the same individual, and the stories were different. Trauma affects memory and emotion. Memories fade and transform. People have distinct perspectives on the same events. Yet deportees' accounts are also the most complete—and often the only—stories we have.

The Men Who Appear in This Book

Of 186 respondents, this book homes in on 158 men, who were deported after living in the U.S. at least a year.[101] We identify all respondents by pseudonyms. When we met, these men had been in Mexico between a day and 10 years. Half had been there more than a year. They ranged in age from 20 to 72, with an average of 35. Most were working in call centers, carwashes, factories, car repair, day labor, or selling things on the street. Half had never gone beyond middle school, and many were unemployed. They lived in shelters (in Tijuana), low-income neighborhoods, and occasionally on the street. In Mexico City, some lived so far from work that they had to commute four hours a day. In Tijuana, the men were especially transient, treating the city as just a point on their journey. Often, a man we met in a shelter one week would be gone when we returned a week later.

These men had deep U.S. ties. They came from 23 Mexican states, but 55 percent were brought to the U.S. as minors, 12 percent came as unaccompanied teens, and 34 percent as adults. They had lived in the U.S. a median of 20 years, with 83 percent having been there a decade or more. More than half were fathers with kids in the United States. Four in 10 had a partner or ex in the U.S. as well. Deportation frayed these relationships. When we interviewed the men, only 20 percent were still married to a U.S.-based partner. Another 28 percent were divorced or separated, and

44 percent were single. Just under half (41 percent) planned to return to the U.S. at some point, a quarter within the year. About a quarter chose to speak English to us, with many more mixing English and Spanish. (See the appendix for more on their demographics).

In most respects, they were comparable to deportees randomly sampled by Mexico's *Encuesta sobre Migración en la Frontera Norte de México* (EMIF, or Survey about Migration at Mexico's Northern Border).[102] Just like that survey, our sample captures a *range* of deportee experiences, letting us explore variations among different people. However, the histories we gathered speak especially to the carceral: the U.S. had put all but four of our interviewees behind bars, with 83 percent detained and 65 percent spending at least a month in prison or jail (versus 40 percent in the EMIF survey). Most had been arrested on migration violations, driving under the influence, traffic violations, domestic violence, gang involvement, or drug charges.[103] Nearly two-thirds (59 percent) said this was their first deportation.

Comparing Carceral Histories

When Fátima, Camila, Ana, and I analyzed the body of interviews, we immediately saw variations based on men's histories of U.S. incarceration and detention.[104] Across our sample, there were men who endured relatively little confinement, men who had been detained, and men who had been incarcerated. It became clear that these entanglements were key to their paths after deportation.

I use these carceral histories as a central comparative framework throughout the book. Another scholar might compare deportees to migrants who returned voluntarily (to the extent return can happen without coercion). Comparing *among* deportees serves a similar purpose. Thus, I look at men who experienced different levels of entanglement in the U.S. carceral system: (1) brief detention; (2) longer-term or repeated detention; and (3) incarceration. I consider *all of* these experiences to be carceral. Yet, some men's histories of imprisonment are far more severe than others. Comparing different carceral experiences helps illustrate *how* policing, detention, and imprisonment erode men's sense of themselves—and sometimes, their ability to feel or make claims at all.

ARGUMENT: HOW DOES IT FEEL TO BE BANISHED?

We argue that carceral deportation makes people feel banished not only from the United States but also from being human.

The force of this system—and its punitive character—is visible in the contrasts among deported men. All deportees today spend time behind bars. Still, they face distinct embroilments in U.S. policing, immigration enforcement, detention, incarceration, and border militarization. Some endure "direct" deportation, without lengthy stays in detention or prison or further run-ins with border patrol. For others, deportation is a repeated process, intertwined with months (or years) locked up, violent abuse by state agents and gangs, and multiple, failed attempts to recross.

The more extensive and severe men's time in the carceral system, the harder it gets to overcome social death. Importantly, men's carceral histories also sort them into contrasting places, funneling those most corroded by prison to more volatile spaces in Mexico.

In banishing men, the U.S. cuts them out of society and leaves them in limbo. Against the odds, some defy this dehumanization.

Cut Out of U.S. Lives and Loves

Carceral deportation inflicts social death by eroding men's spirits, relationships, and masculinity.

First, incarceration, detention, and removal degrade men's psyches. During arrest and confinement, guards and gangs beat men, rape them, and treat them like animals. Many feel that their bodies are no longer theirs. Some lose their orientation in time and space. Others talk about losing their minds, enduring anxiety, depression, insomnia, post-traumatic stress disorder (PTSD), and other unnamed insanity. For those who are locked up the longest, self-blame can help make sense of their fates. These men stop believing they are deserving under the law. Instead, they accept the U.S. state's story that they are criminals who must reform. For all, imprisonment is an emotional assault.

Second, confinement and removal erode men's relationships.[105] Deportation has always ripped migrants from their kids, homes, and jobs. Imprisonment compounds this physical separation by putting intense strain on men and their families in the United States. Prison and detention systems make it hard for family members to visit, such as by transferring men to facilities far away from their loved ones. Often, respondents described the stress on their spouses after ICE locked them up and the tension and fights that arose. Those who spent time in prison also spoke of learning to isolate themselves to stay safe. At the most severe, men lost any trust in people at all. Locking men up did not just take them from their homes in the United States. It also ate away at their ability to demonstrate love.

Third, carceral deportation is emasculating. It deprives men of roles as fathers, brothers, and sons. In the U.S., immigrant men often identify with hard work. Once they are locked up or deported, they can no longer do that. Often, participants spoke of no longer "being a man." Stripped of their roles in family, work, and community, men lose their "place" in a gendered order. In turn, many feel like they lose their place in the world.

In Limbo in Mexico

Men carry this trauma to Mexico. Upon removal, they land in spatial and emotional limbo. I use the term limbo in its fullest sense: a state of uncertainty or in-betweenness, a state of neglect or oblivion, and a state of being trapped, all at once.[106]

It is tempting to think the U.S. deports men "home." In fact, the men we interviewed found it nearly impossible to resettle in their places of birth. U.S. border enforcement had blocked most of them from visiting Mexico since moving to the United States—in our study, an average of 20 years. Starting in the early 2000s, it was common for Mexican families to move to the U.S. *together*, so few respondents had a spouse or child still living in Mexico.[107] Instead, they built families in the U.S. After the men were removed, 90 percent of their spouses and children stayed in the United States. Men went south alone, grieving their families, distrusting themselves and others. Some, like Ángel, also faced rejection in rural hometowns—if they tried to go back at all.[108]

In Mexico, deportees felt betwixt and between: their hearts in the United States and their bodies in Mexico. Most men we talked to thought of the U.S. as "home." About half planned to go back north at some point. Almost all were uncertain what to do next. So, they waited, sometimes indefinitely, until U.S. enforcement eased up or they made enough money to hire a smuggler to help them across the border.[109] When men did try to cross, many were caught, detained, imprisoned, and/or sent back by CBP, compounding their trauma. Some settled at the Mexican border to be close to the U.S. symbolically. Others moved to Mexico City or cities in sending states. Regardless of where they went, most felt out of place.

Disorientation compounded their vulnerability.[110] Having lived in the U.S. for years, few were familiar with Tijuana or Mexico City. Some struggled to remember Mexico at all. They tended to settle in neighborhoods rife with both crime and police. Though many gravitated to cities so as not to stand out, returnees remained visible due to their clothing, tattoos, and/or manners of speaking. Mexican police and cartels fed off this limbo: beating, kidnapping, robbing, extorting, or recruiting deported men. Such experiences reinforced men's sense of erasure.

Being locked up, stripped of their families and masculinity, and sent to places they hardly knew fueled alienation. Men we interviewed often struggled to connect with people in Mexico. A welter of troubles put civic and social life on the back burner, including poverty, unemployment, stigma, organized crime, police and cartel assaults, uncertainty, and the loss of their spouses and children. Those with extensive histories of imprisonment suffered the most. At the extreme, they lost not only their loved ones, manhood, and homes but also their senses of self. Neither here nor there, they had little footing on which to (re)claim their places as men.

Defying Dehumanization

Yet, alienation was not inevitable. Some deportees built radical new ways of being.

In Mexico City especially, many interviewees defied dehumanization. They forged new, transnational identities as *ni de aquí, ni de allá* (neither from here nor there). By *claiming* binationality, they upended the separation between Mexican and American, criminal and citizen, home and away. In the process, they connected with one another. Several secured government resources and bilingual, bicultural work. Some organized at the grassroots to reclaim deportation. Others styled themselves as masculine businessmen, catering to the U.S. Still others challenged the status quo by rejecting "legitimate" politics: joining gangs or cartels, selling drugs, or (re)crossing the border. Though such modes of agency may grate on certain observers, for deported men they are sometimes the only alternative.

Men's histories in the U.S. channeled them into different places in Mexico: border, home state, or megalopolis. Those who spent time in prison tended to feel so alone and debased that they got "stuck" at the U.S.-Mexico border. Men with children in the U.S. or immediate plans to recross often "waited it out" at the border, too. By contrast, those who had not been north for much time more often went back to their states of birth. Finally, those more "directly" deported—especially if they were younger, more educated, more (relatively) class privileged or had organizing or business skills—sustained social ties and self-esteem. Often, they also moved to Mexico City. Sometimes, like Ángel, men sifted among such sites, trying the border and/or their hometown until they realized they might not survive, and only then going on to the capital.

The outcome of banishment reflected the interplay between men's carceral histories, on one side, and the institutional resources and threats they encountered in Mexico, on the other. The border—where ex-prisoners and men in limbo met networks of organized crime—became a "hot spot" of alienation. In sending states, deportees slipped into anonymity, blending in with other returning migrants to avoid the stigma of forced removal. In Mexico City, where exiled men with lighter carceral histories and better resources met the country's most powerful activism, they reclaimed the story of their criminality and invented themselves anew.

MAP OF THE BOOK

The first half of *Banished Men* shows how carceral deportation eats away men's humanity. I analyze the multiple sides of this system: policing, detention, incarceration, and border militarization. The second half considers the system's impacts on men and asks how they try to rebuild. Throughout, I compare men who've faced different "depths" of U.S. state violence.

Chapter 1, "Policed," traces deportation back to law enforcement. Typically, adult men enter the carceral system during arbitrary police stops. I detail the shock and anger they feel at the point of arrest. Then, I consider boys who grow up under policing that targets Latino men. These "sons of the system" often see parents deported. As adolescents, they start getting records themselves, which mark them as "criminals." Thus, they come of age amid longer-term trauma.

Chapter 2, "Locked Up and Broken Down," dives into U.S. detention and prison. I show how most men enter the system angry, trying to fight deportation. But lockup "messes with their minds." The verbal abuse and beatings reduce them to animals. Guards wield *time* as a threat. And, in prison, gangs rule with an iron fist. Over time, men break down. Some resign themselves to their fates. Others come to accept the institutional story that they are (or were) "bad."

Chapter 3, "Forced Out of Families," shows how these institutions ruin relationships. Detention and prison fray social ties. After removal, men also live far from their families. In Mexico, their trauma and habits of self-protection make it hard to relate to new people. Though men tend to be deeply invested in their loved ones in the U.S., carceral deportation strips them of places as patriarchs, providers, and caregivers—in short, of places as men.

Chapter 4, "No Place Called Home," frames deportation as more akin to displacement than to "return." In Mexico, deported men fall into limbo. Their institutional histories structure their movements, mapping U.S. carceral deportation onto Mexico's uneven political economy. The men most degraded by U.S. prisons find themselves stuck at the border. Meanwhile, those with more resources adopt a *strategic urbanism*, opting into Mexico City and its powerful economic and political institutions.

Chapter 5, "Banished," illustrates how men can end up on the precipice of humanity. After deportation, many face crisis. They distrust others. They identify as "American" but cannot reach the United States. Their social isolation leaves them vulnerable to Mexican cops and organized crime, especially at the border. They struggle to advocate for themselves. Exiled from work, family, and even their manhood, few have leverage to claim their own rights.

Chapter 6, "Reclaiming Removal," considers how some deportees forge new, bicultural identities, build communities, and reclaim deportation. I trace three paths to advocacy, the first two in Mexico City: grassroots organizing, acting as masculine businessmen, and joining organized crime. The chapter reveals the kinds of conditions that give life back to deportees, albeit not always in the fashion the U.S. might hope.

The conclusion makes a moral case against merging imprisonment and removal. These institutions assault men's humanity and increase their vulnerability. Punitive approaches to migrants and marginal men—locking them up and throwing them out—undermine not only their manhood but also their ability to show love. To remake this system, the U.S. and Mexico must replace carceral deportation with care.

1

———

Policed

*Acknowledgment: Camila Hernández Cruz helped me see how the criminal-
ization of Latino men like her brother "Ever" is arbitrary and begins from
childhood, prefiguring the story of this book.*

To the U.S. government, Everardo Hernández Cruz was a dangerous criminal. To
his sister, Camila, my student at UCSD, he was just her big brother, Ever, with
fogged-up glasses and a beanie askew on his head.

Unlike Camila, Ever was born in Mexico. Three weeks later, their father left for
Los Angeles. A couple years after that, their mother followed with Ever. The family
settled in a one-bedroom apartment near Hollywood, just above the 101 freeway.
There, Camila and another brother were born. For most of his childhood, Ever
thought that he, too, was born in the United States.

Then, he started getting arrested. Los Angeles police first stopped Ever when he
was 13. He was a good kid, he explained to Camila: "I wouldn't do drugs. I wouldn't
drink . . . I was never gang related, nothing." But Ever loved cars. Sometimes, he
went to the garage at night to sit in the seat of his father's old Honda, his hands
on the wheel. One evening mischief took over, and he got a mind to turn on the
car and go for a drive. A few blocks later, the sirens went on. Then handcuffs. Jail.

That time, the cops let him go. By their admission, he had "never, ever, ever
done anything wrong in your life." But now Ever had a record.

Over the next six years, Los Angeles police arrested Ever 18 times, almost
always for violations related to cars. Camila remembered that when she was a kid,
LAPD repeatedly searched the family's apartment. One night when she was eight,
she told me by email, cops knocked with no warrant and blew past her mother
(who spoke little English). They tore apart the family's one-bedroom home—
especially the living room, where Ever slept on the couch. Camila and her younger
brother cowered back under the bed. As soon as police shut the door, Camila ran
to her mother. Everything was on the floor. Her mother hunched over their broken
belongings, crying as she picked up the pieces.[1]

With each arrest, the cops got rougher and the punishments worse. Sometimes, they beat, insulted, or threatened Ever during arrest. Once, a judge gave him 960 hours of community service (six months of full-time work)—the most Ever's supervisor had ever seen in his life. Then, at 18, Ever landed in prison. When he was 23, even though he had legal permanent residency in the United States, the prison released him to ICE.

Ever got used to being treated like a criminal. He remembered that as a teen, "I'd go in and out of jail, like, all the time since it wasn't a violent crime or anything. Back then, no calls to get deported. It was just like, 'Stop doing that, stop doing that.' I'd just get beat up by the cops every now and then; it was like nothing." For Ever, arrests and abuse became constant, expected—like "nothing." He also grew cynical. Why *not* begin to steal cars?

Eventually, Ever began to think of *himself* as delinquent. He went on, "I can't blame other people for my mistakes, so I guess it's just me not making smart decisions, and I fucked up. . . . I was stealing cars, right? There wasn't like a real reason why I needed to do that. Like, I had a good job. I had two jobs, actually. I would work at a performance shop in the mornings, called Five Star Motorsports, and I was working in the afternoons at a valet parking. So, I had a good income. It was just like, I guess for the adrenaline rush or something. I don't know, like, it was dumb as hell." At 13, by all accounts, Ever was "a good kid." By 18, he was in prison, believing that *he* had done wrong.

During Ever's final arrest, the cops threatened his family. He described to Camila:

Dad calls me, "Hey, where you at? . . . Some officer is here at the house. He wants to speak to you." And I'm like "Oh, fuck." So, I was like, I could have just fled and not shown back at the house, but that was just gonna make me look more guilty, you know? . . . Unfortunately, the 300ZX car, I got it from a used car dealer with my dad, and my dad was my co-signer. And the car was under his name. So, when they raided the house, they started asking for all the stuff, like all the car parts and motors and transmissions, all the shit we had. And dad was getting my back like hard-core, like, "I got this receipt from the junk yard. I got this other thing from the junk yard."

But then there was a laptop in the trunk of that 300 which I had bought off some bum . . . And when they ran the serial number, it had been reported stolen, so the detective was like, "Dude, just tell me the truth, it was you that stole the car." And I was like, "No, I don't know what you're talking about, I want to speak to my lawyer." And he said, "Quit acting, it's time for you to accept guilt for the shit you've done." . . .

He's like, "OK, if you're gonna be in that position, I'll just tell you straight up, like, I know perfectly fine your dad has never stolen anything because in these 20-something years in the States, he only had one speeding ticket." And that was it, like for all them years. And it was like doing 70 on a 65 or something bullshit like that. No other record at all whatsoever. So, he's like, "I know your dad did not steal that computer. I believe you probably bought that off some guy. It would probably be just receiving stolen property, whatever, nothing big, but if you don't sincere yourself up with me right now and tell me the truth, I'm just gonna say that the computer was in that car, and that car is registered to your dad. So we're gonna take him in, and you know what it's been like—you know what it's like to go to jail and to strip butt-naked in front of like 50 other guys and cops and deputies looking into your fucking butthole and flashing the light in there and telling you to cough . . . You really want your dad to go through that?"

And I was like, "Fucking dickhead! . . . You motherfucker." I was not gonna let my dad go through that shit, you know? He didn't deserve it. I was like, "No. You know what? You're right. Yeah, fuck it." He was like, "Man up. Take responsibility for your own acts." He was like, "You know you've done wrong," I was like, "Yeah, I know."

And I just took the rap.

In insisting that Ever admit to his crime, cops also insisted he accept the identity they had *given him* as a criminal. To do this, they threatened his father—another innocent person. And they used his family (and love) as their leverage.

Ultimately, LAPD took Ever to Twin Towers Prison and later to Coalinga. Two years later, ICE stripped him of residency and removed him from the United States.

. . .

In the U.S. and Mexico, many people assume men "deserve" deportation. Even though first-generation immigrants commit crimes at lower rates than U.S. citizens, the media and politicians stereotype Latino men as violent "bad hombres" and gangsters.[2] These racialized, gendered narratives legitimate policing and the use of force on Latino migrants, especially men.

When Camila, her fellow students, and I interviewed deportees, we often heard echoes of Ever's story: of babies who lost their parents to U.S. immigration enforcement, of tween boys who got tagged by police despite "good behavior," of young men who learned about gangs in jail when they needed protection and got out only to face arrest again (and again). In case after case, police (mis)treatment had *made* these men into criminals.

This chapter traces how banishment begins. Long before deportation, police in the United States (re)shape men's sense of themselves and the law. As men encounter police and/or ICE, how do they contend with the institutional story that they are criminals, especially when—in the case of most deportees—they have not committed significant crimes?

Policing triggers removal. Most men enter the deportation system via arbitrary police stops that mark them as criminals.[3] As Elana Zilberg shows, zero tolerance policing in immigrant neighborhoods has helped *create* a population of immigrant "gangsters" through scapegoating, arrest, and building a paper trail of police stops—a record—well before the kids have committed a crime.[4] By labeling immigrant youngsters as "dangerous subjects" and using force against them, police undermine their families and friendships and make it harder for them to survive, let alone to feel and exercise agency.[5] There, gangs step in, offering young men physical protection and even a surrogate family.[6]

Through policing, deportation becomes part of Latino men's coming of age.[7] Immigrant boys grow up under a broad, multi-institutional system that labels young men of color "deviant" and deserving of incarceration and exclusion.[8] This web of punitive institutions begins with the child welfare system (CWS). Rather than protecting or providing for children, CWS polices poor families of color.[9] It sends struggling children to abusive, prisonlike group homes, fueling a pipeline to later arrest. In conjunction, zero tolerance policing punishes people for minor crimes, especially in poor, Black, and immigrant neighborhoods.[10] That is, child welfare workers, schools, families, the media, and police *treat* young men of color as criminals, regardless of what they actually do.[11] In the process, these institutions give young men records and drive them out of school and into the criminal justice system.[12]

Latinx children also inherit migration-related stress.[13] Those who grow up undocumented tend to feel hopeless. Despite the American Dream, they see little space for themselves to succeed in the United States.[14] Regardless of kids' legal status, they suffer when the U.S. removes their parents. Children who fear deportation or have parents deported tend to be poorer, sicker, and more emotionally troubled than children of U.S. citizens.[15] Still, scholars often focus on high achievers (or "DREAMers"), like the students who helped to research this book.[16] Researchers know less about what becomes of boys caught under the dual thumb of overpolicing and family separation.[17]

By dehumanizing Latino men and assaulting their families, we show, police begin the process of banishment. Policing debases men and their families in three central ways: first, arbitrary arrest, especially of men who have not committed crimes; second, intergenerational trauma, as boys watch their parents policed and deported; and third, the criminalization of Latino boys, through serial arrests that start as early as adolescence.

We could hear the effects of arrests and abuse in men's stories. When police stopped adults, independent of any crimes, their targets felt shocked. The arrests sparked a torrent of questions: why were police treating them as criminals, when they had lived with their heads down, staying away from trouble? Men lost their homes, their trust in the law, and their sense of themselves. They often felt rage.

Young men brought to the U.S. as children faced a longer, slower process of criminalization.[18] Often, police harassed, arrested, and/or deported their parents. The state then sent some boys into carceral "care." Boys' own first police stops were equally jarring. Yet for minors, a small infraction did not lead directly to deportation. Instead, it started a record. By the time a boy turned 18 (and could more easily be removed), police had often trolled him for years. Like Ever, such young men began to expect arrests and police abuse. Cut off from family and seeing little way out, some joined gangs or began to steal or sell drugs. In turn, cops frequently kept their most ruthless beatings—and harshest sentences—for members of gangs. I call these men "sons of the system."

THE PIPELINE TO DEPORTATION

Most deportations begin when migrants encounter police, often during minor traffic stops (failure to signal and the like) or stops on pretense (for instance, "the appearance of drunk driving" at nine o'clock in the morning). Police officers disproportionately target Latino men for such stops.[19] For undocumented immigrants, arrest has acute implications. A white U.S. citizen convicted of driving under the influence (DUI) might face community service or mandatory Alcoholics Anonymous meetings, but a migrant can lose his home, job, possessions, spouse, children, and friends. In EMIF, a representative survey, 68 percent of deportees who had been living in the U.S. for more than a year said their deportation began with a traffic incident.[20] Specifically, 35.5 percent were stopped in a routine traffic stop or at a checkpoint, 20 percent for a traffic infraction (an accident, driving without a license, etc.), and 12.4 percent for a DUI.[21] In the same survey, only 8.5 percent were arrested for a nontraffic crime.

In about 60 percent of all deportations, ICE takes custody of immigrants after they are arrested by local police or sheriffs (or occasionally, by the FBI). When police stop someone, ICE can request a "detainer," in which police or jails hold the person for 48 hours until ICE can pick them up. The details of how ICE and law enforcement collaborate vary by city and state.[22] Some cities block police from investigating a person's immigration status until *after* they are convicted of a crime. In many other cities, however, police turn immigrants over to ICE upon booking or even a stop, without any criminal action, trial, or conviction. In such locales, a broken taillight, an expired registration sticker, or a cop's racial bias can set a deportation in motion.[23] At the extreme, some city governments allow law enforcement to act *as* ICE officers, arresting people for immigration violations.

ICE or Customs and Border Patrol (CBP) can also stop migrants directly.[24] ICE agents may stop people almost anywhere in the United States to ask for proof of their immigration status, including in courthouses, trains, bus stations, traffic stops, homes, and workplaces.[25] Because ICE has only about 6,000 agents total, they rely on cooperative local police, sheriffs, and highway patrol. CBP agents, meanwhile, can operate within 100 miles of the U.S. border, including to stop people who have lived in the U.S. for years.

In addition, the U.S. government places virtually all unauthorized migrants convicted of crimes in removal proceedings as soon as they arrive in prison or jail (and many lawful permanent residents, too).[26] As of the 2010s, 100 percent of U.S. jails and prisons submitted inmates' fingerprints to ICE, under the Department of Homeland Security's Secure Communities and/or CAP programs. If ICE agents secure final orders of removal while someone is incarcerated, they deport that person directly from prison. However, if someone's immigration proceedings are incomplete (as is often the case), ICE transfers them to detention after release from prison.

Though the federal government claims deportation is about removing "criminal aliens," this term has no legal definition and is often applied to unauthorized immigrants regardless of criminal activity (note that being undocumented is an administrative, not a criminal offense). Indeed, the U.S. designates *any* undocumented entrant after January 2014 as a priority for "criminal" deportation. Lawful permanent residents (green card holders) are also subject to removal if they are convicted of any of a long list of federally designated "aggravated felonies," which includes virtually any violation that could result in a sentence of one year or more in prison.[27]

In theory, police and ICE target "wrongdoers" for removal; in practice, they primarily arrest men who have no criminal records. Less than half of all deportees have been convicted of crimes, and, of those, most have records of traffic violations, drug possession, or crossing the U.S.-Mexico border. Fewer than 1 in 10 have a record of violent crimes.[28] Nonetheless, more than half spend time in jail or prison before deportation, often *awaiting* a trial, with nearly 30 percent incarcerated for DUIs or traffic-related offenses.[29] ICE also detains people retroactively, after they have already served out a past violation.

THE SHOCK OF ARBITRARY ARREST

Many men in this study, especially those who migrated as adults, described their first arrest as a shock. They spoke of being pulled over on pretense or based on their looks. Police stopped one man for an improper lane switch. They arrested another for lacking a light on his license plate. When detailing these arrests, men often emphasized their meticulous, law-abiding behavior. They had worked hard, they insisted, and respected the law. Yet, officers refused to give them the benefit of the doubt. If migrants asked questions or offered to fix the problem, police would handcuff them or ask for their papers.[30] Such treatment felt racist and inhumane. For instance, Roberto told us about his 2017 arrest in Santa Ana, California. He was riding a bike without lights around dusk, but police pulled him over. Then, they began searching him for drugs. Finding none, the officers took him to the police station. There, off camera, they beat him and planted drugs in his shoe, giving him a criminal record—and grounds for removal.[31] Lautaro, a 41-year-old father of three arrested during a traffic stop, said officers also planted drugs on him and assaulted him. Holding a pen to his handcuffed hand, they then made him "sign" his own deportation orders.

Many respondents felt tricked by ICE or said ICE agents falsely posed as police. For instance, police would tell a man he was being released, only to open a door behind which an ICE van was waiting. Alejandro, for example, had been living in LA a little over five years when he got a DUI. He completed his community service and mandatory AA. A year later, armed men in jackets that said "Police" showed up at the apartment he shared with his sister. She directed them to the Jack in the Box where Alejandro worked as a cook. The authorities called ahead, asking Alejandro to fill out a five-minute survey. When he emerged from the kitchen in his apron, the "police" revealed they were ICE and would be taking him to detention, "to look at your information, to see if we can let you out or not." Ulises, too, was arrested by ICE agents dressed as police. He demurred, "They are mocking the law . . . they dress up to approach you as civil [officers], and then they arrive and they trick you!" Such men felt ridiculed.

In just a moment, arrest ripped men from their lives. The pain was immense. Often, when we met men in Tijuana's shelters—landing points for those just deported—they still felt stunned. Two days before UCSD student Pamela met José Luis in Tijuana, he had been working the blackberry fields of Oxnard, California. He stopped on the way to work to get gas. When he left the pump, an unmarked car lit up, pulled him over, and asked for his license. José Luis did not have one, so the officer took his fingerprints. Then, the computer turned up a record of his deportation seven years earlier. Pamela asked how he felt in that moment. José Luis replied:

> No, I mean, I felt traumatized. In the sense that you're going to work, and they stop you for nothing other than looking suspicious. Because they're looking for someone. I know that I was deported, and I understand that. But to stop me like that because I was Latino, it's racism. And yes, they were stopping purely Latinos. They also stopped Latino people while walking. I asked the immigration official, "Why are you only stopping Latinos?" And he says, "Because we're looking for someone who lives in the trailers. And we're looking at the people coming out of there." I told him, "But I didn't come out of there. I came out of the gas station." . . . "Yeah, but you were in the area." . . . I felt really bad. They stopped me out of nothing. I didn't commit a crime (*un error*).

José Luis felt angry not only about his removal but also that he was arrested for "nothing," by race, having never committed a crime. He cried as he spoke of his fear for his two young children and the hardship they'd face in his absence.

Until their arrests, many men like José Luis had gone out of their way to follow the letter of U.S. laws and demonstrate that they were "good."[32] They insisted that they drove under the speed limit and never drank, smoked, or used drugs. Still, police treated them like criminals. For these men, arrests made no sense. Once, they had believed their actions might earn them fair treatment. But arbitrary arrest stole their faith—in both the state and themselves.

Framed as felons, men clambered to defend their good names and their very humanity. In our conversations, they did this by building a counternarrative about the injustice of their arrests. For example, Leon was 19 and working as a gardener outside Las Vegas when police stopped him on his way home, leading—six months of detention later—to deportation. Over coffee in Mexico City, he said to Ana:

> I was coming from work, and when the policeman saw me pass, it was like he looked at me on my bike. I had my bike and my work clothes on and all, and he thought I was going around selling drugs or I don't know what. And he stopped me because he said I looked suspicious. So, he stops me and asks for my papers, and in a minute, he took me. Since I didn't have my documents with me, he said, "I have to take you in because I don't know who you are, and I need to know where you're from." So, with that excuse they took me to the jail. They transferred me to *la migra* [ICE], and *la migra* has you there imprisoned in a way that—they had me locked up for nothing because they didn't get me on anything, only for being illegal. But they got me in a racist zone—Henderson. Have you ever been there? Henderson is on the edge of the city of Las Vegas, and there are a lot of gringos [white people] over there, and there's one of those jails . . . If I was working hard to earn an honorable living, why did they arrest me? So, I see it as an injustice. And I told that to the judge, but he didn't listen.

The contrast was stark: Leon insisted he had been "honorable," worked hard, and done nothing wrong. Yet police acted like he had committed a crime. Leon believed the treatment was driven by racism.

Others thought cops tagged Latinos as criminals to block them from formal inclusion. Maximiliano, a 45-year-old dad with three children, was stunned at the feeling of having no recourse upon his arrest:

> I was leaving my apartment, my home. I was heading to work. I had my lunch bag. I put my lunch in the car, I got in the car, and I turned it on to heat up so I could go. And when I was about to drive out of the parking lot, a car pulled up on my right-hand side . . . the police, they said, right? . . . They didn't have jackets on that were from ICE; they just said, police. What could I do? They are doing an injustice. They're violating people's rights because we simply don't have any crime. . . . And we can't fix our papers because they are marking us, marking us [as criminals] for the rest of our lives. And that's how it will always be, wherever you are . . . We regret it, we agitate, we want to cry. We are grown men, and we want to cry from emotion, because we lose our children there, too.

As Maximiliano emphasized, arrests drove men into the hands of ICE and labeled them undeserving ("for the rest of our lives"). The emotional impact was stark. So were the practical implications of having a record.

Berto, a 40-year-old father who'd lived in LA, felt branded as well. After stopping him for a traffic ticket, LA police—who "supposedly don't work with immigration [control]"—told Berto he could go, and then—at the exit—released him to ICE. Berto felt wronged, explaining that though he protested, "The [U.S.] government doesn't give a crap, and they do it . . . What can I do, if for them what they want is to stain you (*mancharte*), so that later they have a justification that 'look, here is the guy we're looking for.'" To men like Berto and Maximiliano, it appeared that police were stopping people to *create* a record that led to expulsion. Questioning their removal, men insisted that they were innocent and U.S. police were unjust.

SONS OF THE SYSTEM

For respondents brought to the U.S. as children, whom I call "sons of the system," policing was less a sudden shock than an integral part of coming of age. These immigrant youth faced dual childhood traumas: (1) the mistreatment, arrest, and/or deportation of their parents and (2) their own arrests, typically starting with minor infractions in adolescence. Like Ever, these boys grew up in (that is, they were "sons of") a system that felt designed to give them a criminal record, making them easier to lock up and banish.

Policing shaped boys' formative years and attitudes toward the law. As Latino young men got arrested multiple times, they grew accustomed to police mistreatment. Some came to accept the idea that they had done wrong. In such cases, prison and deportation came as the capstone of a long-term, intergenerational process of criminalization.[33]

When Police Take Your Parents

In the 1990s and 2000s, many immigrant children grew up without one or both parents, thanks to U.S. immigration enforcement.[34] Sometimes, their parents did not have enough money to pay multiple smugglers or were afraid to cross the border with children, so they migrated and left their children behind. Back in Mexico, their sons and daughters were vulnerable to physical or sexual abuse or neglect by other adults. Other times parents split, one taking the children over the border while the other remained, unable to cross. In still other cases, after the children were in the U.S., the state came into their families, arresting and/or deporting one or both parents. Even when children were spared physical distance, the fear of deportation could force immigrant parents to take low-wage jobs that required long hours and kept them away from their kids.

Oscar's youth was marked by such separation. First, his father left the family in Mexico and moved to LA. Then, he sent for four-year-old Oscar. Oscar's first memory was of tears streaming down his face, as a car took him from his mother forever, toward his dad in the United States. Once Oscar arrived in Los Angeles, he wondered what he was doing there, while his mom stayed in Mexico. He wished desperately that he could be back home and poor, rather than have his family split up. When Oscar was 12, his dad gave up on the U.S. (and on Oscar)—returning to Mexico without his son. With no mom or dad, Oscar wanted to study, but he was hungry. So, he began to steal food. A year later, he was arrested for the first time. From then on, he cycled in and out of juvenile detention and group homes, just making do.

Edgardo remembered a similar longing. When Edgardo was six, his father left him behind in Mexico. Edgardo bounced around between houses until, at 12 and missing his family, he followed his dad north. It took Edgardo 22 tries to get through the desert. By the time Edgardo got to Anaheim, California, his father had remarried. His new wife kicked Edgardo out of the house. Edgardo was crushed. To cope, he became addicted to methamphetamines, leading to his deportation.

Even if children lived with their parents, undocumented adults often worked 12-to-14-hour days, nights, or weekends, just to pay rent and buy food. Without legal status, they struggled to find better jobs.[35] The effect was unintended neglect. When Gaspar was 6, his parents moved him to Compton, California. They shared beds, food, and bathrooms with 14 members of their extended family. Gaspar remembered, "My mom and dad worked literally the whole day. I never had an opportunity to see them." To fill the gap, Gaspar joined a gang. He went on, "Being in the gang—or my 'family,' as I said—they took care of me. They taught me; they protected me. They showed me around the city . . . That's where I tried marijuana for the first time, and it was, 'Try this because this is for grown-ups; this is for men.' So, without a parental figure at home, well, what could happen, right?" As sociologist María Rendón shows in her study of Latino young men in LA, gangs give boys like Gaspar protection and space to belong—even as they also expose them to violence or drugs.[36]

Finally, some boys had parents deported, setting the stage for their own removals. Manny is one example. His parents brought him to Chicago when he was a baby, settling in a neighborhood rife with gang and police violence. The threat of deportation loomed over them, too. Manny did well in school. He had spiky gelled hair and a giant smile that made him seem innocent. Yet he was bullied by both teachers and other children. When that happened, as he put it, "I couldn't do nothing. Because, you know, if I told the authorities then they would investigate, and I didn't want my parents to get deported." Manny developed anxiety. At 13, he was close to earning a scholarship to private high school when his dad got arrested, imprisoned, and deported. He reflected, "When my father got deported, I was in school . . . I guess that was the hardest thing, you know, going to prison, seeing my dad in prison and all that . . . Once my father was deported then it was just me and my mom, and that was even harder." The deportation left Manny angry and cynical. It changed his behavior and his feelings about the police. Shaking with nerves, he recalled:

> That made me more aggressive, definitely, because—I mean, my father is one to cause trouble, too, but it didn't make sense that he was deported for that reason. So, for me, it did anger me, because I mean, one, I didn't have a father figure around. And you know, seeing the way my people are being treated, also, that made me upset. It's not like I would lash out at the cops or anything, but . . . To be honest, I think that if my father was never deported or anything, I wouldn't be here [in Mexico]. I would still be over there. I would still be in school and everything. So that definitely changed how my life has been.

Manny did not join a gang. But he gave up on trying in school. And his anger ultimately got him in trouble. Eventually, ICE deported him, too.

Andre's dad's deportation led to the loss of their home, to his mother's return to Mexico, and to Andre taking charge of his two younger siblings at 22. In a blend of Spanish and English, Andre spoke of how they "lost everything":

El chiste (the thing/the joke) is that his work permit expired, and . . . to renew it they were really asking for a lot, and my dad he was like, "I can't afford it right now," so he kind of put it off. But . . . in the end, they found him and deported him. . . . With him gone, we pretty much lost everything: we lost the house, and we had nowhere to go. . . . I was living with them, with mom and dad . . . Well, my mom, in a couple months she went back—she just went back with my dad. And then it was just us three [kids] . . . That just split up everything, and so after that, I mean, it affected us all, I don't know, maybe me more than anybody. . . . I was really upset and mad at the situation . . . and I started to drink a lot. I don't know, I just went a little bit out of control. And in the end, before I know it, that's where it gets a little bit worse for me. What do you think? In the end, I landed in prison.

Traumatized by the loss in his family, Andre lost his way emotionally. He started drinking. Then, though he refused to say why, he spent nine years in prison. In the process he lost touch with his own young child, extending the cycle of separation.

Sometimes, the state also took migrant children away from their parents and placed them in group homes or foster care—institutions known to reproduce carceral violence.[37] Goyo, brought to the U.S. as an infant, was a toddler when a neighbor called child welfare services on his mother, triggering his family's separation. When UCSD student Jasmin asked why the government placed Goyo in foster care, he replied:

[My mother] came from Mexico with four kids, and she couldn't make it. She couldn't make it. The story I was told was that a neighbor, or somebody, called child services on us. But I don't know the true story, and [my mom] wasn't mistreating us. And I guess they told them that we weren't being fed properly, that we weren't being clothed properly, that we didn't have proper nutrition, and that "she can't support them." And you know, she tried . . . I don't remember anything because I was really young. But from what I was told, we were living in a garage in East LA and that's—it was just a garage. It was us four and her. And yeah, I guess that we were living in a garage, and, well, you can imagine what that would be like. And she was trying to feed us, and I remember that it was *frijoles* (beans). I think I was probably three or four at the time . . . when child services took us away.

Goyo then lived in nearly a dozen foster homes. Foster care, he shared, "It changes you. It separates you from reality. It takes you away from a stable home. . . . You get separated from your brothers, from your mom, from your other siblings." The loneliness also led Goyo into petty crime, leaving him vulnerable to police. He was sent to juvenile detention at the age of 13.

Another young man, Leo, was taken from his parents at age 11, after his school discovered his father was beating the children. Leo remembered, "They called us into the [school] office and checked all of us. They took hella pictures of us, made us turn around and everything. Next thing you know, they got my brother from elementary, you know. I was like, 'Damn, this thing is serious.' Next thing you know, me and my brother were in the back of a social service car. I was like, 'What the hell? What the fuck did we do?'"

Law enforcement's response made Leo feel like *he* was the one being punished. He went on, "They took us to a group home, or foster home, I don't know, but I was like, 'This shit is wack.' I wanted to be home. I didn't want to have a fucking stranger telling me when to go to bed or what to do. Oh, hell nah! I was out." Leo ran away. Within two years, he joined a gang. At 14, police stopped him and sent him to juvenile detention, where he spent the bulk of his teenage years. At 18, he landed in prison. He was deported from there. The pretense of care, already thin, ended the moment he reached adolescence—funneling him into punitive institutions.

Raised on Policing: The Criminalization of Migrant Boys

Respondents brought to the U.S. as children grew up in contexts of everyday "illegality," in which police treated them and their families, neighbors, and friends as criminals.[38] These boys watched police stop, detain, or mistreat their parents for no reason other than the color of their skin. They saw officers plant drugs in people's cars or hit them in the face unprovoked. Several came to believe that U.S. police were bored, sadistic, or both.

Police also targeted Latino boys as young as age 10. They often assumed such boys were in gangs or used drugs. They stopped teens for small offenses like graffiti, a fight on the street, loitering in the wrong place, or borrowing a parent's car without asking. The stops added up. Some young men went from institution to institution, from foster care to juvenile detention and ultimately to prison. In the process, most endured verbal and physical abuse.

These experiences made young men feel hopeless, cynical, angry, and distrustful of the law. Some felt impotent. Others expressed defiance, shouting or striking back at police—which typically led to further arrests and beatings. Eventually, some came to think of themselves as criminals, too, whose "choices" had led them to prison.

Ever is one example. Though Ever had U.S. residency, he started getting arrested for small violations. After that first evening joy ride, he got stopped for fighting, street racing, and shoplifting car parts. Casually, he told Camila that cops often beat and threatened him during arrest, just as they would eventually threaten his family.

Manny—who was 13 when his dad was deported—had a similar story. Looking back, Manny attributed his distrust for authority to seeing police abusing his parents: "There was cops that harassed my parents, and I saw that . . . One time they pulled over my father, and they both had seatbelts. And we had insurance, too. But it was a white cop, and he punched [my dad] to see if he would react . . . I mean, they saw my dad as maybe he could have been [gang-] affiliated, so they just wanted to provoke him to cause him to do something, but he didn't do nothing."

Manny felt constantly under threat. He was surrounded by police, on the streets and even inside his school, which hired cops to enforce "security" given the neighborhood's gangs. These police began to stop Manny as well. He remembered his first arrest:

> A fight broke out, and I was defending my friends, but then they arrested us. And the officer arrested us because they were white cops, and we were all Mexicans. They pushed us hard to the ground and everything. But I mean, it wasn't—I kind of understand because they were trying to protect themselves, but also, they were racist. But, I mean, it was something that I was used to by then, you know? Seeing cops throwing swings at us, you know, calling us "wetbacks" and all that, so it wasn't nothing out of the norm for me at that point.

Though it was his first arrest, Manny already viewed beatings and racial slurs as "the norm." After a few more arrests, police turned Manny over to ICE. He was 17. The cops said he could either go to prison ("they were gonna charge me with something that was clearly not right") or sign off on his own deportation. He became one of the few in our study deported as a minor.

Growing up in Johnson County, Kansas, Dylan remembered hearing people yell from their cars at his family, "Go back to Mexico!" or "Learn to speak English!" (This, he said, "was pretty funny, 'cause my English is perfect.") He painted the scene for Ana:

> I believe it is the third-richest county in the United States, so there's a lot of very snobby people there. They tend to look at Mexicans like they're just "help," like you're not humans; you're just here to clean their houses or do whatever. . . . And then the other ones, they looked at us like we were murderers and rapists and drug dealers and all this other stuff. I remember one time I was just hanging out with my friend, and we were sitting in front of this home [on the] porch. We skipped school, and next thing we know, all of a sudden, three sheriffs' cars are storming into this apartment complex. They got out of the cars with their rifles and shotguns, put us down on the ground, and asked us, "What are you doing? Put your hands behind your head!" . . . no reason whatsoever.

Ana invited him to continue:

> Well, from there, I mean, we got an attitude with them. They tried to arrest us. We told them we didn't do nothing, "We're right here hanging out in front of my friend's house, we're not doing anything illegal, we're not drinking, we're not smoking, we're not doing nothing. We were literally just hanging out." And eventually they just let us go. . . . They were trying to get information from us about gang members, but we weren't willing to tell them anything. So that was one bad experience—well, one of many. But other times it's just, pretty much . . . most of the times I got in problems with the police was usually over small things.

Dylan was first arrested when he was 11, for spray-painting. After that, "It was really mostly just petty things at first, just like petty theft, a few fights here and there." Dylan began to lose respect for authority, to see the law as unfair. Defiant, he joined the Sureños gang. He explained, "Once I got older, that's when I started getting bolder . . . I ended up getting involved in the gangs, and it just became a snowball effect. One thing led to another until eventually I ended up going to prison." The metaphor of a "snowball" was apt: policed for everyday actions, Dylan collected a record. When he was 17, police caught him robbing a house, tried him as an adult, and sent him to five years in prison. Upon release, ICE deported him. He had recently turned 22.

THE PATH INTO CRIME

For many young immigrant men, repeated arrests led *into* a cycle of crime that ended in brutality, imprisonment, and, ultimately, removal to Mexico. Of the people we met who had spent time in prison, almost all were brought to the U.S. as minors. Arrested as adolescents, most were incarcerated by the time they were 20. We argue that their criminal histories were products of U.S. policing and immigration enforcement.

Past scholars have shown how being undocumented can make young people feel hopeless, though they say less about how this lack of hope shapes interactions with the police.[39] We learned that as teens got caught in the criminal justice system, they grew cynical and angry. They came to expect to be beaten by the police and believe they could not get out. Some gave up on school or on trying to "be good." Others resisted arrest or berated police, leading to further clashes and spirals of violence. In search of protection and solidarity, some turned to the "blood brothers" they found in gangs.

After a lifetime of experiencing police abuse, Ismael told us, at some point, "I just stopped giving a fuck." Ismael had thick glasses, wide dark eyes, and the word "Chicago" tattooed across his arm, in honor of the place he was raised. Now 26, Ismael told Ana he'd grown up with a single mother, who was just 14 when she had him and had fled the Mexican family that sexually abused them both. She brought Ismael over the border when he was 3. He was always an excellent student, joining the debate team and hoping to go to college. But watching police mistreat his mother added up. He reflected in English:

> I was never like the type that, you know, that was looking for trouble. I guess I was always seen as the good kid . . . until one day when we were—it was me, my mom, and my stepdad. My mother was pregnant, and she was driving. She didn't have a license at the time. . . . We got stopped by the police, and I felt the tension as soon as the officer came to my mom's window. My mom doesn't have the best English. She has a very thick accent. Although she can communicate in English, she's not . . . you can tell right away she's not a U.S. citizen. That's what the police officer said, "You know, you have a very thick accent. You're not a citizen, are you?" And my mom right away was like, "That's none of your business. What did I do? Why did you pull us over?" and stuff like that. You know, my mom was always well educated in that fact, but he

kept on pushing the issue, like, "You guys aren't from here." I mean, just like, really racist, you know? And this is probably when I was like 14, 15, that was really like my first brush with the law. That really set the tone, you know? . . .

The cruisers always say, "To serve and protect," but I mean, what are you really protecting if you're intimidating other individuals? . . . So, I just ended up having a lot of anger toward the police. Any time I would see them or any interaction . . . I was just being aggressive, even though I'm not like that, you know? . . . I always saw them as the enemy just because of that. And I mean, that's just one of many instances, many situations . . . When I would be with my white friends, nothing would happen. We'd be like at two, three, four in the morning, out drinking or just doing whatever, and just because I was with [white kids], like we would even get rides home from the police, or they would take us to the police station and call our parents or whatever. And I would see [the other kids'] parents come, and they would be okay. They wouldn't see them as—they wouldn't treat them as they treated my parents and me. And that just kept adding on to, like, a little basket of hatred and just anger at them.

By the time Ismael was arrested for drinking and driving, he was primed to resist.

That year, Ismael was slated to go to Washington, DC, with the school's debate team. Then, he learned that he was undocumented. He began to give up on "following the rules." He went on:

After that it was a turning point in my life where I was like, "You know what? If I don't have the same privileges as these other kids do, then I'm gonna find my own way, and I'm not gonna listen to anybody or anything. Because if these rules don't apply to me or I'm not able to take advantage of the same options these kids have, then what's the point of me being able to have the same goals as them? What's the point of me setting goals if I'm not gonna be able to reach them?"

And I think that's when I just stopped giving a fuck, like I just stopped caring about what was going on around my life. And I started like, "If I'm not gonna able to go to college because I'm gonna have to pay out of my pocket, then what's the point of me putting so much effort into school? So, you know what? I'm just gonna sell drugs to get some money."

At that point, Ismael recalled, he got caught in a criminal case "with some people that I shouldn't have been hanging around with." It began a cascade of arrests, leading to his deportation.

When the law got me, it's like I couldn't escape from them. I was very young at the time, and I wasn't aware that I could go to jail or prison and get deported . . . I ended up getting caught up in the case, and from then on it was like case after case, and I didn't have the—I guess I didn't have that stopping point in my life where I finally said to myself, "It's done, don't do this anymore." The pain never outweighed the pleasure of having my own things. Because I always had it in my mind, "If I'm not going to be able to get a degree" or whatever . . . I just closed my mind, and . . . my self-esteem just plummeted. So finally, I ended up getting caught—my last case I had was just a DUI, but because I didn't have a state license it was an aggravated DUI.

Knowingly driving a vehicle while intoxicated and not able to present a valid driver's license is, it upgrades to a felony.

Ismael's story reveals how police abuse, the hopelessness of being undocumented, and minor arrests can trigger incredible anger. Going "his own way" helped Ismael feel some sense of control. He could exercise agency, if only to reject U.S. government rules. Defiant responses like his can drive young men into criminal actions, leading to further policing, incarceration, and deportation. But this path into crime begins in state agents' mistreatment.

Gangs as Surrogate Family

Parental deportation, foster care, and parents' de facto absence due to grueling jobs also create a love vacuum. When young men feel isolated, they may seek belonging in gangs.[40] For some, gangs feel like the *only* protection left. Gangs also let members assert masculinity and forge social bonds.

In mixed-status families like Ever and Camila's, the parents were often gone. As Ever put it, "Dad used to work like a slave. He would get up at 5:00 a.m., 6:00 a.m. and go to work, and he [wouldn't] come home till like one or two of the *madrugada* (early morning) tired as fuck, dead as fuck." The kids had to fend for themselves.

Oscar Morales, mentioned earlier, had been taken to live with his father in California at the age of 4. When Oscar's dad returned to Mexico, his undocumented grandmother took him in. To pay the rent, she had to work three jobs. She had a place in MacArthur Park, a neighborhood in LA famous for its secondhand stores and Latinx migrants selling cut-up fruit on the street. But she was hardly around. So, Oscar—then 12—went looking for family and something to eat. Within a year, he had joined a gang. Among the boys on the street, Oscar remembered, "We had like this little family kind of connection, because we told each other, 'Regardless of what we do or how bad it seems, we are family.' And we showed each other that kind of little bond. Because at the end of the day there were times when we didn't have food, so one of us would go and [steal some] . . . or joke around and bring us back to life."

A few years later, Oscar's grandmother had a stroke. With no biological family left, Oscar bounced between group homes and the street. He began selling drugs. By 18, he was in prison.

David, raised in the LA projects, described joining gangs as part of the life course for kids like him: "In the housing projects, if you're not a homeboy then you're not accepted . . . Growing up in the projects with your peers you become a gang member, and you have to do things that you don't want, you know? Like getting high. I got high when I was eight years old . . . You get drunk, and then you fight, and then the older ones give you like $5 to beat each other up." As a teen, David got into crack cocaine. Police arrested him for armed robbery (among other charges), and he spent 25 years in prison.

Gaspar turned to gangs as he struggled to fit into the United States. Brought to the U.S. at 6, Gaspar missed his friends, his school, and his neighbors in Mexico. In his new home in Compton, California ("a neighborhood that's, well, ugly—really barrio"), he shared "my bed, my food, the bathroom, with people I had never seen in my life." Gaspar's parents worked all day long. Then, in middle school, he met "kids my age who had $100 in their pocket"—more than his dad could make in a day. So, he started to join the gangs. He remembered:

> Without a parental figure at home, well, what could happen, right? I tried marijuana, alcohol, drugs, cocaine, and I liked it. It's like a little spiral in which you think you can get out, but it's like quicksand. . . . I would have $200 a day in my bag, right? A child of 10, 12 years old . . . As a child they can't put you in jail, so there are a lot of stores, often on the corner of the streets, and they taught me to sell methamphetamine, cocaine, marijuana, everything was there. We would put it under our tongue in bags, and people would come with their $5, $10, $15, and you'd act like you were shaking hands . . . I was a middle school kid that had the best pair of sneakers in the whole school. I could go where I wanted, and people respected me . . . I knew that I was doing something bad, but I liked coming and leaving those $200 dollars where my dad kept his money, and that he didn't know how they had gotten there . . . I saw how [drugs and gangs] killed a lot of my friends, [I'm] going to their burials. And instead of feeling pain, I felt angry. It was, "If you killed one of my guys, I'm going to go kill three of yours." You enter a spiral that never ends.

On one hand, the gang promised Gaspar respect. It offered belonging (a "family") and money to help his hardworking parents. At the same time, it sucked him in. He watched his friends die. When Gaspar's mother found a gun in his backpack, she cried and cried, repeating, "It's my fault. It's my fault for not being with you." That, he said, was the moment that really broke him.

The spiral of crime also led to greater police brutality. Cops seemed to store up their worst abuse for the boys raised under their watch. They would beat the daylight out of Gaspar and his friends or throw them in the segregation unit (isolation) when they were caught. Eventually, they arrested Gaspar on a drug pickup in Atlanta:

> I was with a friend, and two sheriffs came behind us—[state] marshals, in fact, which are like police above the sheriff. . . And we knew they were following us, and well, they killed my friend. . . . They shot him . . . Literally, they came and started to shoot at me, then all I could do was accelerate the car as hard as I could. We lost them. There are a lot of interstate highways there, and so I turned off onto the side streets, wherever I could. But it's like here [in Mexico City], if you're in a neighborhood [of a rival gang], you can't go . . . So, three marshals were following us, three police cars, like six, seven police in there shooting at us, and I crashed into a corner . . . The marshals . . . found a kilo of marijuana, cocaine (I don't remember how much it was), a revolver, and a shotgun in my car . . . They threw me to the ground. They smashed my head into the concrete, literally. I didn't know what was happening anymore. And

> I ended up beaten to a pulp. And the next memory I have, when I come to, is being detained. My mom looking at me, crying behind the glass.

During his trial, Gaspar remembered, police blamed a rival gang for the murder. Yet in his mind, he was at fault: "I don't consider it racism, because I knew what I was doing, and when a police officer gives you an order in the United States, you have to follow it." Broken by the system, Gaspar internalized the logic that in the United States one must defer to law enforcement, however perverse police actions.

Gaspar had been brutally beaten and seen his friend killed. The deeper the criminal record, it seemed, the more violent the police abuse. Stripping men of their bodily integrity, police brutality marked them as less than human.

CONCLUSION

The process of banishment starts with policing.

Often, the public assumes that police find and filter out those who are "already" criminals. Even observers who admit that a low percentage of deportees have been convicted of crimes sometimes insist that *some* of them really *are* hardened criminals. As Randol Contreras notes in his analysis of drug gangs, it is common to fall into individualistic reasoning and assume that men convicted of crimes (and here: deportees) are evil or sociopathic.[41] This chapter reframes such thinking.

I show how policing *makes* migrant men into criminals. Cops regularly stop Latino men on happenstance, pretense, or for minor violations—like driving without a light on the license plate. Police also initiate violence early in the lives of immigrant boys. These encounters funnel men into jail, establishing the criminal records that eventually get them removed.

Law enforcement also creates the conditions of intergenerational violence, cynicism, and family fragmentation that drive some teen boys into crime. U.S. immigration enforcement fractures families, and boys grow up mistreated by the police. In such contexts, their only recourse may be to reject the law. Often, the most apparently "hardened criminals" are young men like Ever, Gaspar, and Manny—raised without parents and locked up as teens, as police encounters branded them deserving of violence.

Police are the first of multiple U.S. state institutions that use outright brutality to strip migrant men of their agency, dignity, and manhood. Policing in migrant neighborhoods marks Latino men as subhuman, often despite their attempts to be "good." It also erodes their close social ties, from childhood on. Some men, especially those who were not raised in highly policed urban neighborhoods, find these encounters abrupt and shocking. If men are first arrested as adults (over 18), they are likely to be deported directly. For others, especially those raised fearing U.S. police, the impacts of criminalization draw out over time.

Contemporary deportation also targets a generation of children raised amid family separation. Immigrant boys (and girls) grow up with the trauma of parental arrest, deportation, de facto absence, and inability to cross the U.S.-Mexico border.[42] These practices extend decades of racist immigration enforcement, forcible separation of families, and state violence.[43] Watching parents deported, policed, and exploited makes kids feel despondent, eroding their trust in the law. Some children normalize police brutality. Others grow angry at the police or give up on following rules. For some, the clearest path to belonging and agency comes through joining a gang.

On reaching adolescence, Latino teens become police targets themselves. Many get criminal records from the moment they are no longer children—prefiguring their incarceration at age 18 or 19, and ultimately their removal. The U.S. rarely deports minors, so those arrested before age 18 remain in the country and often face further arrests. In turn, police tend to reserve their most brutal abuse for those they've arrested multiple times.

Beginning with police, sheriffs, and child welfare services, the carceral deportation system weaves together a range of state institutions that dehumanize Latino men. These institutions extend penal treatment (of some men as animals) beyond the walls of prisons and jails. Yet rather than inducing self-regulation or taking the "light touch" that theorist Michel Foucault predicted, they tend to rely on force.[44] Often, the men pushed deepest into this system—who spend years in prison and even in solitary confinement—are its very own sons: raised by the dual fists of policing and deportation.

2

Locked Up and Broken Down

Acknowledgment: For our research team, men's harrowing descriptions of detention and prison challenged the limits of "justice." In winter 2019, we spent many emotional meetings talking about how to honor the abuses the interviewees had endured. Early on, it became clear that imprisonment and detention were at the crux of the deportation experience. Later, Ana López Ricoy did important work on this theme, asking in-depth questions in more than 50 interviews and coding all the data to help us better assess the impacts of human caging. I am grateful to students for helping me see the grievous weight on men of being locked up.

In immigration detention, Fernando informed Camila, "They treat you like a cockroach."

Fernando, a friend of Ever, was 25, just deported, and trying to get back to his family in the U.S. when Customs and Border Patrol detained him in the Arizona desert. Though Fernando attempted to run, agents knocked him out with a shock gun. He remembered, "They threw us in dog cages, and they drove really ugly, jumping over the speed bumps, and it beat me up really badly."

Once Fernando got to detention, guards locked him up in what he called "the kennels." Speaking only in English, guards beat the migrants with sticks if they did not understand or reply.

How do migrants make sense of such treatment—or even endure?

Before removal, the U.S. sends immigrants into detention. Roughly 40 percent also spend time in prison or jail. Technically, prison is punitive, and immigration detention is not. They work under different bodies of law. Yet, the two institutions share ideologies, processes, and even buildings.[1] They also use the same techniques of control and dehumanization. Therefore, I frame immigration detention, jail, and prison as interlocked arms of the U.S. carceral system.

In U.S. prisons and ICE detention, migrants endure humiliation, verbal threats, and widespread discretionary violence, above and beyond the scope of their punishments or the law.[2] These facilities regularly deny men's basic needs like food, medicine, water, hygiene, and sleep. Both prisons and detention centers use solitary confinement, a known form of torture.[3] The people in charge also practice psychological warfare, lying to inmates, playing with their senses of space and time, and encouraging men to blame themselves for abuse. Faith, NGO, and government agencies at these facilities also push men to "redeem themselves" by taking responsibility for their actions, adopting strict discipline, and/or turning to God.[4] In prison, guards sometimes wreak the most havoc by stepping out of the way, leaving rival gangs to set and enforce "the rules." Inmates must kill or be killed.

Prisons exemplify social death.[5] That is, like slave plantations or colonial powers, prisons cast their targets out of society, suspend their rights, and attack their bodies and self-esteem.[6] Flirting with full-on erasure, these spaces of violence at once epitomize the law and operate outside of it.[7] For prisoners, the conditions can feel like a "living death."[8] Stripped of rights and punished beyond the bounds of the law, inmates experience "social disintegration." That is, as scholars Keramet Reiter and Susan Coutin put it, "Ties to others are cut off and prior identities stripped away, with devastating consequences for individuals' senses of self."[9] The incarcerated find themselves in mental havoc, unable to understand the world.[10]

For migrants, such violence has double consequences. Through dehumanizing treatment, U.S. carceral institutions also compel them to give up their rights to a trial and acquiesce in their own deportations. Removal comes as a second punishment: the loss of their U.S.-based lives.

This penal system was built on the premise of deterrence. The logic holds that when states put people in cages, they "learn their lesson," whether to avoid crime or refrain from crossing the border.[11] Supposedly, prisoners also serve as examples to others, persuading would-be migrants to obey the law or stay back in Mexico. This penal logic also assumes that prisoners interpret their *own* acts as crimes and their caging as proportionate punishment. Yet, evidence shows that deterrence rarely works, especially in the case of immigration detention.[12] Nor do most inmates consider imprisonment just. Instead, like most U.S. prisoners, the men we met condemned U.S. carceral practices as violations of human dignity—unfair by even the state's own standards of treatment.

In this chapter, I explore how getting locked up before deportation changes men's psyches, shaping their sense of themselves and the law. I show how prison, jail, and detention wear people down emotionally, producing crosscutting despair. Men we interviewed described going crazy, breaking down, or losing it. They began to ask not only "Am I part of the United States?" (as one might expect of a migrant) but also, "Am I human?" and "Am I a man?" The treatment in such facilities, they often insisted, was more fit for bugs, pigs, or dogs.

The torment made men feel powerless, eroding their will to fight.

Men also sought ways to cope. Yet their strategies varied by the facility and the time spent locked up. Their reactions also tied back to their histories of policing, with men detained after first arrest expressing most shock (and anger) while those criminalized in youth had to struggle just to survive.

Those who spent less time detained were often *defiant*. They refused to accept mistreatment or sign off on their own deportations. The longer men spent in cages, however, the more they *resigned* themselves to abuse by the carceral state. They began to believe that violence was "just how it is." After years in prison, men often felt *broken*. They struggled to keep a hold on reality and simply to stay alive. Some came to believe that they, themselves, were to blame. Few imagined a future aside from removal; for them, deportation came as relief.

TECHNIQUES OF DEHUMANIZATION

Though few deportees are convicted of serious crimes, all face carceral deportation. That is, before removal, they spend time in prison, jail, detention, or some combination thereof. While officially administrative, U.S. detention centers look and feel like prisons, with bars, cells, guards, and barbed wire fences. Most of the facilities *used to be* prisons or jails. Unsurprisingly, participants often referred to both interchangeably as *cárceles* (jails) or *prisión* (prison).

Conditions in U.S. detention and prison routinely violate government standards of treatment.[13] Copious scholarship and the accounts of men in this study outline a set of practices that leave men physically and mentally broken: (1) deprivation of food, medicine, hygiene, and sleep; (2) psychological warfare, including distortions of time and space, deceit, gaslighting, and solitary confinement; (3) verbal and physical assaults; and (4) ceding control to gangs, especially in prison.

Deprivation

Respondents reported that ICE detention centers and U.S. prisons were frigid and filthy. They frequently went without toilet paper or access to showers, and fewer than half had access to private toilets. Many wore the same clothes for days or weeks at a time. These reports are verified elsewhere: in one survey of more than 600 migrants detained in the U.S. in 2019, four out of five could not shower, clean themselves up, or brush their teeth; up to 85 percent reported insufficient food or water, spoiled food, or dirty or foul-tasting water; and 85 percent reported issues related to sleep, such as having to sleep on the floor or having the lights on 24 hours a day.[14] Often, their cells had no windows, and facilities blasted cold air.

In the words of one interviewee, "The conditions were really bad. The showers, they were really moldy. They had flies coming out of the drain. And, well, it smelled bad. We didn't get to go outside and see the sunlight at all. It was 24 hours inside. . . . There weren't any windows; it was all concrete. And the guards, they were mean . . . They talked to you like you're an animal or something. They slammed the doors really hard, like just to annoy you."

The institutions also left men hungry, malnourished, and sick. "You're hungry as soon as you eat," one respondent remembered. "They give you three sandwiches [a day], one in the morning, one in the afternoon, and one at night, and a child's juice [box], but the sandwich is white bread and bologna . . . There is your food." Other times, guards withheld food altogether. In one case, after one detainee stabbed another with a comb, the guards starved everyone on the block for three days. Many men also lacked medical care.[15] Interviewees told of being refused insulin for their diabetes. One was left paralyzed when guards would not treat his staph infection. ICE released others back into the general population the day they had surgery or shipped them posthaste to Tijuana when they began to fall ill.

Psychological Warfare

A second technique of dehumanization was psychological warfare. Officers played with men's sense of reality. They fed them misinformation, misled them, and messed with their senses of time. They also gaslit men and sent them to solitary confinement. Gaslighting refers to psychological abuse aimed at making victims feel "crazy."[16]

Ángel, introduced at the start of this book, had a ponytail and a melancholic penchant for describing his inner state, particularly when speaking of the 12 months he spent in jail and six more detained. The treatment wore at his sanity, he told Ana:

> They break you down . . . The whole drama of being inside, having to watch your back or you might get beaten up. The getting up too early [3:00 a.m.], trying to eat. You lose sleep. They hit you with information, legal words, and you don't understand at that very moment what's going on. So, you become, like, I don't know, a number, like a walking—a numb walking person. You're talking and you're listening, but you really don't know what's going on. If I think back . . . *Why didn't I say something? Why did I allow them to just manhandle me for no reason?* I mean, you get numb, and you actually don't know what's going on, until you just accept any offer just for the sake of "leave me alone." . . . They break you psychologically.

The process of "breaking men down" entailed a barrage of mistreatment: lies, threats, sleep deprivation, and plays on their understanding of time. Like Ángel, men began to feel numb—disconnected from their bodies and their emotions, as if they were walking dead.

Distortions of Time and Space.   ICE facilities, especially, used time as a tool of torture. Because detention is administrative (or "civil") by law, individuals held in this manner do not have a right to counsel.[17] Nor are there constitutional limits on how long they may be detained.[18] There is no requirement of bond, and if offered, bond can be set at $20,000 or more. Ironically, this "nonpunitive" designation often means *worse* delays and violations of due process than found in prisons.[19] For 95 percent of detainees, getting a date in court takes more than a year.[20] As of 2021 the average immigrant waited 54 months (four and a half years) for a hearing.[21] The only way to shorten the process is to relinquish one's right to a hearing and sign one's own deportation papers—legally marking *oneself* as a "felon."[22] While migrants and guards often talk about "fighting your case," in fact, this term simply means waiting it out for a hearing. Policymakers blame delays on long "backlogs," but respondents' stories suggest that ICE also uses delays as a tool to push migrants out of the country.

In detention, agents wielded prolonged wait times and uncertainty to pressure people to give up their rights to a trial.[23] Officers threatened to give people more time if they fought their cases or exaggerated how long migrants might have to stay: "If you don't sign now, you may *never* get out of here." As warnings, guards pointed to examples of people languishing in detention. Ángel remembered, "You just keep hearing the same stories of different people who are fighting their cases. I've met a few people that were there for four, five years fighting their cases. They keep delaying it and delaying it with the immigration courts. [And you think], 'Oh my God, how can you do that?' . . . I was like, 'Am I gonna be stuck for a long time?' . . . They want you to leave voluntarily, they make it hard." The threats played with detainees' sanity—pushing many to sign and get out.

ICE agents also withheld legal information, lied to migrants, or tried to intimidate, coerce, or confuse them into signing off on their own deportations. Guards mocked detainees, jabbering in English or in legal jargon the prisoners could not parse. They refused to provide information about migrants' cases, deliberately obscured the facts, or feigned ignorance. They (falsely) promised some people legal papers or a chance to appeal, *if* they signed deportation orders. They held pens in detainees' handcuffed hands. Under such conditions, migrants often caved in and signed. In the end, fewer than half of all hold-outs got their cases heard by a judge.[24]

In prison, sentences were more fixed, though some facilities used extensions and commutations as punishments or rewards. For bad behavior, men stayed longer in prison. Studies also show that jails detain migrants with ICE holds significantly longer than citizens on the same charges.[25] Men told us time was also used as a carrot, with commutation dangling like a bonus for "good" behavior, which could include anything ranging from attending church to agreeing to their own deportations.[26]

Both prisons and ICE also used space to isolate and disorient prisoners and their families and legal counsel. As carceral geographers highlight, the U.S. Department of Homeland Security intentionally locates detention facilities in remote areas, far from most detainees' advocates and loved ones.[27] Like prisons, they also use frequent and unannounced transfers between sites as a tool of repression.[28] Respondents in ICE detention described being spontaneously moved into new facilities, while their lawyers and family members scrambled to find them.[29] Likewise, prisons often moved inmates to institutions where they knew no one— and thus had to build their social relations and senses of safety anew. One man, arrested in North Carolina, rattled off an atlas of sites:

> In the federal prison, I was in South Carolina, so I went from South Carolina, they took me to an ICE detention [facility] in South Carolina, like an hour apart. From there they sent me to another ICE detention [facility] in South Carolina, even more south, and from there they sent me to Atlanta, Georgia. I was just all over the place. It's really stressful. The food is not that great, and when they put you in the bus or in the van they tie you up, your hands, your legs, like you're an animal. And once I was in Atlanta, Georgia, that was like my last ICE detention, they flew me to McAllen . . . , no, Brownsville, Texas.

Transfers often felt like their own form of punishment, whether for undesired behavior or for *being* undesirable.[30] They left men deeply disoriented: in time, space, and even reality.

Lies and Gaslighting.   Both penal institutions and prison-based "redeemers" used stereotypes, structural vulnerabilities, and institutional inequalities to erode victims' sense of reality and make them "take responsibility" for their own suffering. Guards misrepresented the length of men's stays, the information relevant to their cases, or the lives awaiting them post-deportation. The accumulation of lies led inmates to distrust their own moral compass. Sociologist Paige Sweet calls this gaslighting.[31]

One such technique—especially in prison—appeared on the surface to have a genuine rehabilitative function. That is, a series of groups, ranging from evangelical proselytizers to NGOs to Alcoholics Anonymous, stepped into prisons to fulfill state mandates for "programming," but for free. For cash-strapped, overcrowded facilities, such offers could be too good to pass up.[32] Following prominent sociologist Reuben Miller, I refer to these groups as "redeemers." As Miller argues in his book *Halfway Home*, U.S. prisons widely embrace the idea that incarcerated men have gone wrong and can save themselves from state violence simply by committing (on an individual level) to a life of personal transformation.[33]

Both prisons and external organizations offer men a narrative of redemption or of God's love, premised on their willingness to "admit" they have sinned and obey authorities (including those in penal institutions). These moralizing lessons can change how men perceive and respond to the violence they face, both behind bars and out in the world. The idea of redemption implies that men have invited mistreatment by choosing to be bad or sinful, but that they can, by the force of their wills, become productive members of society, even men of God.[34] In the process, these organizations sometimes reverse men's own understandings of themselves as good people trapped by oppressive institutions. Instead, they urge men to concede guilt and internalize the state's accusation of criminality.

Solitary Confinement.   Solitary confinement is another common tool of abuse. In prison and in detention, men described being sent to solitary for minor misbehavior, their own "protection," or little reason at all, sometimes for months or even years.[35] As criminologist Keramet Reiter explains, solitary confinement arose as a technique to undermine Black inmates' radicalism in California prisons in the 1970s.[36] Even though solitary was originally meant to be brief and exceptional—a parsimonious punishment—many facilities now hold inmates for 23 hours a day in featureless cells, with no visitors or human contact and no end in sight.[37]

One participant, in prison for selling drugs, spent a month in "the hole" for making what guards said were inappropriate gestures. Likewise, at the California Correctional Institution in Tehachapi, outside of Bakersfield, Isaac, a 37-year-old man with gelled, black hair and tattoos down his arms, said he was threatened, cursed at, beaten, put in a circle of naked men, and then instructed to see who could grab a set of prison-issued underwear first ("and that was just the reception"). Later, when Isaac started giving other inmates tattoos, guards threw him in solitary for six months.

Even when guards used solitary confinement for obvious retribution, they would claim that it was protective—for a prisoner's "own good." Challenging guards' authority, being threatened by other inmates, and experiencing mental health episodes could all get people sent to "the hole."[38]

Physical and Verbal Assaults

A third technique of erasure was verbal and physical abuse.[39] Among 69 interviewees who spoke in detail of their time in detention or prison, 24 said they faced verbal abuse, 31 witnessed beatings, and 24 were beaten themselves. A few spoke of being tied up in their cells or forced to give sexual favors to guards.[40] They said they were screamed at, sworn at, insulted, called "wetbacks" and pigs, beaten, tripped while handcuffed, and thrown into doors and walls. Correctional officers forced others to sign things. Guards told men that they were assholes, that they'd ruined their lives, that they would never find work again, or that everyone outside hated them. Lazaro, a 38-year-old man who'd been detained in the Adelanto facility outside Los Angeles, remembered, "A lot of us didn't speak English, and so sometimes people would tell [the officers] they didn't understand, and they'd grab them, and they'd say, 'Stop fucking around here. You are not going to be here with your bullshit. We are going to beat the crap out of you . . . There are cameras all over the place here, but we'll take you where there are no cameras and beat the shit out of you.'" This violence went beyond beatings to mistreatment like waking people in the middle of the night, imposing "routine" and arbitrary pat downs and cavity searches, and destroying detainees' scant property.[41]

While abuse occurred in both detention and prison, the violence was more routine and extreme in the latter. There, inmates' criminal convictions gave guards extra impunity. For instance, Ever (Camila's brother) had his arm dislocated by a prison guard. He remembered, "You're in [hand]cuffs. Even though you're cuffed up already, they're still kicking you, tripping you, spitting at you, yelling at your face."

Ceding Control to Gangs

In prison (and, to a lesser extent, in detention), the state often did the most harm by stepping out of the way, leaving men to the whims of gangs. In the process, guards also deflected the blame for violence.

Not everyone who served time in prison spoke of abusive guards, but most had a lot to say about gangs. Often, they told us, gangs viciously attacked other inmates. Some men said they'd been raped, stalked, beaten, or otherwise abused; a few showed us scars from being attacked. Others told of having to kill in prison. Gangs forced some to act as violent enforcers or risk death themselves, even when they wanted out. Gaspar, the young man raised in Compton whose drug dealing ended in a deadly car chase, spent 42 months in prison. He explained:

> In prison, everything is ruled by gangs. In the street, everything is ruled by gangs, but in jail, the gangs *rule*. That is, you can be alone in jail, not join anyone, but literally you have to be watching your back and your ass 24/7, all the time. You can't even go to the dining hall, even though there are guards watching you. Literally, I had to sit down and be like this [looking around] . . . The guy in the cell next to me, they stabbed him because he owed a cigarette, and they killed him! They cut his throat . . . I tried to keep a low profile in there, but like I told you, if you don't join a gang everything gets really ugly, really complicated. There were 18-year-old kids who had killed three, four people, and they tried them as adults. And when they got in, someone would show up and say, "You're going to be my bitch, because I want you to." Literally, it was rape him and rape him and rape him and rape, rape, rape, rape, day and night, day and night. I try to leave out those parts, but yes, it's—you can't sleep. When I would sleep, I slept with—I put magazines on my chest underneath my uniform because, well, if we had problems with another gang, well, the gates are open, and you didn't know who would come in [and stab you]. Even if you fell asleep, you kept one eye open, waiting for someone to come in.

In prison, gangs regularly overshadowed the violence (and role) of the carceral institutions themselves.

When men spoke of getting used to "how prison works," they usually meant the rules of the gangs, not the guards.[42] One man who spent nine years in prison for robbing a bank explained, "The gangs have their regulations: get up early, clean your cell, bathe daily, cut your hair, don't let your mouth smell, be clean, make your bed, clean the bathroom, don't spit anywhere, things like that. And there are people that don't follow them, and the regulations of the institution don't interfere with those guys. What applies is the regulations of the gangs, and that's what sticks . . . The gangs are the ones who rule in there, and you have to obey." From this inmate's perspectives, what "stuck" were the rules of the gangs, not of the institutions.

Yet, institutions facilitated gangs' control by turning a blind eye (at best) or actively encouraging violence (at worst). Some guards enabled gang violence by staying out of the way. For instance, David explained that when fights erupted,

"They [guards] stay away from it. As long as you don't mess with one of the cops they stay away." Other times, prisons actively fueled gang affiliations. Teodoro, who grew up in Escondido, California, spent two years in prison for his participation in the Sureño gang. He explained, "You get to prison and they [guards] say, 'Are you Sureño, Paisa, or Other [gang affiliation]?' Basically, the police [prison officials] themselves classify you in which group to put you in." Since Teodoro was with the Sureños before being sent to prison, the guards sent him to live with them. Then, when Teodoro's gang insisted he assault other inmates, the guards did not intervene.

Many times, prison authorities compounded gang violence by punishing participants (including victims) or sending them to solitary confinement. For instance, Dylan was 17 when he got tried as an adult and sent to prison. He wanted to stay out of gangs, but a rival recognized him from the streets as Sureño. To punish Dylan for hiding his affiliation, the Sureños jumped him and beat him. He added, "After that, they pretty much told me like, 'You either get with the program or we're gonna kill you.' So, well, when those are your two options, you know—I'm going with the program." The "program" meant Dylan was made to fight. After five fights, the prison sent him to the gang unit—and isolation—for a year. Just as that year was ending, a fellow Sureño got jumped. Angry that Dylan had not defended the man, his gang arranged to stab him. Dylan remembered:

> One day I went to lunch, and I'm standing in line to get my juice, and next thing I know I'm feeling like somebody punched me in my back . . . I see this guy I recognized, a little kid they called "Danger" . . . about 18 or 19. And I took a step back to see if he was gonna follow me, and he kept coming toward me. So, that's when I started fighting. And I knocked him out, and from there the police came up behind me, slammed me to the ground, and started cuffing me. . . . There was about two feet of space between two of the guards and another Sureño . . . He ran toward me, dove at me, and I felt like somebody had punched me in my face, until I see all the blood on the floor. That's when I realized that they stabbed me. They had stabbed me right across my eyelid . . . And then after that, administration decided to leave me in the hole for a[nother] year. I kept telling them to let me out, but they wouldn't let me because they were afraid that either [the Sureños] would do something or I would do something. So, they're like, "In order to avoid an issue, we're just gonna leave you in the hole" . . . They believed that I was going to be a "menace to society," you know, their favorite words to use with people.

Guards were complicit: they slammed Dylan down and cuffed him right as opponents stabbed him. They compounded the assault by throwing him in the hole for another year. Later, Dylan added, "The warden ended up sending out all the gang leaders . . . They ended up putting all those guys in the same camp [prison section] so that way, they could just do whatever they want to each other."

At the time, both Dylan and the men who assaulted him were teens. The brutality they faced behind bars compounded the policing they'd endured growing up.

Though prisons *are* officially punitive, such beatings are well outside of the scope of punishment under the law.[43] Often, the U.S. government attributes prison brutality to uncontrolled, evil, "menacing" gangs (as Dylan insightfully put it). Yet, men's stories made it clear that prison guards enabled and even *employed* such violence, so as to "sic the dogs on each other."

"I AM NOT AN ANIMAL": HOW INMATES ENDURE

Together, these techniques put men's humanity on the line. Men often felt they were losing their minds—their selves. Many invoked the word "trauma" or said that detention and prison "ruined them." Others insisted that these institutions "psychologically crush you," make the world close in, or leave men "mentally bad, bad, bad, bad." Some felt like the guys all around them had turned into monsters— as if demons had gotten inside them. Their survival in danger, many acquiesced in their own removal. In turn, they lost their jobs, children, families: all that had made them men.

Gaspar—raised in Compton—came to feel in prison like "less than an animal"—as if he were going insane. Ana met Gaspar in 2019, on a smoke break outside a call center in Mexico City. He was tall with a light moustache and single expander "plug" earring. He had spent four years in prison, replete with gang violence, mistreatment, and everyday deprivation. Staff turned the lights on at four in the morning and kept him locked up for 23 hours a day, with just an hour outside "in a cage." The meals were disgusting: "Like they ground up the food a week before, and that's what they give you. It's just a gray, green, or red mass. You don't even know what's in it. Literally, it just barely keeps you alive." Guards toyed with the men, saying things like "If you don't stay standing right there for five minutes, I am going to add another day to your time for bad behavior." He remembered:

> They would come in to review the dormitory, and they would punish you if it wasn't clean. Your bed had to be made, your clothes had to be folded, and everything had to be put away. There were times they would come in, and we had just fallen asleep or it was two or three in the morning. The police [COs] would come in and they would take apart your whole bed. They threw it down, and they would throw things at you. I had a photo of my mother, and various times they ripped it up because they said it was contraband, and I couldn't have it there. So yes, it was just being in a room of white stone, with the lights on all day long, two or three hours to sleep . . . You get one blanket and your uniform, and if it's cold, well, [they say], "You're in jail and I'm not going to treat you like—" That is, we were animals. We weren't people who made a mistake; we were animals. And I think that not even animals are treated like that in some places, right?

Literally and symbolically, guards "tore up" men's ties to family, leaving them isolated and grieving. To call his parents, Gaspar needed special permission and $50 to buy him a few minutes' phone time: "It was literally, 'Mom, I am OK, I'm sorry,' and hearing her cry on the other end of the phone." Meanwhile, his mother had been through the ringer, just to figure out if her son was still living. The gang members whom Gaspar had called "brothers" did not visit either; they were now on the run. The loneliness made Gaspar "leave my soul."

How men endured and how they held onto humanity shifted with the time spent locked up, the extent of abuse, and the level of isolation. Deportees we interviewed fell into three approaches. Some were defiant, others resigned, and still others broken down to basic survival. Those whose lives had been saturated with police apprehensions and carceral control (often since childhood) fared the worst. At the extreme, men internalized the state's dehumanization and resigned themselves to their banishment.

The Defiant

Men who spent a few months or less in detention were typically angry. Though they suffered less abuse than the other two groups, they resisted the most. Often, these were the same men who had felt shocked at their own arrests. Still rooted in their communities and a faith in their goodness, such men were far more likely to picture themselves as innocent and hold out for a hearing before a judge (behavior known as "fighting" their deportations). They insisted the U.S. should treat them as human.

For example, Berto, the 40-year-old chef and father of five introduced in chapter 1, was incensed after a month of detention in Orange County. The deprivation and disrespect made Berto feel like an "animal." He believed that ICE put good people through hell intentionally, "to kill you psychologically":

> They humiliate you so much that, psychologically, they destroy your dignity. So, they put you in a cold room, and they turn up the cold air so that—and they got me with a T-shirt like this [a tank top] . . . like fucking animals. And the agents, if you even look at them or you look over there, they think you are doing something to them. They beat you, and even though there are cameras, it's like a closed circuit and someone manipulates the cameras. And if you call your family, look, here they punish you too . . . I would understand if we were bad people, if we deserved it. I myself would say, "OK, I deserve it." But for 25 years I was working hard, you could say, so I don't have a record. But they treat you the same as any criminal—but we aren't criminals.

Since Berto still saw himself as an upstanding person, the treatment made him indignant. Enraged, he hired a lawyer (unsuccessfully) to fight his case.

Jesús, a 57-year-old contractor who had lived in Phoenix for nearly two decades, was also in disbelief. Jesús had gentle, dark eyes and a thick, salt-and-pepper moustache. Though his three eldest children were in their twenties, his youngest daughter, "the love of my life," was only 13. Jesús had been deported before, in 1998, after drinking and driving. He returned to Phoenix the following day. This time, things were not so simple. When a friend's neighbor called the cops on Jesús for drinking, he spent 109 days in detention, predominantly in Florence, a notorious

Arizona facility. Like Berto, Jesús was livid. He saw the United States as a mess, and he wanted his family out. He tried to fight his case. Yet, he faced barriers. ICE unexpectedly relocated him to California, sowing confusion as his family and lawyer frantically tried to find him.

Jesús insisted that the U.S. government was breaking its very own laws:

> They took me to four or five courts there, tied up like an animal. It's a violation of human rights! . . . The only thing left is for them to put a chain in your mouth, because they take you around like a horse. Because you go shackled at your feet, your waist, and your hands—you go like that [shows hands chained to waist], and a little box that goes here like this [over the hands]. . . . You can't even scratch. There is no bathroom on the bus from Florence to Phoenix. You don't have a seatbelt. And when the bus would brake, we almost broke our noses there [on the seat backs]. They treat us worse than swine! Pigs get a protective box; human beings don't.

For Jesús, detention felt like a cage. Men were housed in 15-foot rooms that the guards referred to as "chicken coops," ten or more at a time. "And they lie to you," Jesús insisted. "'I'm going to give you five months' . . . that's a lot of time! . . . If they paid me for the time I was in there unjustly, how much would it be? They didn't just do psychological damage, they hurt me on all sides, all sides."

When I asked Jesús what kind of damage they did, he replied:

> Emotional. Lost money, lost time, distrust in the "law," in quotes, when you start realizing that they themselves are breaking it. So, I go to Arizona, to the federal detention center, and they put up a bond of $250,000 dollars. Well, who did I kill? . . . With $250,000, I would stay in my country with a house in a neighborhood on the beach—on one of those beautiful beaches where American tourists go to have fun. $250,000! I don't know who set that amount of money and who approved those laws.

A religious man, Jesús began quoting biblical prophesies of evil and doom, saying that the United States was about to "go down in flames" for its treatment of human beings—many of whom, like him, had committed no crime.

Defiant respondents often denounced the U.S. immigration system for being driven by profit. They criticized the "business" of detention, questioning how much the U.S. paid private detention centers per inmate and the mismatch between such earnings and the toxic bologna sandwiches these facilities fed to inmates. One man reasoned, "We're nothing but dollar signs, you know?" Leo, a 29-year-old from Oaxaca, was raised in the U.S. and spent a year in prison and three months in ICE detention before his removal. He described being "tied up like a dog," stripped of all his belongings, and made to sit in a hot bus for hours. He called the detention system "some bullshit," protesting to Camila:

> The [officers] in immigration are fucking assholes. They look at you like you're a fucking cockroach. You ask them for something—and that's why I never asked for shit because they would come all pissed off . . . Those niggas get paid enough money to attend people, you know. Like what the fuck? Personally, I feel like this is a business

for them. If niggas [migrants] don't continue to flow into America or keep getting deported, those fools won't make any money. And put that on the record! Those motherfuckers get paid some money, for every head they get paid some money. All they give us in there is a sandwich with ham and a water.

Like Fernando, Leo felt reduced to an animal: a dog or a cockroach. And like those shocked by policing in chapter 1, he saw a disparity between his good behavior and the brutality of the authorities. Yet he was still mad—and still critical of the system. Such men's anger revealed they had not yet been broken.

The Resigned

After more time locked up, most men grew resigned to removal. They spoke of humiliation and degradation—of feeling desperate and scared, of weeping, of wondering if they'd begun to go nuts. Many believed officials *wanted* to break them emotionally, as a form of deterrence. Disorientation, despair, and the threat of indefinite confinement eroded their will to continue pursuing their cases. They felt powerless to protest injustice. It was better to give up everything than lose their sanity. Almost universally, they wept as they spoke of all they had suffered, all they had lost.

Take Ismael, the earnest Chicago debate star who gave up on studying when he learned that he was unauthorized. At 21, Ismael got 18 months in jail for driving under the influence without a license. When ICE agents came to the jail, he thought, "'Shit! Whatever, you know? I'm gonna play the best U.S. citizenship shit I have in my deck.'" In answer, ICE held Ismael in a tiny "reception" cell for more than two months. They also threatened to give him five more years behind bars. Ismael believed they were trying to upend his grip on reality and on justice:

> I felt like slowly they were mentally breaking me down, they were trying to break me, because I wasn't supposed to be there for that long, like in that cell . . . It's like they knew everything, my favorite color even, you know? So, I'm like, "Whoa, shit! If you guys have all that, why are you asking me [for a social security number]?" Everything that says there, whatever, you know? They gave me a thing to sign, and I read it all, basically signing my deportation papers, and I'm like, "No, I'm not gonna sign this. I'm not going to sign this." And they're like, "You can appeal this later."

Ismael felt they were messing with him, asking questions they already knew the answers to and misleadingly saying he could "appeal" his deportation after he signed it.

Meanwhile, Ismael did his time for the DUI. The day he was slated for release, he got a letter saying he would be picked up by Homeland Security. The guards hadn't told him. They let Ismael grow hopeful that he might not be deported, acting like they knew nothing. But when Ismael walked out of prison, approaching his uncle's waiting car, "The officers stepped in between us . . . they basically put me in a truck, and we drove probably like four hours to a different state." On the way, ICE picked up other migrants, whose English wasn't so good. Ismael recalled:

> They were ignorant of the fact that you didn't have to sign anything if you didn't want to. They were getting kinda punked around by the officers. And I didn't like that. I remember we were . . . it was just a picnic table with laptops and a fingerprint machine and cameras. And we were sitting next to each other, all of us. And I told everybody, "Do not sign anything, don't sign anything." I'm kind of advocating for them. And obviously the officers didn't like that at all. They didn't like that, and I pretty much got a cell by myself, and they waited until everybody else got processed in and everything and finally I was let out.

Ismael saw guards mislead other migrants. Then, as soon as the guards realized Ismael was trying to inform fellow prisoners about their rights, they cut off his human contact—isolating Ismael and blocking others from learning their options.

Ismael sat in Wisconsin detention for almost two months, inside a federal prison with an area roped off for immigrants. His mother hired a lawyer, who pulled all the documents and witnesses they could think of to help his case—his schoolwork, his therapist, his high school teachers:

> They spoke and everything, but it wasn't enough. Just because I got caught up with a little bit of weed and a DUI, I was—my "moral integrity" wasn't intact for me to perform as a U.S. citizen in America. So, it didn't matter that I volunteered a lot, 'cause I mean, I did, you know? Even though I was a little rowdy when I was a child, I was involved in a lot of things because of the school I was in. But that wasn't enough. The state—the county's attorney or whatever, he just basically kept painting a horrible version of me: "He doesn't care for the law. He was driving while drunk. He didn't have a license. He didn't care. He could have killed somebody." He was just painting it hard. I was just like, I spoke with him, and I told the man, "You know what? I understand that I messed up, but we all mess up. I've been here since I was three years old. My native tongue is English. I know everything you want me to tell you about the Constitution. I know—I passed my Constitution test. I went to school; I have my high school diploma. I was in community college. I was doing something. And I wasn't just—it wasn't just a history of mess ups. Everybody messes up; everybody makes mistakes. But that's not me anymore. That was in the past." But they ended up—just, they didn't care, and I got like a five-month continuance for my next court date. And at that point I'm just like, "Man, you know what? No. I can't do this anymore, I've been incarcerated way too long." And I finally just broke, and I said, "You know what? Fuck it. Just give me the papers." And I signed them. I put my fingerprint on both of them, and probably like two weeks later they shipped me out.

As Ismael pointed out, the system had little space for immigrants to be human or make mistakes. Compared to U.S. citizens, Ismael was held to extraordinary moral standards. Just for driving under the influence, U.S. police framed him as a broken man. He grappled with the disconnect between his self-image and the ways state agents described him. The discrepancy messed with his sense of fairness. Israel had no one in Mexico; even his grandparents had moved to the United States. But, as he put it, "Finally I just broke." After all that fighting, all that money on lawyers, he agreed to his deportation.

Misinformation, abuse, and intimidation left men emotionally battered. They talked of sobbing, depression, and suicidal thoughts. One described how immigration agents kept him awake for days, mocking him and showing their belts as if they would beat him. Then he started having anxiety attacks: "They get into your head. You can't focus your brain after not sleeping for so long . . . and they treated me like a crazy person." Julián, detained in Fresno, California, after a DUI, underscored how even the manliest men broke down. Though Julián thought of himself as mentally and physically strong, he said, "Nothing can prepare you, no one can prepare you for an experience like that. I saw guys—almost all of us cried, everyone cried. Gangsters, people who are there for drugs or for serious crimes, crying, crying, as manly as they think they are (*por más hombres que se creen*)." The state seemed determined to strip them not just of their sanity but also of their masculine pride.

Alone and degraded, men felt impotent. Julián went on, "You can do almost nothing. That's why I say 'I *tried* to defend myself' but well, how can you defend yourself? What can you do? They have you locked up . . . My parents don't know how to drive. They don't know English; they don't understand the system. What can they do? . . . Who is going to defend me? No one." Emasculation was entangled with isolation, separation from loved ones, and symbolic ejection from humanity. Often, men could not talk to family for weeks. During those long stretches, ICE agents dangled deportation as a way out: "You want to go, you want to get out quicker? Sign here, and as soon as we can, you can go to Mexico." Ultimately, the only choice left was to go. Feeling powerless, Julián gave up and signed.

Twenty-seven-year-old Memo got to the point at which one more moment detained felt like throwing his life away. He explained to Ana:

> They put us like in a room with like 300 people sleeping on the floor. There was no toilet paper . . . Like that, without bathing, without talking to your family for weeks . . . Then, they took me from Kentucky to Louisiana, and from Louisiana to different states . . . Various places. I lost all the things I had—my toothbrush, my food, my pencil. It was like a desert, like, "You don't have nothing, you ain't worth nothing." . . . The court dates came to fight your case, and they would give you another six months. So, I told my mom, "Look, mom, the truth is that I am—at this age, I am 25 years old. Mom, look, the truth is that it's not worth it to have them humiliate me like this, just to have documents or, I don't know, to stay with you guys and be happy."

Memo expressed a common ambivalence: while he did not think he had done anything "bad," ICE took away his belongings, human contact, and ultimately, his worth. Others, likewise, calculated that detention was like "years of my life thrown in the trash." As one put it, "They already detained you anyway; you're not going to get free of them. They have you in their hands and it's better to just go voluntarily." It was a Faustian bargain: to gain a future, they had to leave their whole lives in the past.

The Broken

If men responded to the degradation of detention by accepting removal, how did they cope in prison, when they could not get out and had to struggle to stay alive? How did they hold onto a thread of their own humanity?

The third group of men, who felt broken, endured more systemic violence. They were sons of the system, often locked up as young men. In prison, they endured years of the emotional and physical abuse that drove those detained to the brink. They spoke of being stalked from one prison into another, being stabbed and beaten by gangs, or being stuck for years in "the hole." Several became suicidal. As one said, "A lot of people can't even take it. I've seen people hang themselves because they can't take the situation and they—and, ugh, yeah, it's ugly. It's ugly." Prison threatened both their survival and their will to survive.

In a common trauma response, some hung on by giving in to the brutality. Gangs' dominance and sheer violence made guards seem almost humane. Many lost sight of legitimate human treatment. Instead, they came to see prison violence as "normal" or even fair.

In search of agency, other men practiced self-discipline. Unable to change the institution, they turned to changing themselves. Prison staff and the nonstate actors I call "redeemers" encouraged such practices. If men performed as "good" prison subjects, they could avoid solitary confinement ("the hole") and even get early release. Thus, prisons framed both getting out and "getting time" as upshots of individual actions, instead of as the caprice of an unjust state.

As men used their minds and bodies to *practice* "personal responsibility," many internalized the government's story that they were "bad." They blamed themselves for imprisonment or started to think they were sinners in need of reform. These narratives helped them make sense of state violence and find hope for their future, after release. The idea of redemption also reframed deportation as a relief, a second chance, and even a form of "rebirth," rather than as the punitive loss of their families and homes.

Normalizing Violence.   In prison, inmates grew habituated to violence. Officials were "just doing their jobs," said some. According to other interviewees, "You're in jail, and a jail is a jail . . . You're in jail, and jail is ugly." When Camila asked Pascual, a 30-year-old man from Oaxaca, if he saw abuses in prison, he replied:

> Listen, I didn't see abuse—almost none. And if maybe I saw [violence], it was because, well, obviously you're a prisoner, but you're under their rules because you're a prisoner . . . But there are people who don't obey. Obviously, I think they have to take their—get everyone to follow the rules. And when someone opposes them—but I think that's all normal, like anything, right? I think that they are authorities. And you might not want to obey them, but, well, they're authorities for a reason, and, well, I think that was normal.

Pascual's description flip-flopped. First, he said did *not* see abuse. Then he admitted he *did* see abuse but called it all "normal."

Others used the word "normal," too. When Tavio was 20, he drunkenly crashed a car, and cops beat him up. When Lorena asked Tavio how officers acted in jail, he said, "Normal, that's what I would call it, you know? I don't know what's normal, what's not normal. I was only used to mistreatment with officers. I never had a good experience with officers. I don't think nobody has a good experience with officers—I guess that's normal." Having grown up under police mistreatment, men like Tavio just expected abuse.

Similarly, Humberto came to see beatings meted out by the guards as his fault. Arrested for shooting a rival gang member, Humberto spent ten years in prison before his removal. The prison system moved him from California to Oklahoma, hundreds of miles from family. On three occasions, guards threw him into a room with no cameras and beat him. At one point, after fighting on gang leaders' orders, Humberto did a year and a half in solitary confinement: "24 hours a day in a tiny cell, like 3 meters long or less . . . always hungry because that plate of food didn't last me [the day]." Nevertheless, he told Camila, "There were some [officers] that treat you well, but others really were a bit mean, because you're inside and sometimes you behave badly. If you behave well, they almost don't mess with you, but if you act like someone who likes problems, there are times when they yell at you . . . and there they beat you." When Camila expressed surprise that Humberto was beaten for answering back to guards, he pushed back: "I think they were right. Because the truth is that *I* acted badly [my emphasis]."

Humberto internalized the prison's perspective that questioning guards was "bad" and warranted further abuse. While the treatment jarred him at first, Humberto got used to it. Over the years in prison, he said, "my mentality was changing." Before his arrest, Humberto thought he had a good life. In prison, he came to believe that "everything I lived is worthless, and it's like I hadn't lived at all." After getting out, he promised that he would live differently.

When prisons enabled the gangs to take over, men's sense of the law also shifted. Compared with gang brutality, guards' violence struck them as tame and even "acceptable."

For example, Brayan, a 27-year-old who had worked as a mule (carrying drugs across the U.S.-Mexico border), suggested that in *contrast* to gangs, when guards used violence, they were "just doing their work." Brayan had been deported multiple times, most recently spending two years in prison and seven months detained. He underscored to Ana, "Inside we hit each other among us. Sometimes people have even fought in prison for a Maruchan ramen soup, because in there if you owe something you have to pay it . . . for five dollars, even for a dollar, for a lack of respect. If you look at a person the wrong way." Each time something like that happened, he added, the prison sent COs with pepper spray and batons and "a lot of people get hurt." In such incidents, Brayan felt, "they're just doing their work, and everything's fine."

Instead of blaming the prison for COs' brutality, Brayan welcomed the lesson in discipline. The last time he was locked up, he embraced it: "I started exercising, I started working, I started doing my thing from the first day 'til the last. And it helped me a lot."

Self-Discipline and Self-Blame.   To cope with the violence of prison, many respondents turned to exercise, books, work, or God. Offers of early release, as well as religious groups and other "redeemers," encouraged men to discipline *themselves*. Respondents talked about studying, learning languages, getting their GEDs, and reading hundreds of books. Others worked outside the prison, in places like farms or factories, making chairs for judges or putting up light posts. Still others devoted themselves to physical fitness. Through such practices, men exercised a circumscribed form of agency. But they also reinforced a story in which their suffering was no one's fault but their own.

For some men, self-discipline offered something to focus on other than loneliness, pain, or the time that stretched out before them. Milton, a self-described former gangster, found purpose in reading 1,000 books. For Gaspar, reading and drawing became an anchor that "kept him sane":

> The only relaxation you have, or the only chance to breathe fresh air is to read, right? To take your mind off that [prison]. I didn't used to like reading. But when I was in there, I got some books by Stephen King. I remember *The Shining* was the first book I read, and I remember that unleashed my imagination, my ability to draw, and I would do it all day, every day, right? Ten hours of my life were just drawing and pages and pages and pencils and pencils . . . and my papers—that was—I think that's what kept me sane was that "I want to make something out of this, that I know how to do."

As Gaspar got used to deprivations, violence, arbitrary rules, and retaliations, like the guards tearing up his mother's photo, creativity helped him keep a sense of himself.

Christianity also promised a narrative of salvation. Christian organizations proliferated in prisons. Groups ranging from Alcoholics Anonymous and Narcotics Anonymous to evangelical churches offered baptisms, *limpias del pecado* (cleansing from sin), and printed "certificates of rebirth." According to interviewees, such "redeemers" constantly pushed the Bible. In turn, Gaspar recalled, "I saw a lot of people become real fanatics about that and get [Jesus] tattoos and things." As Reuben Miller suggests, charitable groups in prison "can't change the reality these people face, so they try to change how the people who face those realities see, understand, and respond to them."[44] While U.S. penal institutions are not officially religious, several respondents believed that going to church earned them better treatment, like access to snacks, time outside, or even early release.[45]

Turning to God (whether for the first time, or to reinforce past beliefs) pushed men to "take responsibility" for their suffering. Converted men said in serious tones, "I was with the devil, but now I am coming to God." Such beliefs often went hand in hand with self-blame. While religion helped many respondents endure imprisonment, it let the system off the hook for their trauma. In this view, men's pain wasn't the fault of police, violent prison officials, or gangs. Rather, *men themselves* had been in the wrong.

For instance, Santino, now 32, was first sent to prison at age 17 for selling meth. He got locked up on and off after that. In prison, he found religion:

> I start to read the Bible, and when I started to ask God for things, he would respond to me in my dreams. Even now he responds to me in dreams. But I started to have a lot of faith, to believe a lot in the word of God . . . I started to read . . . books about God, about my bad behavior . . . . And it made me understand a lot of things. It made me understand that I was bad/doing wrong (*yo estaba mal*). It made me understand that I was a selfish, arrogant, proud person. It made me understand that if I . . . continued that kind of life, only two things could be waiting for me: prison again, or death.

Santino's conversion reframed his life story. "Before I went to jail," he said, touching his heart, "I was really broken inside, here." He went on, "I learned that I have hurt many people. I hurt my wife, and I hurt my kids. And believe me that if I don't try to remedy this with them, they are going to believe the same as I [did when I] grew up . . . Maybe they'll be drug sellers too, because someone is going to come and tell them that this is easy money, and they are going to say, 'Well, my dad did it.'" Religion made Santino feel *he* was bad. He said nothing of the obstacles or abuses that he had endured. Instead, he channeled his energy into changing his *own* life. By moralizing, men could make sense of the beatings they'd faced (physically and metaphorically) and feel they had some control.

Interestingly, men who felt defiant and resigned also spoke of God. Yet those men asked God to save them from the violence of detention. By contrast, men in prison tended to expect religion to save them from *themselves*.

Where the defiant group questioned the state's dehumanizing treatment and insisted on their core humanity, broken men accepted dehumanization as justified. For instance, Goyo, who in chapter 1 described his transit in and out of foster care and prison, came to feel that "I deserve it, you know. Whatever happened, happened because it was the choices I made. So, I accept it. I wasn't very smart; I wasn't dedicated, and I wasn't putting in the effort to my life and to being successful." His path, he believed, reflected his personal choices and failures. After Alcoholics Anonymous and Bible classes, Romeo, likewise, said, "I was being ignorant, and I didn't want to be ignorant anymore . . . I wanted to know God." As Oscar put it: in the past he "made bad decisions," but in jail he "had to become a man."

At the extreme, some men expressed appreciation for the "opportunity" to "learn discipline" from prisons, religious groups, classes, or even gangs. Sentenced to three and a half years in prison for selling drugs, Ulises endured constant hunger and months in the hold for lewd gestures. Yet when Natalia asked if he'd faced abuse, he said "no." He insisted that he valued following rules: "The guards, the prisoners themselves, they teach you what respect is. [They might say], 'If I have a uniform, you have to obey me. I'm not interested in who you were on the outside, I am here. 'You see this black wall? I say it's black, so it's black.' There are rules here, order. This is not a hotel." In Ulises's description, guards demanded he alter his own reality: see the world as they told him to see it. These were not shared rules, but arbitrary control.

It is important to be clear that men's gratitude did not reflect true opportunities for rehabilitation. Reams of evidence demonstrate that incarceration does not reform inmates but rather makes their lives more difficult. Educational programming is in desperately short supply.[46] Yet such programming plays a symbolic role, marking the supposed "beneficence" of prisons and the individual responsibility of inmates to seize opportunities for their salvation.

The idea of redemption also encouraged men to reframe deportation not as a punishment but as a "second chance," a rebirth, or an opportunity to "become men." Sometimes, accepting removal allowed people to commute their prison sentences or avoid immigration detention post-prison. Carlos, for instance, told Itzel that when he was deported, he felt "really good, actually, happy and content." The U.S. had sentenced Carlos to life but reduced his time to eight years when he agreed to go back to Mexico. So, it seemed to Carlos, "I'm getting out free!"

Emilio, who spent years in Theo Lacey Jail in California, where he was beaten and had to work to keep basic hygiene, felt that in the U.S., "You always have a criminal record," but in Mexico, you can "become a man." He went on, "You know everything that you did, all that life that you lived on the other side [the U.S.], that's gotta stay there and bury it. And uh, I had a really bad life. Because of my fault, you know? I lived a bad life over there, you know, doing stupid stuff . . . But right here [in Mexico] I'm free." By agreeing to start anew, men could hope for a certain (deeply limited) "freedom."

In practice, as detailed in chapter 3, men's mental degradation came with them, undermining their ability to reconnect with people and start over in Mexico.

CONCLUSION

U.S. detention and prison erode men's mental welfare and moral core. The deeper people get in this system, the more of themselves they lose. Perhaps counterintuitively, those who spend the least time in detention, jail, and prison are most enraged and resistant. A few short months can leave them resigned to injustice—as well as to their removal. Not surprisingly, more than half of immigrants in detention survive by getting the hell out, signing off on their own deportations. Meanwhile, those who stay in prison for years grow inured to abuse, and some of them blame themselves for their fates. Under such conditions, men can see deportation as a chance at redemption, even though imprisonment has disrupted their lives, eroded their family connections, and scarred their moral, emotional, and mental well-being.

Anti-immigrant policymakers might argue that these group-level differences prove that imprisonment "works." Men go to prison, come to see themselves as responsible for their plights, and excuse the system of violence because they have committed worse crimes than those who are only detained. Yet, this logic does not explain why men who spend years in immigration detention show similar patterns of thought, when they have committed no crimes. Rather, the stories in this chapter reveal how the carceral system debases men regardless of their criminal histories. Insanity and self-blame are also forged *inside* the system itself.

Very few of the people the U.S. deports are the "hardened criminals" of media and political rhetoric. Yet, a logic of deterrence legitimates terrifically brutal treatment.[47] Across the deportation system, men felt reduced to animals and robbed of their loved ones and lives. Some became habituated to violence and deprivation or so disoriented that they no longer knew what was "normal." Many felt powerless. Only the most racist and inhumane observers would argue that such techniques are worth it, simply to drive people out of the United States.

There is a longer-term toll as well, as the trauma of imprisonment follows men back to Mexico. In the chapters to come, I explore how U.S. prisons break men's connections to people and remain lodged in their hearts.[48] Men often come out of detention and prison with mental illness, diagnosed or not. They are stigmatized as "crazy" and "criminal"—even in Mexico. They arrive in their "homeland" cut off from society, justice, and their humanity.

3

Forced Out of Families

*Acknowledgment: A preliminary version of this chapter was published in
Social Problems in 2022.[1] The chapter also benefited from the outstanding
BA thesis written by Pamela Elguezabal, who shared important ideas about
what happens to fathers amid deportation. Indeed, all my students—so many
of whose fathers had been deported or feared deportation—helped focus my
attention on the pain that immigrant families endure.*

U.S. immigration control is notorious for separating families. The Netflix docu-
series *Immigration Nation* is one illustration.[2] In the pilot episode, an ICE agent
drives through dark streets. She tells viewers, "Luckily for us we haven't really been
involved in any of that family separation thing. We don't rip children out of families' arms and things like that. We don't do that. It's just—that's not what we do."
Minutes later, the agent and several colleagues forcibly enter a building. At their
loud knocks, a woman opens her door. The agent tells her in Spanish, "We're doing
an investigation. Can you tell [your husband] we're here? We need to talk to him,
to ask him a few little questions we need to know." To the camera, the agent says,
"This is not gonna be easy."

Out comes Gerónimo, a salt-and-pepper-haired man in a dark blue shirt. As he
steps through the door, the agent says, "We are from the Department of Homeland
Security, Immigration. We have an order for your arrest." Ashen-faced, Gerónimo
drops his gaze. A child wails inside. Then, a girl in a pink sweatshirt, perhaps four
or five years old, bolts into the hallway. Gerónimo takes her into his arms as she
cries. Stroking her hair, he soothes her, "It's OK, it's OK." The child shrieks: already,
she seems to know that she won't see her father again.

Men we interviewed also faced heartrending moments of family fracture. One
sobbed as he spoke of how ICE agents broke down his door at dawn, seizing him
before his children woke up. Another went to get gas, was arrested, and never
came home. In the U.S., 4.4 million citizen children live with unauthorized parents
and more than 10 million people live in mixed-status families.[3] When ICE deports
parents, children endure anxiety, depression, isolation, and trouble in school,
along with sudden drops in income and housing security. Even *fear* of removal

undermines mental health, driving tension between spouses, making parents afraid to lose custody of their children, and forcing children to act as adults.[4]

Without question, deportation harms families. Yet, a focus on physical removal decontextualizes those harms from the carceral side of contemporary removal. From the 1950s to the end of the 1990s, under the apartheid-style immigration system, Mexican men often lived and worked in the United States while their spouses and kids stayed in Mexico. Indeed, apartheid *relied* on men to take masculine identities both as workers in the U.S. and as husbands and fathers in Mexico. By contrast, banishment assaults men's masculinity, and with it, their human ties.

In this chapter, I trace the mechanisms by which carceral deportation damages men's family relations. I look at how detention, incarceration, and border militarization erode men's places as breadwinners, fathers, brothers, and sons, undermining their relationships in both the U.S. and Mexico.

While extensive research looks at the impacts of parents' deportation on children, scholars rarely consider immigrant men's emotional lives as caregivers.[5] Likewise, politicians often split immigrant parents by gender, dividing deportable "criminals" from their own "deserving" spouses and children. Men we talked to expressed overwhelming love, sorrow, and loss. Yet such feelings rarely appear in studies or public accounts of immigrant men.

In addition, scholars often study incarceration separately from deportation. Immigration scholars tend to focus on removal, rather than examining families in the *context of* policing, detention, and imprisonment.

A vast scholarship shows that incarceration harms the bonds men need for emotional and material reintegration.[6] As detailed in chapter 2, U.S. carceral institutions mark men as outside of humanity, in what scholars call social death. Confinement keeps them physically removed from their loved ones, forces them to rely on women economically and emotionally, increases care work and economic burdens on partners, triggers marital tensions, and makes it hard for men to work or support their families.[7] As a result, many romantic and fatherly relationships dissolve. Some men also turn to "on and off" parenting or serial fatherhood, focusing on recent children and partners at the expense of earlier families.[8] Their children undergo negative impacts as well, from poverty to behavioral problems in school.[9] Removal and border enforcement compound such effects.

Carceral deportation not only rips men away from their families in space, it also strips them of their relationships. From across the border, men cannot provide or care for their spouses and children. Family roles get upended. Couples divorce. Fathers lose touch with their kids. Thus, men come to feel that they have failed as migrants, as grown-ups, and ultimately, as men.

Family fragmentation is a multi-institutional process. For men we talked to, there was rarely a single event, or "Gerónimo" moment, of rupture. Instead, detention, incarceration, and repeated border apprehensions intensified tensions with loved ones and wore down men's hope for family reunification. The impacts extended to family members on *either* side of the border.

The effects of detention, prison, and border militarization are clear through comparison: the deeper men's entanglements with U.S. institutions of coercion, the more their relationships deteriorated. When deportees got apprehended more times or spent longer locked up, they struggled more to engage with people they loved. Extending the analysis from chapter 2, I group these entanglements into three categories: (1) direct deportation, when men have been removed but not (yet) faced extensive detention, incarceration, or encounters with U.S. border enforcement; (2) complex deportation, when removal is combined with one or more additional border apprehensions and the attendant detention and/or prison sentences; and (3) imprisonment, in which men are expelled after longer stays behind bars.

In relation to family in the United States, men who were deported directly sustained more intimate ties. They spoke with their loved ones often and focused single-mindedly on family reunification, in defiance of U.S. border regimes. By contrast, those caught attempting to recross the border were more acquiescent to institutional constraints. Such men still identified strongly as fathers and sons. Yet, their institutionalization and the difficulty of return made them depend on women for empathy, money, and practical ties to their children. For them, the *illusion* of reclaiming a place in the family was stronger than the practice. The third group, men who had been imprisoned, resigned themselves to the loss of their loved ones in the United States. Incarceration undermined their marital intimacy and erected barriers to contact with children, as it does among inmates more broadly.[10] Behind bars, some built habits of self-isolation, distrust, and emotional suppression, which cut them off from would-be social support. Afraid of returning to prison, few ex-prisoners planned to risk crossing the border again. Instead, they struggled to "restart" in Mexico.

Carceral deportation also undermined men's ability to relate to people in Mexico, too. Two decades of U.S. border militarization meant that few men had visited that country since they entered the United States. Because we interviewed people who had lived in the U.S. at least a year (many for over a decade), few had family left on the Mexican side. Almost no one "went home" to a wife or children in Mexico, as many Mexican men had done in the 1990s. Generally, their closest relatives had also moved to the United States. If men had distant family south of the border, most had not seen those people for years. For younger migrants, return was laden with the shame of failing to "grow up" and send money back from the United States. Mexicans also stigmatized deported men as criminals or told them they didn't belong. Traumatized, some deportees could barely engage with people at all. They ended up alone in the world.

LOSING FAMILY TIES IN THE UNITED STATES

Removal and border enforcement compound the dehumanization men face under U.S. policing, detention, and prison. By leaving men jobless, disconnected, traumatized, and stigmatized, these institutions undercut men's relationships, along with their identities as providers, protectors, and patriarchs.

Removal almost always means separation. When immigrant men are deported, in about 70 to 75 percent of cases, their families stay in the United States.[11] In our study, less than a dozen men planned to bring spouses or children to Mexico, and none had acted on the idea. One dad explained that in the U.S. his kids had citizenship, good schools, and dreams—"everything their mom and dad don't." He did not want to take that away.

Visits were rare as well. At the time of our interviews, more than half the respondents were separated or divorced from the moms of their kids. These men relied on siblings or parents to bring their children to visit. Of married respondents, 72 percent had undocumented partners, making it risky for their spouses to come to the border, let alone cross to visit. Their families also lived scattered around the U.S., and few had money to travel.

Still, men we interviewed showed abiding love for their families. Defying racialized stereotypes of absent, "criminal" fathers and sons, they strove to reunite with their spouses, children, or parents in the U.S., working to earn money for smugglers and risking life, limb, and prison to recross the U.S.-Mexico border. Some went above and beyond to stay in touch from afar. Fathers were especially—indeed, heroically—committed to their children.

Yet, men acted differently on these sentiments. Though many people we interviewed tried to return to the U.S. and family, when they got apprehended by U.S. Customs and Border Patrol (CBP) (often repeatedly), they struggled to stay in contact. While such men still identified strongly as members of families, their ties grew more illusory as they acquiesced to institutional constraints.

Men's family connections—and ability to reclaim traditional, masculine roles—were especially weak after prison. Confinement drove rifts in families. While behind bars, men fought with their partners, and many separated or divorced. Removal deepened the distance. Some men had not talked to their children in months. At times, they coped by giving up on their U.S.-based families. The more detention, prison, and border arrests men endured, the harder it was to practice their love.

Direct Deportation and Defiance

Men deported "directly," without jail, prison, long-term detention, or additional border arrests, remained *defiantly* committed to family in the United States. Despite their distance, they kept in near constant contact. They also worked tirelessly to reunite with their loved ones in the U.S. (or occasionally to move their families to Mexico). They hung onto identities as family men. In this, their emotional experiences echoed the strains described by earlier generations of Mexican migrant men, who moved circularly to the U.S. while their families remained in Mexico. Still, removal made it hard to provide for their families, upending traditional breadwinner roles.

In January 2019, when UCSD student Zianía Ruiz met Tonio, a 45-year-old construction worker and father of six, he'd been away from his family for less than a week. Tonio had lived in Orange County, California, for almost 29 years. The day before he was arrested, his U.S. work visa expired. The next day at dawn, ICE agents stopped Tonio en route to work. They left his car on the road, keys still in the ignition. Tonio couldn't read English, and the next day, misled by ICE, he unwittingly signed his own removal papers. He remembered how the guards called him by number, rather than name, and tossed him his bag saying, "Here is your trash." Then, they asked him to sign something: "'Sign for your belongings: phone, wallet, credit card.' So, I say, 'OK,' and I sign it. But it wasn't for my belongings; it was for deportation." Tonio felt desperate, unsettled by agents' calm lies as they ripped him out of his life.

Tonio planned to go straight back to California to reclaim his family. He explained to Zianía, "When you're already married and you have children there, you don't look out for yourself. You look out for your children." When Zianía asked of his wife, Tonio said, "She is constantly telling me that she misses me already, not to take too much time, not to go and look for another woman." He laughed and then stopped, saying, "No, but seriously, I told her, 'No. How could you think that?'" Tonio felt he had to get back, "so that [my children] can realize their dreams, study—or if they don't want to study, then to work—whatever they want to do, but help them on the path that they want." Though Tonio's wife was worried, he felt strong in his role as caregiver, loyal husband, and provider of opportunities for the family.

Still, even the most direct deportations triggered costs, fear, and stigma that weighed on men's families and senses of manhood. Virtually everyone we interviewed identified with a traditional migrant masculinity, in which men were considered providers who went north to earn dollars.[12] Removal subverted these roles. When men could not show up for work, they lost income and U.S. employers' trust. Most also lost their jobs. In Mexico, where deported men were stigmatized and it often took months to get documents, it was hard to find well-paid work, and the pay in pesos was never enough to remit to families up north.

Detention and deportation were also expensive. Attorneys and bail cost tens of thousands of dollars, leaving families in debt.[13] Deportees had rarely accumulated resources in the United States, and any money they'd saved went to cover the loss of their income. Men also had to pay for phone calls to keep in touch. And, if they wanted to recross the border, they needed money to hire a smuggler—to the tune of thousands of dollars.

For interviewees, it felt hard, even heartbreaking, not to be able to work. They felt ashamed they had "failed" as income-earners and migrants. Losing their standing as breadwinners also strained marriages. For one thing, it flipped the traditional relationship of dependence, as women took on new hours or jobs and new roles as workers and heads of household.[14] Men, once the wage earners, now relied on their wives or families to send them funds to survive.[15] In the process, men feared they were losing their "place" in the family.

Berto, the 40-year-old LA chef encountered in previous chapters, fretted over signs that his family was changing. Berto was a father of five, and all but his eldest (age 15) had been born in LA. When we met in Tijuana, he'd been gone for five months. He spent a month in detention attempting to fight his removal and four months stuck at the border, trying to earn the money to hire a smuggler. Berto pined for his children. He called his wife daily. When UCSD student Janet Miranda Hernández asked Berto about his family, at first, he told her, "Absolutely nothing has changed . . . The only thing that has changed is the distance. I think that staying united is the base of the family. My children still call me every day, just like if I was there. I don't think it's changed. I think they value a little more what they had when I was there." To Janet, and perhaps to himself, Berto reasserted that his family remained intact.

At the same time, Berto admitted that his inability to provide was compromising his role as husband and father. Even though Berto worked in Tijuana, he could not send money north, so his wife had to get a job. He went on, "My wife always used to spend her time taking care of the children. Right now, everything turned over, and she has to work to get my children ahead . . . So [my deportation] did affect her because she didn't know what to do." He worried: "Maybe it's not like it was before. [My wife] is learning to make her life, and she's learning to get ahead without me. So as long as the devil doesn't get to her head, as they say, so that once I return, she can't take orders from anyone—because before she depended on me, and now she only depends on herself. So, yes, there could be a problem of separation, because now we won't share the same ideas. And before that happens, I have to do something." Though Berto appreciated his wife for sustaining the family, it troubled him that he might no longer be boss.

Seeing his children online felt painful as well. Berto feared they'd forget his love and care. He explained, "[Video chat] is hard for me. I prefer not to see [my kids] so much, because it reminds me. You see, if I'm calm and I see them, it makes me long to go back there any way I can." He worried that the children would become distant, going on, "I've been here four or five months, and my fear sometimes is that time—just like you cry for someone who dies but then after three months you forget the loss because they don't call you on the phone . . . It's already changing the family vehicle." Before this happened, Berto was determined to reclaim his position as patriarch.

Men also felt guilty imposing strain on their wives. As one put it, now "[my wife] has all of the burdens—she's just working and working, and she stresses a lot." Juan Diego, a 28-year-old father of two, felt ashamed at his loss of both income and marital intimacy. For 13 years, Juan Diego worked in LA construction while his wife stayed home with their kids. After his arrest, his wife got a job at a local factory to cover rent and buy groceries. Whatever was left, she sent to support him in Mexico. Juan Diego was touched by her dedication. But he didn't want to depend on her anymore. Though his wife was undocumented and could not come visit Tijuana, they talked every day, swapping texts, voicemails, and phone calls and "telling each other everything." Sometimes they'd reminisce about the good old days, like the night they met in a cumbia dance club. Other times, they spoke of their six-year-old's love of french fries and trampolines. They still hadn't told the kids of his deportation. In Tijuana, Juan Diego felt anxious about imposing on them and forsaking his role and his pride. He decided he would keep attempting to cross—pulling the trigger of Russian roulette, as he put it—until he got back to his kids. Yet with no Mexican credentials, he struggled to find work in Tijuana or save the money he needed to cross. Missing his family desperately, he said, he was "rarely in a good mood."

For men like Berto and Juan Diego, deportation alone did not sever relations with loved ones in the U.S. Instead, the (seemingly temporary) loss of their roles as providers and patriarchs reinforced their resolve to return.

Complex Deportation and Acquiescence

A second group of respondents tried to reenter the U.S. after deportation and got caught, leading to detention, additional removals, and sometimes prison. If removal stripped men of their jobs, repeated border apprehensions undermined their ability to be present as caregivers, leading them to acquiesce in family dissolution. As among people stuck in ICE detention for months, their will began to erode.

Starting in the mid-1990s, the United States radically increased the budget for border enforcement, placing officers, walls, drones, and other technology along the U.S.-Mexico border, particularly in urban areas. These fortifications pushed most migrants to cross in the desert of Arizona, at much higher cost and risk of death.[16] They also meant that more migrants were caught. Estimates suggest that in the 1990s, CBP stopped fewer than 25 percent of border crossers. By 2018, they caught between 50 and 67 percent of those trying to enter the country.[17] Once apprehended, migrants now face steeper punishments, too. The U.S. imposes 3-, 5-, 10-, or 20-year bans on most deportees, blocking them from applying to visit family legally. If a migrant is caught recrossing after a deportation, he can be charged for reentry and imprisoned for up to two years, even if he has no other criminal record. If he does have a record—including for things like drunk driving or prior reentry, he may be incarcerated for up to 20 years, depending on the seriousness of the crime(s).

The more times interviewees were stopped by CBP, the more ambivalent they became about their places in families. Apprehensions extended their absence from loved ones and made their return more uncertain. Sometimes, U.S.-based partners got tired of supporting a man behind bars or across the border. Contact grew sparse, or the woman found someone else. Spouses also had to mediate fathers' contact with children, absorbing everyone's pain as kids or dads sobbed on the phone. Many people fought with their loved ones. In such cases, men felt they'd lost their roles not just as providers but also as caregivers, protectors, and loving fathers and sons. They grieved being with their loved ones, especially kids. Yet, after getting caught at the border, several had not spoken with family in months. Many fantasized about reconnecting, without in fact being in touch. Several separated or divorced.

U.S. border enforcement wore down these men and their spouses. Now 38, Raul was brought to California as a toddler and had three teenaged children in Los Angeles. Though his (now ex-) wife was a U.S. citizen, he had never applied for a green card, out of pride that he was "not in it for the papers." In 2016, ICE agents came to his home and deported him. Prone to depression, Raul longed for his kids. He had been the breadwinner. Worried for his children and his own well-being, he tried to get back to LA. He recalled:

> I felt so much pressure toward—like I told you, I tried to give my children the best, whether in clothes, or giving them the joy they deserved, the attention of my time, too—just being with them, teaching them, chatting. All of that started to stress me out, that I was no longer giving them time. I was no longer teaching them. I didn't see them the way I used to . . . Thirty-four years there, and I don't have family [in Mexico], you understand? Yes, it made me afraid. It's like saying I was going to be alone, empty. And I thought my depression was going to hit even harder . . . I was thinking about my kids, and I said to myself, "I'm going [to cross] because I'm going. If it sticks it sticks, and I want to be with my kids." To fight to be with your family, above all, the kids. But it didn't stick, and here we are again.

U.S. border agents stopped Raul and sent him to detention for another month before they removed him. He waited almost a year, then tried again. When Fátima met Raul in 2018, he had just come back from another failed attempt. In between, he lived in Tijuana, working as a security guard and staying in shelters to save up money. With no stable work, he fell deeply in debt. He went on, "I got into debt of $15,000 dollars. I had to pay that. I just felt this pressure, and I couldn't find a way out—plus rent, with me as the only one working, plus the bills, and depression is—how should I say it? I don't know how to explain it because you feel ugly. You feel sad. Sometimes you don't feel like getting up or bathing. You feel afraid. And four times I tried to take my own life." Jobless and far from the people he loved, Raul struggled to find will to live.

As Raul fought to get back to LA and get by in Tijuana, he began to fight with his wife. After his second deportation, he remembered:

> She said, "enough." I understand her, because as a woman she has all the burden . . . So, when she would say [mean] things to me, I would say, "She's mad about this and that—about what we're going through." But with all of that, it started breaking. In

less than a year she left me. I thought she was going to support me, but no. And that's why I stopped calling her much, because instead of motivating me it was negative . . . She told me that I should stay here [in Mexico], that I should find someone, that I should make a new life. And I told her, "Before I start a new life," I told her, "I have to be sure that my children are OK . . . because I am not planning to have a life here, be OK here, and my children over there."

As communication broke down and Raul's wife sought comfort elsewhere, he grew angry about what he considered betrayal. By the time of our interview, Raul no longer spoke to his wife. Occasionally, he talked with his eldest son on the phone. Those days, he told Fátima, "I feel bad. I feel sad, I feel—I don't know, sometimes I get mad at myself. I get mad that I'm not there with them. I'd like to have communication, hug them, kiss them, teach them like I used to teach them." He missed being there for his kids.

Though Raul longed to keep up with his children, his absence, debts, depression, and marital conflicts made it nearly impossible. Raul felt empty inside. He explained, "On a normal day here I always think of my kids, my family, my parents, my mother. Like I say, you live [here] but you feel empty, you feel like something is missing." With his kids still in the U.S., Raul could not imagine a future in Mexico. Still, after what he'd been through, he was not (yet) ready to try for the U.S. again.

Similarly, Enrique moved to Los Angeles as a teen in the 1980s and worked for AT&T. Because of a teenage misdemeanor, he could not become a citizen. Now 50, Enrique had four kids, ages 17–29. In 2008, when his children were between 7 and 19 years old, he decided to return to Mexico to visit his dying mother. He never got back to his family in the U.S. He attempted to cross 12 times, once getting so desperate that he rode his bike through traffic at the San Ysidro port of entry. On the final effort, the U.S. sent him to prison for 24 months, for reentry and past transgressions. By the time of our interview, Enrique considered himself divorced. When Fátima asked how his deportations and two-year imprisonment had reshaped his family, Enrique replied:

> When something like that happens, so that you separate, things are really hard because everything comes in a chain, bam, bam, bam . . . My chain was having left the country and that they deported me, and I couldn't come back. And from there came the separation . . . My children never wanted to come live here. They were very little, and my kids told me, "No, you're crazy; you're crazy. No. Not to Tijuana nor to Mexico." . . . Then things [with my wife] started with, "Hey, are you going to come [visit]?" "No, I can't go that day." "But why not?" "No." And then pretexts and things, and then—bam—then you run into lies . . . [So I said], "You know what? I don't want you to come back to visit me." And from that moment, our relationship ended. There, the marriage of twenty-some years just died. That easily. Forget about me, just forget. In the end I'm just worthless.

Enrique suspected his wife had taken a lover, so he refused to see her again. Without her help, his contact with their children grew sparse. Though the eldest were grown, he didn't like asking them to help him or visit. He wanted them to come but thought he had to "have patience," adding, "And if not, well, too bad, right?" Enrique had no one left. His mind on his kids in LA, he felt unable to restart a family in Mexico and, ultimately, not just alone but "worthless."

Though men like Enrique loved their children, (ex-) wives now mediated their interactions with kids. Under the strain of distance, many such women were angry and/or overburdened with care work and earning money. One man, for instance, called his wife daily. But whenever he asked to speak with his three-year-old daughter, the child started to cry. He added, "I'll say, 'pass her to me,' and my wife says, 'You know what? No, because you'll leave her crying with me, and it lasts the whole day, and I can't calm her down at all.'" At that point, he felt, "I'm better off hanging up because [my daughter] starts to cry, and I cry too—and it's just better not to."

In some cases, men's efforts to rejoin their families ended in their doing time, triggering (again) the trauma of incarceration.

Imprisonment and Resignation

The combination of removal and incarceration was most damaging. Prison ate at intimate relationships, imposing stigma, trauma, and barriers to connection. Often, men deported after prison resigned themselves to little, if any, contact with their U.S.-based families.

For one, imprisonment inhibited communication. As I've discussed, prisons and ICE detention facilities place inmates in isolated, rural locales and frequently moved them over state lines, making it hard for family to visit or track them down, especially if the family members are also undocumented or do not own cars.[18] Visits entail expensive travel and harrowing waits, only to see men behind the plexiglass of prison booths. ICE and prisons also regularly confiscate men's cell phones and money and charge their families exorbitant rates for calls. The costs of calls, visits, lawyers, relocation, and applications for waivers and visas add further financial strain.[19] For instance, the man who told us his family and lawyer had to track him down after an ICE transfer from Arizona to California noted that his wife ended up hospitalized eight times in the three months he spent detained. The anxiety, coupled with her diabetes, was just too much.

Time behind bars also stigmatized men as criminals, sometimes within their own families. When men went to prison, family members' treatment of them often changed. As one participant put it, "There's a lot of us that have done a lot of jail time and that their families—they just throw you in the trash. They say, 'You know what? Stay in jail. And we don't want anything to do with you.'"

To protect themselves from violence and psychological torment in prison, many men developed habits of self-isolation, distrust, self-doubt, and emotional suppression.[20] While behind bars and after release, they struggled to maintain sanity, let alone healthy emotional ties to their spouses and kids. Many came out depressed. "You end up at an extreme mentally," said one respondent. "You get to a state of shock. A shock because you say to yourself, what have I lost? If I'm locked up a year . . . You lost a lot of time. You abandoned your children. You didn't see them grow up. You weren't there for graduations, birthdays, parties, time together, weekends—you lose it all."

Confined and then removed, few men could keep up contact with spouses, parents, or kids on the U.S. side. Their loved ones grew frustrated with their absence. Some gave up. Men's own hope dwindled as well. While these men imagined themselves as brothers, fathers, and sons, after prison, few kept up practical ties. Marriages dissolved. Communication with children withered. Even when spouses *did* want to stay together, young children struggled to understand their fathers' absence or relate to their dads on the phone.

The story of Carlos, a mild 29-year-old with a baby face, exemplifies this multifaceted process. Carlos had been in Tijuana for three months, where he rented an apartment and used his fluent English to get a job at a call center doing surveys for U.S. corporations. Previously, he lived in Los Angeles for 14 years, 8 of those in prison. He arrived in LA as a teenager "in a rebellious phase," as he put it. Lost, he looked for support in a gang. His involvement in drugs and violence broke down his relationship with his parents, and when they got papers, Carlos "got left behind." His family tried to help, but ultimately, they got fed up with his crimes and repeated arrests. The first several times, as a minor, Carlos escaped deportation. Then, when he was 20, his girlfriend got pregnant and gave birth to their daughter, Luna. The baby made Carlos want to retire from gang life, so he took on one last big "job." A few months later, he was sent to prison for murder.

In prison, Carlos lost contact with his siblings. He explained, "The [sibling] relationship has a certain shame . . . I think I embarrass them. I don't know, with all these things . . . You act badly and use drugs, join a gang. It's really hard for them to believe in you again . . . My siblings say, 'No, that guy, I don't want to hear about that anymore. We're tired of that." Carlos wanted to be close with his brother and sister (an undergraduate student at UCLA), but he wasn't sure whether they wanted to talk to him—a "criminal"—anymore.

His relationship also broke up. Carlos's life sentence left Luna and her mom on their own, and Carlos fought mercilessly with his girlfriend from prison. After seven years of fights over money, the baby, and everything else, their relationship died. By the time Luna was a toddler, her mom had found someone else. Carlos cried as he considered that if he hadn't been incarcerated, "I would have gotten married to my girl, and I'd have my daughter with me. I did my time in prison, and, well, I lost my girl, I lost my daughter, and I lost my family . . . I lost everything." Prison left Carlos alone.

Carlos coped by framing returning to Mexico as a "reset" or "second chance," echoing the idea of "redemption" that some men adopted in prison. When Carlos agreed to accept deportation, the judge commuted his sentence. The early release made Carlos feel "happy," "free,"—or at least less depressed.

At the same time, removal made it harder for him to see Luna. Carlos went on:

> [My ex] doesn't come to visit me. It's because it's hard for her to cross. She's [Guatemalan] not Mexican, so she would have to get another visa—I don't know. Yes, it's sort of a shitshow—it's—she's not going to come. My daughter, yes, because she is a [U.S.] citizen . . . Well, it's a project. [My ex] won't, on her part, and I don't want her to. With my daughter right now we're planning how my mother can bring her, but my mother doesn't speak English and doesn't understand my daughter. And the girl doesn't speak much Spanish. There's not much communication with my family. My mother and father speak passable English, but the only way to communicate is my sister or brother . . . There are always intermediaries to our project of bringing [Luna] here to the border so I can say hi to her and hug her and tell her I love her. [Do you talk with her?] No, it's very hard. She [ex-wife] only talks to my brother because she doesn't want to talk with me. . . . That she takes the initiative so I can talk to my daughter, no. It's not going to happen.

Carlos wanted to see his daughter, but he wasn't willing to risk getting locked up again. Giving in to his failed relationship, he felt little choice but to give up and start anew. He went on, "I have a lot of plans . . . I might form a family, get myself settled here, have children, and go on." Though Carlos said he thought of his daughter daily, he felt that helping her in any concrete way would be "going back to the past." Unlike those holding out for return, Carlos no longer saw the United States as part of his future—only his "past."

Armando, 35, told a similar story of stigma and family erosion. Armando grew up in Compton, California, and started selling drugs at 13. He ended up in and out of prison and in and out of relationships. At a Tijuana soup kitchen, Armando met and confided in Jasmin, whose brother had been locked up and deported, as well. He shared that he had a nine-year-old son with a woman he met in jail. But after years in lockup, he and his son's mother no longer spoke. If Armando tried to call, he said, "She yells, and I just listen. I'll be on the phone, and she says, 'What do you want?' She says, 'The only reason I don't hang up on your ass is that: one, God knows when you're gonna call again. Two, it may be that you never call again.'" Armando's son grew hostile as well. During their last conversation, the boy told Armando, "You ain't shit . . . You always in jail and shit." Armando regretted missing out on his son's childhood and recoiled from this disdain. But now, he felt, the U.S. "contains nothing but the past. And I hate to relive the past . . . If I can't do anything about it or change the situation, I try not to think about it." Unable to reclaim his family, Armando relegated it to his past and resigned himself to being, in his words, a "bad father."

At the extreme, post-prison deportees rejected their U.S.-based families or denied they had family at all. Dante, now 34, had migrated as a teenager, leaving a first wife and daughter in Mexico, neither of whom he spoke with again. He then married and had four children in the United States, living with them until he was convicted of robbing a bank. After eight years in prison, Dante was deported to

Tijuana. A week later, Camila met him at the Casa del Migrante, where he was staying until he could find work and a room for rent. Dante talked as if he were no longer a father, looking away when Camila asked of his children. He could not even remember their ages, except for the eldest: 14. His second wife was a white U.S. citizen with a well-paid job, adding racial, economic, and citizenship inequities that made Dante feel unneeded as a husband or dad. That wife now wanted him out of their lives. He explained:

> She told me, please, she is trying to rebuild her life, and she doesn't want me to know about my kids. You think she needs me? She doesn't need me. And she's like 20 times whiter than you [Camila]: white girl, white girl—her hair, everything . . . I can't return because she has a [new partner], and that person is going to do everything possible so that she doesn't separate from him. If I get near the state where they live, what do you think happens? He would report me . . . To avoid that, it's better that I stay here.

With two ex-wives and five children in two countries, Dante flatly stated, "I don't have a family." Emotionally, he'd given up. He wouldn't attempt to cross to the U.S. again. He believed he should restart his life, but he was not sure how. The one thing he knew was that it would be hard.

Men who did not have kids felt just as alone. Ashamed of failing to come of age and earn money, they, too, stayed isolated from any family, especially after prison. For instance, Abelardo, now 42, was born in Zacatecas and brought to Oregon when he was two. In 2016, Abelardo was arrested and deported on drug charges. He spent six months in Tijuana, tried to cross back to the U.S., got apprehended, and spent 18 more months in federal prison for reentry. Abelardo had been in contact with his U.S.-based siblings only once in those three years. He explained to UCSD student Nick (in English):

> I think most of it is just me being stubborn and having some type of pride . . . Even my eighteen months that I'd been in federal [prison], throughout that time, I'm not gonna ask for help, financial help. I only talked to my sister once during that time, and I made it a point not to ask for money. You know, I just struggled it out, or whatever, if that's what you want to call it. Now I just want to do things on my own. I don't want to ask for money. I feel like if I call, they're gonna think I want money, and that's not why I'm calling. You know what I mean? That's not why I wanna call. But I just feel like embarrassed, or I feel bad . . . I know the right thing to do is like at least call and just say, "I'm not calling for money, you know, I love you guys and I miss you guys, and I'm all right, and how you guys doing," and just stuff like that . . . But the other part of me just wants to not call them and just keep struggling it out here in TJ [Tijuana] and do the best I can. Just be a man about it, you know.

For Abelardo, "being a man" meant independence: not asking others for money, "struggling it out" on his own. Shame deepened isolation, and Abelardo avoided calling family at all.

ALONE AND ADRIFT IN MEXICO

Instead of finding relief in Mexico, men tended to feel more adrift. Few had close family left. They faced stigma among other Mexicans, especially if they had tattoos. For many, the ordeal of prison, detention, and deportation made it hard to relate to people at all. Men's focus on returning to the U.S. could also get in the way of (re)connecting with people in Mexico.

Casual observers often assume that deported Mexican men go "home" to a wife or family, like many migrants did through the 1990s. But as Doug Massey, Jorge Durand, and Karen Pren demonstrate, border militarization has stopped migrants from going back to Mexico to visit.[21] Instead, undocumented Mexican migrants now tend to bring their spouses, children, and parents to join them up north. Once there, if people remain undocumented (as most do indefinitely), few dare to cross the border again. By the time of our research in 2018–2020, most men deported after living in the U.S. (versus crossing) had not been to Mexico in years. Some could not remember Mexico at all. Their relatives left on the Mexican side were usually distant. Take Abelardo, for instance. Though his mother and cousins still lived in his home state of Zacatecas, they had not seen one another since Abelardo was a baby. He did not have their numbers or know where they lived. Others just said they had "no family in Mexico." Of 171 respondents, only three returned to spouses or parents on the Mexican side.

For the small group of interviewees who did leave spouses or children south of the border, by the time they got back, those people no longer felt like family. Bruno, who was 55, left his children in Oaxaca in 1999 to work in Seattle and send money home. During the 13 years Bruno spent in Washington State, his marriage disintegrated. Upon return, he told Samantha, "My wife was really changed, really . . . Right now, we're definitely separated. My children don't speak to me anymore. I separated from my wife, my parents are no longer alive, my siblings are off on their own. Everything changed too much . . . You give all you can to your children. But you can't get back that time that you lost, that should have all been different . . . Instead, I lost everything." Others came back to find their spouses wanted nothing to do with them or had shacked up with other men. One man's wife would not let him move back into their house, so at the time of our interview he was sleeping in their garage.

Some men felt so desperate for family in the U.S. that they could not make friends in Mexico. One explained that even though his sister lived in Mexico City, he could barely bring himself to interact with her. His heart was with his wife and young daughter in Vegas. He recalled, "I didn't want to go out. I *didn't* go out for two months. I fell into depression and the truth is they'd say, 'Come, we're going out,' and [I'd reply], 'No, I'll stay here on the cell phone [with family in the U.S.].' And that's the only thing I would do—be on the cell sending messages to my wife, my friends . . . It's like I couldn't accept that I wasn't still with them." Separation from family impeded interactions in Mexico, too.

Men's instability also made it hard to bring loved ones from the U.S. to join them or visit in Mexico. Participants often framed getting their finances (and "themselves") in order as a prerequisite to sending for, hosting, or even contacting family. For example, Esteban, a 34-year-old single father who remodeled homes, was pulled over driving in Arizona. When he could not provide a license, police turned him over to ICE, and he spent two years in a two-by-two-meter cell, trying to fight his case. After that, he did not want to go back. Esteban was a devoted dad. When he got to Mexico, he wanted to send for his two U.S.-born daughters (then in the care of an aunt). He waited, though, because, as he put it, "I had nothing here in Tijuana. I had nothing. *Venía en blanco* (I came emptyhanded). I had nowhere to land, no stable place where I could bring my daughters, and that's what I'm looking for now. I'm trying to establish myself here in Tijuana." Only once Esteban found work did he plan to send for his children. Others, similarly, hoped to bring their families to Mexico but not until they had stable houses and jobs. Some were too ashamed about their financial status to even have family come visit. Until they could reestablish their income (and manhood) in Mexico, such men subsisted on phone calls.

Economic shame could also lead men to avoid their families, especially if they did not have kids. Unmarried men often left their Mexican hometowns as teens to show they were independent and efficacious as men. After getting deported, such young men were deeply embarrassed that they had failed to earn and send dollars from the United States. They felt emasculated, anxious, and depressed. As one participant put it, "[Deportation] wasn't the way I wanted to come [back] here, because I arrived with nothing. Everything I had worked for and lived through there [in the U.S.] went into the trash, because I arrived here with nothing. Imagine, starting from zero. It's brutal (*está cabrón*) . . . they really take down your life." To avoid losing dignity, some hid their deportations from family or refused to go back to visit their places of birth. Benjamín, who left his hometown in Veracruz to send money to his parents and eight younger siblings, continued calling his family but never told them that he'd been deported. He did not want to worry them, he explained.

Alfredo, likewise, tied financial independence to "being a man." Born in the state of Sonora, Alfredo had migrated to the U.S. at 12 and spent many years "in the system": foster homes, juvenile detention, and then prison. The last time Alfredo got sent to jail, his sister offered to help bail him out. But he said, "No, don't waste any money on me right now. I put myself in this situation, so let me deal with it. Let me be a man about it . . . I want to be independent, so I don't want to depend on you." Though Alfredo was struggling to subsist in Tijuana, he was too proud to ask for help. He *claimed* he stayed at the border to be close to his U.S.-born siblings. In practice, they did not even know that he'd been deported.

For Alfredo, the lack of work in Tijuana also forestalled the possibility of starting a family in Mexico—and thus, his coming of age as a man. Alfredo said he would not feel ready for a relationship until he had a job he felt proud of:

Right now, I'm not thinking about having a family. I would like to, but I can't afford it. I mean, I'm not gonna be able to support a family with this salary [at a Tijuana call center]. With the minimum wage, what future am I gonna give my family? . . . I would want to give my family things I never had. Of course, I want to feel love and care, yeah, and give love and care. I'm a sweet person—treat that person with love and care. But I have to be in a better, stable position before—have my own place, maybe, or have a good job, a job where I know I'm gonna be working there for the next 20 years. Keep that job, and that job is gonna give me the, you know, financial stability to be able to afford a family . . . First, I would like to be stable and on my own. Like, she is gonna introduce me to her parents, and her parents are gonna say, "What do you do for a living?" "Dad, he's a motel manager for Holiday Inn, he deals with tourists," "Oh, yeah, nice to meet you, son," then I'd be welcomed to the family, but if she says, "Oh, he's nobody," her family would probably reject me.

In Alfredo's mind, a job made the difference between being "nobody" and being a son-in-law who deserved love and care.

Alfredo's story was common. Without income, several respondents felt unready to start new relationships. Many avoided seeking or rebuilding family, even in Mexico. Some of them stalled at the border, hoping to earn money before they went back to see loved ones in other Mexican states. In the process, they further lost touch with the people they loved.

Ironically, by undermining ties to family in Mexico, U.S. imprisonment and border enforcement pushed some deportees to seek to return to the United States, often at serious personal cost.

CONCLUSION

Carceral deportation does not just rip people away from their families; it also strips them of their identities and relationships as men, leading—at worst—to social and family death.

Men we interviewed felt they could no longer "be the man" in their families. They resented feeling that they were "no longer needed" either as providers or for their love. Their relationships became ridden with tension. Economic and emotional strains led to fighting and often divorce. Fathers lost touch with their kids. Young men could not check off the markers of coming of age: migrating, working, marrying, or sending home money. Many began to feel hopeless. Some coped by giving up on U.S.-based family and talking of starting over. Others grew wary of family relations in general.

Family degradation is not just an unfortunate side effect of an immigration system focused on getting "bad people" out of the country. On the contrary, current U.S. immigration enforcement *depends* on family separation. By stripping men of their places as fathers, brothers, and workers, it effects their removal from social relations in both the U.S. and Mexico.

Separation is a process fueled by multiple carceral institutions. The U.S. immigration system targets men whose families have already been degraded by systematic arrests and parental deportation. Being locked up in prison and ICE detention degrades relationships further, leaving intimate ties on thin ice by the time men land in Mexico. In turn, border enforcement may "seal the deal" on family division. Whereas U.S.-born prisoners often return to their families after release (however episodically), for deported men, marital tensions and the threat of more prison tend to put return out of reach.

The combination of removal, joblessness, border enforcement, and incarceration undermines fathers' emotional and practical ability to invest in their kids or fulfill masculine roles. Uncertainty, confusion, and the cost of communication—both inside U.S. institutions and after release—make it hard to remain connected. The trauma of detention and prison also reinforce men's distrust, so they struggle to connect with family anywhere, whether in Mexico or the U.S. This process triggers incredible sadness. Grieving their families and breadwinning roles, men grow isolated and depressed.[22]

Family tensions intensify with men's entanglement with border enforcement and U.S. carceral institutions. Deportees who spend less time detained or incarcerated tend to have more intact family ties, which help give them strength and hope. By contrast, those repeatedly apprehended by CBP feel ambivalent about their roles or even give up on family, reinforcing their isolation. When deportation comes after prison, it compounds men's sense of emotional limbo, clinching divisions introduced while they are locked up.[23]

U.S. politicians often distinguish immigrant "felons" from "families"—to use Obama's words—or imply that Black and Latino men are not "responsible fathers."[24] Instead, I find that the U.S. *creates* such divisions. Men move mountains to return to their families. Yet, U.S. policing, detention, incarceration, removal, and border enforcement impede them at every turn, marking them as criminals and eroding their capacity to forge social ties.

Confinement and removal leave men untethered. In Mexico, they struggle with the weight of emasculation, financial troubles, and isolation. These feelings shape their decisions about whether to remigrate to the United States, return to their hometowns, or settle at the border or somewhere in urban Mexico. Thus, the emotional limbo of losing family echoes in a second, geographic limbo, as deportees fight to figure out where to go.

4

No Place Called Home

Acknowledgment: As always, students' interviews helped me trace men's ideas and plans about place. In particular, the four RAs—Ana, Fátima, Camila, and Samantha—did important comparative work to understand deportees' relations to the U.S., Tijuana, Oaxaca, and Mexico City.

When ICE told Ángel he was headed to Mexico, he could not believe it. After two years behind bars—and a whole life in California—he thought, "Okay, whatever, stop messing with us." In the van, Ángel asked for his stuff. He thought back (in English):

A lot of men were complaining, "Where are our belongings?" [The guards replied], "Oh, we'll just put a paper in—or do you wanna go back to jail? Because we can take you back, but it's gonna be a *long* time and we're gonna put you in county. You're not going back to detention." It was in San Diego: "We're gonna put you in county jail for this. If you wanna wait, we have no problem, if you want to. Or you can just get out right now, free."

Nah, Ángel thought to himself, "I want to be free."

At the border, the fear hit. Ángel continued, "You don't know what's gonna happen next . . . So, you're always in fear. I was shaking. I didn't know what was coming up. And then I started seeing the Mexican flag just flying far away, and, wow, it hit me, like, 'This is a reality.'" In a gray, prison sweatsuit, Ángel walked over the busiest land border crossing in the world and into Tijuana.

ICE releases 96–99 percent of Mexican deportees at the U.S.-Mexico border, and virtually none to their home states or towns.[1] As immigration attorney Nora Phillips put it, deported men "get arrested one day, shoved into a van, driven to a concrete wall, and forced through a door into a foreign city—the psychological equivalent of getting pushed off a skyscraper."[2]

Cast off at the border, deportees meet a tangle of cops, prostitutes, thieves, and scouts for cartels, who recognize them by their clothes and sometimes tattoos. With few contacts and rarely much money, men also face a decision: Should they try to reenter the United States? If not, then where do they go in Mexico?

Symbolically, deportation "puts migrants in their place," sending them "where they belong." Likewise, scholars often assume that migrants move "home" upon return. In the twentieth century, Mexico-U.S. migration *relied* on a symbiotic relationship between hometowns and destinations, as men (for the most part) went to work in the United States and women raised families on Mexican farms—á la apartheid.[3] By the end of the 1990s, that pattern was fading. Yet, scholars, policymakers, and the U.S. public still tend to think in binary terms. To date, most studies of deportation look either at how migrants reintegrate in their hometowns or at why they cross back into the United States.[4]

Banishment upends this binary system. Now, when deportees land in Mexico, they carry the scars of U.S. policing, detention, prison, and/or repeated border enforcement. These institutions undermine men's families, jobs, and manhood in the U.S. *and* in Mexico. They crush men's spirits. They also mark deportees as "criminals," even back in their homeland and threaten further dehumanization should the U.S. catch them recrossing the border.

Men end up disoriented. Their bodies in Mexico, their hearts in the United States, they feel dislocated (*desubicados*), as if they belong to nowhere.[5]

In this chapter, I trace how banishment shapes where deportees go. First, I show, prison and detention leave men in limbo toward the United States: wanting return but wary of taking the risk. Many wait to go north. Some wait forever. Second, I look at where deportees end up in Mexico. I explore why they rarely go back to their hometowns, with a focus on the state of Oaxaca. I consider how those who wait get trapped at the border. Finally, I look at how some men overcome limbo by strategically opting into big cities, like Mexico's capital. By comparing who ends up where, I show how men's uncertainty and isolation map onto place.

Imprisonment, detention, and border enforcement inhibit reentry to the United States. Until the mid-2010s, more than 80 percent of deportees recrossed the border within a year.[6] They were especially likely to cross if they had kids in the U.S. or thought of that country as home.[7] Today, by contrast, less than 20 percent plan to reenter the U.S. right away.[8] In interviews, men were torn about whether to risk reentry. Like deportees surveyed elsewhere, virtually all of them *wanted* to get back to the United States.[9] More than half had U.S.-born kids, and most considered that country home. At the same time, stricter enforcement and punishments for reentry threatened more penal trauma. After prison and ICE detention, their U.S.-based families also felt distant.

While deportees weighed these impossible choices—and struggled with forced displacement—they waited. Even the most determined had to stay in Mexico until they could raise enough money—or conditions seemed "right"—to attempt a crossing. In the meantime, they had to decide where to go.

Though we met our interviewees in Mexico, barely any of them planned to go back to their birthplace to live.[10] Like Ángel, few had nuclear family left. Villagers shunned deportees and passed them over for work (if there was work at all). In some regions, cartels attacked returnees. Those who moved back to their states of origin tended to end up in cities, not in the *pueblos* (towns) of their birth. Resettling in one's hometown was a last resort, reserved for the old or the sick.[11]

Instead, men often got stuck at the U.S.-Mexico border, exemplified here by Tijuana. Released at the border, many deportees were so shattered after prison that they did not know how to proceed. Alone and often depressed or anxious, they lingered in indecision. Some stayed in Tijuana because it felt close to their U.S.-based lives. The border was also the obvious place to *wait*—sometimes for months or years. Thus, the temporal limbo of waiting and the existential limbo of indecision mapped onto the liminal space of the border.

A few men escaped the border by moving to big cities—notably, Mexico City— in what I call "strategic urbanism." Sometimes, they moved after other possibilities failed: when they could not recross to the United States, return to their hometowns, or stay sane at the border. This was also a choice that only comparatively privileged migrants could make. To move to Mexico City, men could not be tethered to the U.S. (or hometowns) by children. They needed enough mental stability for a move. If they were younger, more educated, spoke English, or had experience in business or organizing, it was easier to find jobs in the city and to connect with people "like them."

In short, varying entanglements with U.S. detention and prison "sort" deported men into unequal spaces in Mexico. For decades, Mexico has exploited and neglected its poor, rural states (including Oaxaca), driving half a century of outmigration. Politics and economic activity are centralized in Mexico City, a metropolis of more than 22 million people. The U.S.-Mexico border, in turn, expresses the contradictions of being close to the United States: it is at once an exporting powerhouse and a place deeply impacted by drug cartels and the "wars" both countries have waged against them.[12]

By cutting men off from both the U.S. and "home," U.S. enforcement shunts the most degraded to this zone of social precarity.

TEMPORAL LIMBO: AWAITING RETURN TO THE UNITED STATES

Most men we interviewed hoped to get back to their families in the U.S. Yet, prison, detention, and border apprehensions weakened the ties that might pull them north. In the early 2000s, the U.S. also stiffened penalties for reentry. Today, a deportee caught crossing spends 18 months in prison, on average, and up to 20 years if he has a record. It is also harder to get over the border. In the 1990s, U.S. Customs and Border Patrol apprehended less than a third of migrants while they were crossing. Today, estimates are up to two-thirds, thanks to new drones, cars, infrared cameras, and agents.[13] Enforcement in urban areas has pushed migrants to the deadliest parts of the desert, where they must also pay more for *coyotes*, or guides.[14]

Under such conditions, the men we interviewed often waited to recross, deferring their hopes for a future (however distant) in the United States.

The longer and more dehumanizing men's U.S. carceral histories, the deeper their uncertainty toward the U.S. and the longer they had to wait. Men who spent the least time locked up (direct deportation)—and whose family connections stayed strong—remained *undeterred*. They insisted, "U.S. or bust." Those who spent more time detained or were stopped on a prior crossing (complex deportation) felt *ambivalent*. Facing tension with loved ones, risks in the desert, and more time in prison, these men grew uncertain whether, when, or how to attempt to return. Finally, men coming out of prison often *gave up*, consigning return to the realm of dreams.

The Undeterred

Men who did not go through prison, long-term detention, or repeat border enforcement were determined to go back to the U.S. as soon as they could, no matter the cost or the risk to their lives. Think back to Tonio and Berto, enraged at U.S. detention and still deeply tied to their spouses and children. In winter 2019, Zianía met Tonio in Tijuana, a few days after he'd been removed. He had six kids and one goal: to get back to California. He was quoted $16,000 for a coyote, double the price we heard in conversations with other migrants and astronomical compared to the $300 he paid when he first crossed the border in 1990. Still, he told Zianía, "I am going to try to cross. I don't care how. Well, the safest way, so that they don't detain me, but safe. It doesn't matter what I have to pay . . . What's important is to get there." Tonio's family ties still ran deep. Though he felt terrified of the border, his plans had not (yet) been ruined by struggles to get back across. On the contrary, he evaluated the prospect of crossing based on his memories from a far easier time.

Likewise, the minute 40-year-old Berto landed in Mexico, he could not wait to get "home" to LA. In Mexico no one called him. He felt like he "didn't exist." Planning to go back to LA gave him hope. Berto told Janet:

> I was depressed when I had just arrived [in Mexico]. For about two months it was really hard. And right now, I am getting over it, precisely because I'm fighting to be able to see my kids. And if I were weak, or I went to do drugs or alcohol or do whatever—well, I think God has given me the strength to get over this [deportation], and I know that I'm going to succeed. I'm already here; I already have work and the will, and it's just a question of waiting.

Pining for his children, Berto found work in a restaurant in downtown Tijuana. He was saving his tips to hire a smuggler across the border. When we met, he'd been at it for almost four months. To him, it was a phase ("Just a question of waiting"). He would not succumb to U.S. enforcement. "I'm not one to accept (*conformarme*) and to live a life I don't like," he added. "Over there [the U.S.] is my future."

Studies estimate that 45–75 percent of people who say they'll remigrate actually try, and, of those, 33–50 percent make it across the border.[15] That is, less a third of deportees who plan to reenter the U.S. make it through. The physical risks, plus the high rate of apprehensions and incarceration, can interrupt or scuttle men's plans. As they scrounge to make money or try again, they must bide still more time.

The Ambivalent

Men who tried (and failed) to recross the border were often resolved to get back to their loved ones at first, like Berto and Tonio. But after getting caught crossing—and/or spending months in prison or ICE detention—they grew ambivalent toward the U.S. Incarceration and detention also drove rifts in their families, as detailed in chapter 3. Men lost contact with children, parents, and siblings. Many separated or divorced. They also hesitated to risk further time behind bars. After failed attempts at recrossing, they began losing hope. Some decided to stay in Mexico "for a while," until "things calmed down," or until, they hoped, they got legal papers in the U.S. Ambivalence lengthened their limbo.

Just like the undeterred, ambivalent men longed for their children. But they did not want to die in the desert. And they did not want to go to jail for reentry—its own form of (social) death. They worried that if they got caught again—either by CPB or, worse, by *narcos* (cartels)—they could be beaten and face further pain. Locked up in the United States, they might have even *less* ability to reach or support their families than they did in Mexico. Sometimes, "thinking of family" meant avoiding such fates. As one man put it, "My son needs me out," even if that meant staying in Mexico.

For instance, Raul, who attempted to recross numerous times, had been married when first deported. By the time we met in Tijuana, he'd lost all practical ties to his wife and kids. After several failed efforts to join them in the United States, he was also more pessimistic. He'd gone into debt and grown deeply depressed. He attempted suicide four times. Though Raul missed everything about the U.S. (especially his kids), he was not sure if he could risk it again.

Vicente, a 53-year-old dad whose wife had multiple sclerosis, expressed this catch-22 as well. Vicente had lived for 44 years in Oxnard, California. After Vicente's removal, his daughter, an aspiring nurse, had put college on hold so that she could earn money and care for her mom. Now, she was on prescription medication for stress. Vicente grieved her normalcy. He wished he could see her date or go off to college. He felt lonely without his family, adding, "Family is what makes you fight. What do you do when you come here [Tijuana]? Be in a room alone, go out to work. You distract yourself, but it's not the same as coexisting, sharing, relaxing, or talking [with family] . . . It's lonely." Every message from his daughter made Vicente feel worse.

Yet, Vicente feared he could not get back intact. On his latest attempt, Vicente had been kidnapped by a coyote who robbed him of all his belongings and held him for ransom. Then, CBP caught them both. The coyote escaped. Vicente did not. Instead, border agents threatened him with beatings, slurs, and ten years in federal prison (a common tactic, even though border patrol does not have authority to sentence people to prison). Vicente felt broken. He was uncertain if he could withstand such stressors again. Even if things went right, he figured, he'd have to survive the desert: a long three-day walk and severe dehydration. He waffled over whether to try again. Emphasizing the threats of physical and/or social death, he added, "You have to keep living." Though Vicente wanted to go north, he was no longer sure it was possible.

Others added that though they were heartbroken to be ripped from their kids, they could not face detention again. Uriel, a loving, sensitive dad to a five-year-old girl, sighed:

> I don't have that heart . . . to keep suffering what you suffer there [under ICE]. . . . I keep having—if I can put it this way—a psychological hangover from all that I lived through. You are hurt, really resentful, really sensitive. Any small thing—a movie, something like that—something happens, and you relate it to something, and like *that*, "Ay!" You get sad. It makes you want to cry. Or you see how they treat other people—racism, discrimination—and it bothers you because they treated you like that.

Uriel was still straining to overcome his short stay in U.S. detention. He did not think his heart could handle another round.

Caught between love and the U.S. carceral state, men felt "indecisive, uncertain, confused." Manuel, a 43-year-old father of three, was deported after a few years in prison. He was devastated. Arriving in Mexico, he said, he got stuck in a rut, thinking, "What am I gonna do? I want to get out of here. What's my next step? And desperation sinks in, and you don't know what to do." Manuel missed "*everything*" about the U.S. Yet he was scared to go back to prison. He wanted to *live* (and not endure emotional death behind bars). He thought about going back, but stopped himself:

> I can't be stuck on that . . . This time, [if] I get caught, I can be facing time in jail for illegal [re]entry. I mean, I've seen people do years for that, and it's not worth it. I'm getting too old to be doing time. The years I have, I have to try to live them . . . I want to go back, but it's the same thing. I go back, and it's not really a life you have there because you can't have nothing under your name. We just live in the shadows.

At first, I took Manuel to be saying he'd given up on the United States. Yet when I asked at what point he decided *not* to recross, Manuel replied, "I still haven't . . . I'm taking it a day at a time. For tomorrow, I have to survive and work. I have to pay rent." Manuel added that he "never really thought about" his future. He hedged, torn between rejoining his kids and resigning himself to removal. In the meantime, he lived just a day at a time.

Often, such waiting dragged on for years. Many men hoped to go back to their children but feared U.S. prison. So, they waited and worked, and bided their time. As one 29-year-old father told us, "[It's] a filler job, because I'm not interested in working hard here or—I'm just, like, in transit . . . Right now, I'm still confused. I still don't know what I want. I'm still not a person that has my future defined or that knows where I want to be. I'm one of those people who lives one day at a time—I don't like to make plans." Unsure how to weigh risks or imagine *either* possible future, men lingered in indecision. They also got stuck amid short-term planning.

Other men's ambivalence manifested as stalling. They waited for political conditions to change, for a chance to get papers, or to rest and recover. Amaris, a 40-year-old, had lived in the U.S. since he was 13. He reflected, "As soon as I stepped here, I stepped on Mexican soil, I was happy to be out of jail, but I was like, 'No, I need to go back to my son, my family, my wife.'" Amaris did not even visit his mother in Mexico City before he tried to recross. Desperate, he tried twice to rejoin his family. Both times, he got deported again. Now he was unsure when he could get back to his kids. By the time Ana met Amaris in Mexico City in 2019, he was in a prolonged state of waiting. He told her, "To be honest with you, I don't think I'm gonna stay here for that long . . . What I wanna do, I just want to wait until, maybe until mid-next year, until this South American caravan moves away from the border or whenever it gets a little bit colder, when it's not as hot as it is right now and I'm gonna try to sneak back in [to the U.S.] to be with my family."

Though Amaris was living in Mexico, he thought of his time there as short-term. Others who unsuccessfully tried to recross got depressed, telling themselves they should "rest awhile and see what happens, and then in the future if you want to cross, we'll try it . . . let the waters calm, and then you can go through again." To face the border, they said, they had to "get in shape" mentally and physically, especially after all they had just survived.

The Ones Who Gave Up

Men who'd spent time in prison rarely tried to enter the U.S. again, though they still fantasized about returning one day. Perhaps ironically, these men were the *most* likely to have grown up in the U.S. and think of that country as "home." Even so, few were prepared to repeat the anguish of prison.

Many men in this group had lost touch with their families. Only 6.6 percent remained married. While many were dads, few had contact with their U.S.-based children. Sometimes, building on narratives peddled in prison, they crafted an arc of "redemption" in which they imagined overcoming "their" criminality and proving they deserved to get back to the United States.

Though Enrique attempted to return to the U.S. 12 times, he quit after serving two years in federal prison for illegal reentry. When Fátima asked why Enrique kept trying, he said, "For my kids—not so much because I want to be over there. Right now, my ex told me, 'Look what you're missing! Your grandchildren are at the age where you like children,' and I told her, 'Yes, lucky you that you're there.' It makes me sad, and tears fall. I don't want to cry here, but yes, yes it makes me sad, and that's what made me [keep trying]." In Tijuana, Enrique had no one. He'd lost his old Mexican accent. He could barely remember the customs. He went on,

"Here, I feel really alone. Here I *am* alone (*Yo aquí me siento bien solo. Yo aquí* soy *solo*). I don't have anyone here, it's like—you're not OK in your mind. [You think] Why is this happening? It's because your mind is over there—even more when you've left your kids, your mind is over there." For Enrique, limbo meant living in Mexico with his mind on the United States.

Eventually, Enrique gave up. His last deportation (from prison) was in February 2017, a year before our interview. After that, he said:

> At this point, I have erased the United States from my mind . . . Because if they catch me again, it would be five or six years [in prison]. So, what am I going to do? Prison doesn't kill, but psychologically it hurts you, yes, yes it hurts. . . . From the time you enter it's psychologically traumatizing, first with the sentence. Then with the prisoners themselves, the rules, that "Look, you can't spit here." "Look, you can't go to the bathroom here." No, it's something traumatic, traumatic, that "look, you can't talk in the afternoons, at these hours you can't laugh." . . . So now, to avoid all those problems, I'd rather stay here in Tijuana. I'd better stay here and wait for the will of God.

Enrique figured it would take an act of God to spare him from prison again. When his daughters looked into legal paths for reunification, they learned that, quite literally, their father could only go back to the U.S. dead. Wistfully, he said he'd return to LA when he died, so his children could throw a flower on his grave.

Andres, 35, felt resigned to removal as well. After he spent four years in federal prison, his family ties had dissolved. Now, he said, "Practically, I am alone. I more or less consider myself—that I am alone in this world . . . I am not going to be able to return there, and if I want to return, they're going to lock me up. And if they lock me up, it's like they're taking—it's like they're putting your life on pause. Like, your life just stops there until you get out." For Andres, prison was short-term death, life on hold. With no family left, he had little cause to risk that again.

Others believed that in Mexico they could redeem themselves—as promised in prison. If they took responsibility, overcame "their" criminality, and proved themselves to be good, they hoped, they might "earn" their way back to the U.S. down the line. After the hopelessness of prison, for instance, Ignacio turned to God for a second chance:

> I was locked up, and I said, "I want to change my life . . . I want to get out and have a different life." Because you get mad. You get to a point where you can't find a meaning in life, to keep doing the same, doing harm to people. I had to change. And that was my goal since I got out: to change. And, thank God, I'm more or less going in that direction . . . God gives us another chance to do things right, we have a second chance. And I, at least, have a second chance to do things differently and to teach myself to have a life like a normal person.

Now, Ignacio wanted to stay away from the U.S.—and "all that [crime]." In Mexico, he was no longer labeled a criminal. As he put it, "I got a chance here [in Mexico], and here I don't have no record . . . It feels good, it feels good not to look behind you wherever you go." Ignacio believed he'd been deported "for my own mistakes." But he hoped that in Mexico he could free himself from an association with crime. *This* was his "second chance."

Others believed that if the U.S. marked them as "dirty" (criminal), in Mexico they could be "clean." One explained, "I'm not dirty in my country. In my country, I'm a clean man, I don't have penal antecedents. I don't have anything. Here I am a clean man, and I am at a really good point to start my life. And I'm going to do it, and I'm doing it." Some suggested that they had screwed up in the past but had learned to have morals, to be a good person. Still others spoke of leaving drugs, their homies, and the life of gangs in the past. Having found God in prison, they sought a "rebirth" in Mexico. They hinted that if they proved to their children (and perhaps to us, the interviewers) that they had reformed and were "good," they might one day reclaim their families and get back to the United States.

SPATIAL LIMBO: HOW U.S. IMPRISONMENT SORTS MEN IN MEXICO

If deportees were too isolated or afraid to go north right away, then where *did* they go? Where did they "wait out" the chance to return? Where did they land, as they figured out what to do—or dreamed of the U.S. lives they'd once known?

Carceral deportation muddled the home-away binary. After detention, prison, and leaving families in the U.S., most deportees could find *no "home" in their hometowns*. Instead, ambivalence toward the U.S. kept many stuck at the U.S.-Mexico border—*a space of limbo*. Prison left some men too traumatized or depressed to go anywhere after the U.S. released them. For others, the border was the obvious place to wait (sometimes indefinitely) and decide if reentry was worth the threat of more prison. Still others stayed because the border—although in Mexico—felt close to their lives and loved ones in the United States.[16]

Finally, younger deportees who spent less time in prison were sometimes able to adopt a *"strategic urbanism,"* finding their way to cities (especially Mexico City), where they saw a chance at new lives.

No "Home" in Hometowns

When we met deportees on release at the Mexican border, almost none of them planned to go live in their places of birth.[17] As detailed in chapter 3, two decades of U.S. border militarization had severed their ties on the Mexican side. In a *rancho* (village), it was hard to find jobs. Many people in Mexico assumed deportees were "criminals," making it hard for them to settle—even survive—in their rural hometowns.[18] In some parts of the country, cartels also threatened violence.

Many men ruled out their natal homes for a lack of work—the reason their families had left in the first place. In Mexico, the areas that send the most migrants are rural zones of federal extraction and neglect, with few stable jobs. Neoliberal restructuring since the 1990s has undermined such states' farming and manufacturing sectors, leading to wage stagnation. States in the south like Oaxaca have been especially hard hit, with up to 77 percent of people living in poverty, compared to just 1.1 percent in Baja California.[19] The stigma of deportation makes it especially hard for returnees to find work, reinforcing their feelings of having failed to earn money as migrants. On top of this stigma, some of them come home with debts—only to face their unhappy lenders.[20]

Take Benjamín, a 24-year-old Nahuatl speaker raised in a family of seven in a 200-square-foot wood house in the mountains of Veracruz. The family had little to eat, sometimes subsisting on just tortillas and salt. As the eldest, Benjamín migrated to send money home. After removal, he felt he had to stay in Tijuana to keep up that role. Similarly, Ulíses, whom we met in Oaxaca City, explained that though he'd moved back to his state of origin, "I would not go back to my *pueblo* . . . there is nothing there. How do you survive there?" In a village, men saw no way to subsist, let alone start anew.

Men who did "go home" felt emasculated, powerless, even subhuman, for failing to make ends meet. Isaac, age 37, for instance, went back to Oaxaca but did not plan to stay. He explained, "I get really fucking depressed . . . I do three jobs, and sometimes it's not enough money. So, I say, maybe if I am in a, like, a better city, I can have more. And that's part of what I want. I don't know. They say that money doesn't buy happiness, right? But being poor doesn't buy anything." Scraping to get by, some men came to resent their places of origin. When Christopher got to his hometown at age 29, he started to work at his cousin's carwash, for 50 pesos a day (U.S.$2.50). Unable to save even the money to buy his child back in the U.S. a box of diapers, Christopher said, "I didn't see my future. I felt like I was stuck; I was my cousin's slave." When Christopher started complaining, his cousin kicked him out of the house, "'Cause supposedly I was like a bum: 'I didn't wanna work; I'm one of those lazy Americans,' that's what they would say." Expelled from "home" in *both* the U.S. and Mexico, Christopher added, "I felt horrible. Like the end of the world. Like the whole world that I knew, loved, and had was gone in the blink of an eye." Arriving back in their pueblos with U.S. ideas about money intensified such men's frustration and social rejection.

Men also faced deep disdain in their states of birth, as illustrated by our experience in Oaxaca. A rural, migrant-sending state of 3.4 million, Oaxaca is one of the top three states of origin of repatriated Mexican citizens. Yet, when Camila, Samantha, and I asked around in Oaxaca City, we struggled to find deportees. Long overlooked by Mexico's federal government, the state had very few deportee-serving organizations. Its reintegration services (such as they were) faced constant shaming for working with "those delinquents." When we did meet deportees—mostly through students' families or friends,—they kept a low profile, letting few people know they'd been forced to return.

Rural villages elsewhere rejected deportees, too, dismissing them as *cholos*, or gangsters. Ramón, raised in gang-ridden Dallas, was in his mid-20s and fresh out of prison the first time he got deported. For a year, he tried to "go back" to his cow-herding village in San Luis Potosí. He had no close relatives left there and only vaguely remembered the pueblo. Nevertheless, he gave it his all. He got a job. He fell in love. Still, people in town told Ramón that he did not belong, insisting, "Tú no eres Mexicano . . . Tu eres del gabacho" (You're not Mexican; you're from the U.S.). In a jumble of Spanish and English, Ramón confessed, "That, for me—it bothered me. 'Cause you're telling me I'm not something that I know I *am*." Though Ramón showed neighbors his Mexican ID, they retorted, "That doesn't mean that you're Mexican." Hurt, he said, "That's when it hit me. I'm not a Mexican 'cause *they* say I'm not a Mexican. . . . I'm a freaking American." To cope with the isolation, Ramón started to drink. He got into fights. Eventually, at a *fiesta patronal* (an all-village party), the locals attempted to kill him. Broke, estranged, and depressed, Ramón left his "home" for good.

Ramón's words echoed in other interviews, too. One after another, respondents told us they felt like outsiders in their hometowns. Judged "wrong" or marked strangers by distant family, some were overcome with shame, isolation, and fear.[21] To avoid this feeling, 20-year-old Tavio did not even tell his family when he went back to Oaxaca. He did not want to face their scorn.

In regions with active cartels, deported men also faced threats of violence. States like Michoacán, Guerrero, and Jalisco (not incidentally, the highest migrant-sending states) had grown more dangerous in migrants' absence, their villages wracked by extortion and sometimes spectacular brutality. Frequently, men from such states were too scared to even pay them a visit. Berto, for instance, explained that though he'd never been incarcerated or convicted of crime, he could not go back to his home state of Guerrero. He elaborated, "There are no police. There, it's the world of whoever has power. So, there are a lot of people being destroyed. Because they [cartels] come and say, 'OK, you have a nice car. Give me the keys.' I want to bring my family, but I don't want to bring them to a world like that." Likewise, Esteban owned a house back home in Colima, but criminal organizations had since overrun his town. His sister warned him not to come back, fearing cartels would take him and hold him for ransom.

David, 47, also detailed risks he might face in his birthplace in Tamaulipas. Once a gang member, David spent 25 years in prison in the U.S. He knew that if he tried to go home, his tattoos would make him a target for cartel recruitment:

> The cartels are really tough over there, and I have a lot of tattoos on me. So right here [in Tijuana] I can be on the street with like a slingshot [tank top] and also have tattoos. Nobody cares because everybody has tattoos here. But if I have tattoos over there and the cartels see me, then they're like, "Oh we got a new guy." . . . They'd kidnap me just to see who I'm working for, and if I say I'm not working for anyone, they wouldn't believe me. They did that to my brother; my brother got kidnapped over there so I learned from that when he told me.

If deportees in Oaxaca suffered poverty and exclusion, those from some states—like Tamaulipas—also risked being kidnapped and killed.

As a result, deportees rarely settled down in their pueblos unless they were old or sick. Of 171 men we interviewed for this book, only two returned to their hometowns out of pride—or even saw those places as "home." All those who did stay in villages were older than 55 or disabled. Some had advanced diabetes or had lost limbs in accidents. Others were addicted to alcohol or to drugs. Instead, most respondents who returned or planned to return to their states of origin lived in the central city. Even there, some stuck around only because they'd fallen in love or had kids. Ever, for instance, went back to his parents' pueblo when he was deported, to get his bearings. He ended up having two kids. Though he knew he'd get better pay fixing cars in Mexico City, he stayed in Oaxaca to be with his children—and "only" for that. As one man put it, the hometown was a place "to live when you're retired . . . a little house where you can stay and wait for death, nothing else."

The Border as Space of Limbo

Instead of going "home," deportees often stalled at the U.S.-Mexico border—sometimes indefinitely. Tijuana wasn't a city men chose, they said, but a place they stayed in between other destinations. Yet carceral deportation left them untethered, often with nowhere to go. Released at the border, many stayed as they weighed what to do.

Tijuana has long been a staging ground for migrants entering the United States. Today, it is also a stepping stone back. Many men we met in Tijuana had just been removed from the U.S. and were on their way north or south. Yet the border was not just a short-term waystation. Some deportees had lived there a decade or more. They stayed because the border felt close to the U.S., because they were waiting, or because there was nowhere else they could go.

The border was the obvious place to stall. Of the deportees we met who intended to return to the U.S., 90 percent were currently in Tijuana. While a few of these people (27 interviewees) had concrete plans in the coming weeks, most were biding time until the "right moment" came, their reentry bans expired, or they made enough money to hire a smuggler. Their limbo may have been indefinite, but it occurred in a finite space—near the U.S.

The border was also a space of illusion, indecision, isolation, and slowed-down time—where men stayed when they *felt* close to the United States but could not go back. Manuel, who was "taking things one day at a time," hung around in Tijuana for years. He knew no one in his birthplace in Guadalajara. He was ambivalent about going back to the U.S. again. At the border, there were other people who had been through the same kinds of things. Manuel also hoped to reconnect with his kids, with whom he hadn't spoken in months. Perhaps if he stayed nearby, he figured, he could convince a sibling to bring them to visit. So, Manuel took a job in Tijuana and found an apartment, staging his uncertainty from the border.

Similarly, Gerardo told Fátima, "Why did I decide to stay in Tijuana? The truth is I have not decided if I'll stay or go. I'm still in the process. But now that you just asked, you know what? I don't know if I *should* stay or go . . . Why Tijuana? Look, in the first place, I have the hope that—I have that illusion of continuing to fight my case, the process, and my ex-wife is a U.S. citizen and she can come with my children to Tijuana, and I can see them." Gerardo was 37, a gardener, and recently separated from his wife. He had zero family in Mexico. He adored his two kids in California. When Fátima asked where was "home," he replied, "If I told you, 'In the place I was born,' I'd be lying. If I told you 'Tijuana,' too. There is nothing that makes you feel safer and happier than being with family, wherever that may be." At the same time, Gerardo acknowledged that legal return to the U.S. was an "illusion." To get as close as he could, Gerardo hung out in Tijuana.

Other men also stayed in Tijuana based on a (distant) hope that their families might visit. Alfredo, raised in LA foster care and juvenile detention, never met his father and grew estranged from his mother and sister while he was in prison. They did not know that he'd been deported. Still, Alfredo said "pretty much the only reason" he stayed in Tijuana to was to be close to his brother and sister, in case they got a mind to come see him. Raul added, "I have hope that maybe [my ex's] heart will soften all of a sudden, and they'll surprise me—a dream that my family will arrive here, my kids." Another man said he stayed because "I was still holding on to that thought, like, 'No, no, you're close, maybe they'll come visit you.' . . . I was still talking to one of my exes, and she'd be like, 'Yeah, one of these days I'm gonna go visit you,' so I was holding onto that feeling. It was a personal feeling—or maybe an illusion of me being closer. It was horrible 'cause I was like, 'Oh, they're so close from here, it's like a two-hour drive.'" Deep down, men knew the visits were dreams. Still, the fantasy—and the geographic proximity—had powerful impacts on men's directions.

Border life offered another advantage: it had a similar culture and lifestyle to California.[22] Tijuana appealed to those who had little connection to Mexico but feared returning to prison in the U.S. As Alfredo put it, "I don't know nowhere else. It´s like being in LA." David, likewise, joked that in Tijuana, "sometimes I wake up in the morning and I'm thinking I'm in LA. I wake up, and I see the roof top: 'Damn!'" Another man said that after 25 years in prison—and the threat of life behind bars if he tried to go back—he stayed in Tijuana because "I don't know nowhere else. It's like being in LA. It's like-[multi-]cultural here, and everyone is bilingual. They speak English, and you know your friends. I have a lot of friends here from California and from prison, so we kind of know each other. So, when we see each other here we would help each other find jobs, and that's why I like it." It wasn't family, but at least in this in-between space, men could hang onto elements of their old lives.

Others were so depressed, anxious, or stressed that they struggled to make decisions at all. Deposited at the border, men who suffered the longest penal histories in the United States—and the attendant trauma and family disintegration—tended to end up stuck where the U.S. government left them. Disoriented and detached from family on either side, they did not know where else to go.

Populated with so many uncertain and displaced people, the border could be difficult. NGOs and the Mexican state actively pushed deported men out of Tijuana, afraid their presence would negatively impact municipal finances. Border cartels, police, and drug dealers also targeted recent deportees, as explored more in chapter 5.[23] Thus, after staying at the border a few months or even years, some men came to want out. They lost hope that their families would visit. They decided the border was "dangerous" or felt they "did nothing good there." Unable to reenter the U.S., return to their hometowns, or resettle close to the border, they had to figure out where in Mexico they could live.

Strategic Urbanism in Mexico City

In lieu of getting stuck at the border, some deportees strategically moved to Mexico City or other urban areas. Nearly half the deported men we met in Mexico City had tried living elsewhere first and then chosen to move to the capital. In cities, they found social, economic, and political support. There were communities of migrants, deportees, and others with experience in the United States. There were jobs that required English-language skills. There was also more room to cultivate a bicultural identity, bridging the cultural gap between "here" and "there."

Yet, men needed the wherewithal to make such moves: mental stamina, youth, education, English skills, experience in advocacy or business, and/or a lack of tethers to children. Compared to men we met in Tijuana, those who moved to Mexico City were not as worn down by the violence of U.S. prisons.

For instance, Ramón, whose village in San Luis Potosí rejected him, headed to Mexico City after his second deportation. In the city, he explained, "They don't understand what I'm going through, but they don't reject you [like in the pueblo]. Yes, it's better there." In the capital, Ramón sought out people who appreciated diversity and identified with his experience growing up in the United States. He added:

> Mexico City has the biggest—just in Mexico City alone it has over a hundred thousand Americans living in Mexico City . . . I said, "There is something there they want, and if they want it, I should want it too." . . . and I start coming to the city because of the beautiful things—there is a metro here. You can get around. There are facilities. . . . I mean, cool, if you want to return to your rancho . . . but if you're looking for culture, people, home? Mexico City. Because here there is a huge diversity of culture. You don't stand out. Everyone stands out! Because everyone has their own lifestyle, it's normal to be different. Where else are you going to want to be? . . . So, I say before you try to return [to the U.S.] and risk your life, try Mexico City first.

For Ramón, Mexico City was *the* alternative to both his hometown ("a place to retire") and going north. Its size and diversity allowed him to be "himself" and hang around Americans, without the risks of reentry.

Other deportees went to Mexico City to get jobs, build community, engage in advocacy, and find "big city" adventure. In contrast to Oaxaca or Tijuana, where we did not meet anyone planning to advance their career by studying or gaining new skills, several interviewees in Mexico City were attending college, studying, or preparing for new careers. One said, "There is more work here, they say, and they pay better than up there [at the border where] . . . the work is killer (*matadito*)." Another added, "There's always work for bilingual people . . . here [in Mexico City] I think that the people who are bilingual are idiots if they go around living in the streets or stealing." Others joined organizations that trained bilingual people for jobs or helped get deportees back on their feet. In addition, as I explore later in chapter 6, Mexico City was the only place we met activists fighting against deportation. As one such advocate put it, "Mexico City is strategic for doing a lot of things."

When we asked men how they *got* to Mexico City, most said they browsed the Internet, seeking support and people like them. As Ramón told it, "I did research . . . I'm on Facebook all day, because that's my only way to be in touch with my people." Alone at the border or in rural pueblos, those with English or Internet skills realized that Mexico City had opportunities for people who felt "in between." Yet searching the Internet required education, facility with computers, and often English. The average deportee has a middle-school education. By contrast, those who made it to Mexico City tended to have finished high school (often in the U.S.) and know English.

Only about half the respondents we met in Mexico City had spent time in prison (compared to three-quarters in Tijuana), and those people spent an average of two years locked up, versus four at the border. One in five had graduated from college, and almost three-quarters had finished high school. Nearly two-thirds had been raised in the U.S. (migrating at a median age of 9), giving them familiarity with English and U.S. culture—critical skills for jobs.

Take Ángel, who grew up in the U.S., spoke English, went to college, and was an activist—arrested at a protest in favor of DACA. Seeking an alternative to his birthplace in Guadalajara, Ángel found an NGO on the Internet. It taught coding to deportees. He explained:

> You start looking for help, start looking for other people you can actually connect with, that went through the same thing . . . I started searching for resources online, and I connected with some people that started telling me, "You know, there's more to deportation, there's more to returning." . . . You start to reconnect with other returnees, deportees, so you get that sort of foundation . . . People that you can actually—know what you've been through, or you can sort of connect and say, "Oh, that's true, it is a horrible feeling, the whole system needs to change."

Ángel's English and computer skills helped him connect with others like him, recognize alternatives to life in his hometown, and escape the "prisons" of his memory.

In Mexico City, Ángel started to feel like he had a future. He added, "I'm trying to actually have some solid—a solid life here, meaning to just be here in Mexico, continue my career . . . to actually make something myself . . . I'm trying to stay very positive, very optimistic, not waste time that I feel had already been wasted." Other migrants we interviewed in Mexico City were optimistic and proactive, too, especially compared with those in home states or at the border. Being able to have a career, make friends with other deportees, and build a binational space was critical to their hope.

While deportees in Mexico City did not escape limbo altogether, their ideas about the U.S. took a different tone. They hinted that in Mexico City, they could *earn* a right to reenter the U.S. one day. Some hoped that by building careers, getting education, and/or and waiting out their bars on reentry, they could refute the U.S. image that they were "bad." If they worked hard, finished school, or made enough money, they hoped, they might be able to get a visa to go back to visit or live. For instance, Manny, introduced in chapter 1, had been deported two years before. Now in Mexico City, he said his goal was to finish school and make money, "So I can go back . . . with a visa or try to get papers over there." Others, too, believed they'd stabilize, get a degree, then seek a way to return. While the move gave men a chance to "start over," they, too, had to prove themselves *within and against* U.S. stories of criminality and redemption.

CONCLUSION

If U.S. immigration control once enforced a symbiotic apartheid, with men in the U.S. and women in Mexican hometowns, carceral deportation breaks that interrelationship. Prison, detention, and border enforcement dissuade men from reentering the U.S. right away, forcing most to wait for further migration.[24] Though deportees typically want to go back to the U.S. at some point, less than one in five now try crossing within a year, and only about a quarter of those get through.[25]

One might argue that carceral deportation "works" to deter reentry. But at what cost?

By merging removal with prison, detention, and border enforcement, the U.S. weaponizes trauma. To keep the unwanted out, it severs emotional ties. If there is a deterrent effect, it comes from dehumanization and family disintegration. Only by beating men down does the U.S. convince them to fully give up on reentry.

Banishment also severs men's ties to their hometowns. Thanks to decades of U.S. border enforcement, few deportees now have close family left. In their places of birth, repatriated men face stigma and a lack of options for work. Instead, most think of their pueblos as places to retire or die. Feeling alone and "homeless" in Mexico then *drives* some men to want to migrate again.[26] Though deportation ostensibly sends Mexican migrants "home," their liminality does not end when they leave the United States.[27]

Shunting men away from both the U.S. and hometowns marks a shift in the geography of Mexico-U.S. migration. Instead of being another form of return, banishment extends the purgatory that undocumented immigrants face in the United States, where legal violence can undermine their well-being and make them feel they do not belong.[28] As a result, deportees look less like other returning Mexican migrants and more like the stateless.

The limbo of deportation also maps onto precarity and inequality within Mexico, where the rural south and west are deprived, the border caters to the United States, and resources and power concentrate in the largest cities, especially Mexico City. Deportees most traumatized after imprisonment often land in the no-man's land of the border. Vulnerable to stigma, police, and organized crime, these men struggle with existential dislocation and ambivalence about their "place" in the world. By contrast, the "lucky" ones escape to the capital.

Mexico's urban contexts then interact with men's U.S. carceral histories to shape their erasure and agency. In chapter 5, I explore the lived experience of alienation at the U.S.-Mexico border. In chapter 6, I turn to Mexico City and the possibilities for forging new space to belong.

5

Banished

Acknowledgment: In Tijuana, students insistently drew my attention to men's isolation. Jasmin Divas, whose brother was deported, did outstanding work at the city's major soup kitchen, connecting with men caught deepest in limbo. Breanny Andrade and Nick Sabia helped flesh out the "reset mentality" on my office whiteboard. I am also in awe of the courage with which Camila Hernández Cruz and Ana López Ricoy engaged men struggling with mental illness, physical debility, and addiction, despite what I later realized were significant risks to themselves.

Tijuana's flagship migrant shelter, the Casa del Migrante, sits a 35-minute drive from my front door in San Diego. It feels like a world away.

On the rutted road to the shelter, men line the sidewalks. Some sleep on the cement, their hair matted down with dirt. The Casa kicks out its "clients" during the day, so both guests and hopefuls linger nearby on the street. Their belongings mark them as migrants. Shoes worn thin. Ziploc bags stuffed with papers—the few remaining artifacts that tell the state who they are. The just-deported are especially easy to spot, with their ICE-issued sweats. Often, police beat up migrants nearby. Sometimes, deportees get recruited or kidnapped by border cartels.

The Casa del Migrante opened in 1987—with the encouragement of U.S. and Mexican NGOs—to help Mexico's labor migrants during their journeys north. It was the first of now more than 30 migrant shelters around Tijuana, most run by churches and NGOs, housing several thousand migrants per day. The Casa hosts up to 160 people a night, taking them for a few days at first and up to six weeks if they look for a job and don't cause trouble, drink, or use drugs. In the 1990s, the shelter served mostly those heading north; in the 2010s, 90 percent of its guests were deported men.[1] Compared to the average deportee, people who stayed there were poorer, older, and less socially connected—the ones with nowhere to turn.[2] From 2017 to 2020, the Casa del Migrante also served as the base for our Tijuana fieldwork and training ground for 35 students a year.

A metal grate guards the Casa's front door, echoing the bars of U.S. prisons and ICE detention. Just inside stands a wall-sized bulletin board. The right half is pinned with snapshots of men who are banned from the shelter. Captured at intake, their dark eyes stare out from the wall: tired, sad, angry, grasping. Under each image, someone has scrawled a label in Sharpie: *borracho* (drunk), *drogadicto* (drug addict), *ratero* (thief), *violento* (violent), or *narco* (drug trafficker)—naming the men by their crimes. On the left, there is just one label: *Se busca* (seeking), for those who've gone missing. It feels as if the men are eternally lost.

Ostensibly, the wall is for staff: to keep out troublemakers and addicts and help find those who have vanished. Yet, its labels echo the stigmas that mark migrant men beginning in adolescence. Students in the Mexican Migration Field Research Program dubbed this the "wall of shame." For me, it was the wall of the banished: people exiled not just from the United States or from the Casa but from humanity as a whole.

I think of Oscar, whom I met one night at the shelter while waiting for dinner. He was just 21 and seemed tender and vulnerable—a kid with a backward cap. When we talked, I learned the story that now features in chapter 2: he'd been taken away from his mother at 4 and left by his father at 12. He began selling drugs. When he was 18, the U.S. sent him to prison and then—a few weeks before we met—deported him to Tijuana. Oscar and I later spoke for more than two hours, under the florescent lights of an unused office. He insisted that he'd left drugs in his past. Casa, he said, was helping him find decent work. Yet when I returned a week later, Oscar was gone. I never saw him again. Rumor was he'd been tossed out for boozing. I hoped he'd made it back to LA or gone south to rejoin his mom. Maybe he ended up on the streets. Perhaps he joined up with the narcos or was taken by local police. As one shelter worker told me, "Every day, people just disappear."

The eyes of those disappeared stayed with me on nights I returned from my Tijuana fieldwork, shaming me for the ease with which I could speed back over the border. What becomes, I wondered, of men the U.S. tries to erase?

Researchers know that deportation is devastating. Upon return to their countries of origin, deported men and women face stigma, criminalization, police abuse, and detention and imprisonment. They are vulnerable to criminal violence, especially at the U.S.-Mexico border.[3] Most lack strong social networks or income. They face high rates of mental illness, homelessness, and drug abuse.[4] Often, they describe return to their homelands as exile.[5]

In scholars' terms, deportation is social death, marking people as disposable and subhuman.[6] Stripped of their deep interpersonal ties, people lose their sense of belonging to a group or a place; their roles in work, family, and community; their autonomy; and even their faith in themselves. As their physical and psychological condition deteriorates, some can no longer function as social beings. They become "disintegrated subjects," pushed out of society and barely able to fight to belong.[7] Some scholars go so far as to suggest that life after deportation is "outright inviable."[8] Yet, analysts say less about how U.S. incarceration, Mexican police, and cartels intensify this rupture.[9]

In addition, erasure is not a foregone conclusion. As I explain in chapter 6, some people rebuild their lives and communities after deportation. Assuming social death is universal can reinforce fearmongering by U.S. (and Mexican) politicians, such as the claim that deportees will carry "their" crime from place to place.[10] The idea that men themselves are a threat also deflects attention from the ways *institutions* degrade their humanity, on both sides of the U.S.-Mexico border.

In this chapter, I trace how institutions leave deportees feeling banished, not just from the U.S. but from society as a whole. I find that alienation is most acute when men have endured U.S. prison and/or long-term detention and when they are left in limbo at the U.S.-Mexico border. Those who spend the most time behind bars have the weakest social connections, feel most emasculated, and are most likely to face PTSD. Some survive violence by isolating themselves. Others struggle to function outside of prison at all. As detailed in chapter 4, such men tend to get trapped at the border when they have nowhere to go. Others also stay near the U.S. to prepare to recross. Focused on the U.S. and waiting (sometimes forever), both groups struggle to be present in Mexico.

At the border, Mexican cartels, police, and military agents reinforce deportees' erasure.[11] These institutions make up the "Mexican side" of what is, in fact, a *binational* system of banishment. U.S. border militarization fuels cartel violence, creating a profit motive for smuggling drugs and people.[12] Under the mantle of the War on Drugs (and stopping migration), the U.S. also arms and trains Mexican military and police. Some cartels, such as the Zetas, now use U.S. military tactics as well, learned from members trained in the U.S. military and/or in special units of the Mexican military overseen by the United States.

Mexican authorities and cartels benefit from the vulnerability, isolation, and skills of men coming out of U.S. prison. After prison, deported men land in Mexico traumatized, disoriented, and visible. To cops and cartels, they're walking dollar signs. They can also be easy scapegoats for border police to fill quotas and recruits for cartels in search of cheap labor. Criminal organizations also covet deported men for their English, familiarity with the border, and/or experience exercising violence (whether as members of gangs, or as past U.S. military).

These institutions re-mark deportees as criminals and targets of violent abuse. They add to the degradation wrought by U.S. state institutions, crippling men's capacity to rebuild relationships, homes, and a sense of themselves. Under such conditions, men feel profoundly alienated.[13] They are cut off from people, place, and sanity. They struggle to rebuild connections and trust their own goodness. Time and again, they describe a deep loss of hope. Many are haunted by the visceral prospect of dying.

THE MEXICAN SIDE OF CARCERAL DEPORTATION

U.S. border enforcement gives Mexican institutions a model for violence and an incentive to use it. In turn, Mexican police and cartels extend the erasure of deportees.

Respondents' experiences in Tijuana exemplify this convergence. The second largest city on the West Coast of North America (after LA), Tijuana is also a major commercial hub between the U.S. and Mexico, the busiest land border crossing in the world, and "one of the great control points between the affluent and developing worlds."[14] Its factories (*maquilas*), call centers, armed forces, and traffickers cater to the United States.[15] Despite this economic power, most of Tijuana's residents face deep precarity, economic and otherwise. No Mexican city has absorbed more deportees. In this space of limbo, people are conditioned to the rapid mobility (and disposability) of human beings. As political newcomers within Mexico, local government leaders are arguably more oriented to the United States than to Mexico City. Civil society remains weak, built mainly on charitable, Catholic organizations focused on basic needs.[16]

The context is ripe for cartels and cops to exploit men post-deportation.

Cartel Assaults, Recruitment, and Exploitation

At the border, U.S. demand, prohibition, and enforcement fuel a vast illicit traffic in drugs and migrants, among other things. By some estimates, the drug trade makes up as much as 5 percent of Mexico's GDP.[17] In this context, cartels (narcos) are both notorious and ubiquitous. While the U.S. frames cartels as external threats, in fact, the fortification of the U.S.-Mexico border *enables* organized crime, making it profitable to traffic drugs and people.[18] Mexican federal policies have also intensified violence among cartels. Since 2006, Mexico has waged a "war on cartels," debilitating the organizations' most powerful leaders but triggering intense and widespread fights for control. Today, as anthropologist Shaylih Muehlmann reports, it is hard to exist at the border without getting involved with or falling in debt to cartels.[19]

When deportees cross into Mexico, cartels often recruit them as foot soldiers, sentries (*halcones*), mules, and *burreros* (who smuggle cash on their bodies).[20] Organizations like the Zetas, the Sinaloa Cartel, the Knights Templar, and the New Generation Jalisco Cartel kidnap deportees for ransom (assuming U.S.-based loved ones will pay), force them to work, or recruit them to take drugs or people to the U.S. (exploiting their desire to get back across a difficult border). Loosely affiliated with U.S.-based gangs, cartels also stave off rivals by obliterating and sometimes absorbing deportees who have ties with opposing groups.[21] In our interviews, more than 50 of 171 men (especially at the border) brought up cartels without prompting. They spoke of being beaten; attacked; kidnapped; tortured; and robbed of their trucks, watches, wallets, and jewelry. Some had friends killed by cartels.

U.S. imprisonment and removal leave men vulnerable to such violence.[22] For one, ICE often uses "lateral deportation" to release deportees in cities they've never been to before. Men arrive in Mexico disoriented. Most have never been to the border, and many have not seen their home country in decades. Robbed of their social connections, they are easy to kidnap, extort, or coerce. If men are or were once affiliated with U.S. gangs, they can also be seen as rivals—a threat to local cartels unless they are killed or brought into the fold. Particularly at the northeastern border, which has been hotly contested since the early 2000s, cartels seek to neutralize possible enemies. Often, the U.S. deports men straight to the territory of opposing cartels, as if intending to have them killed.

At the same time, U.S. incarceration, military experience, and gangs (including prison gangs) *train* men to endure and exercise violence. Many deported men have withstood harsh conditions in prison. In addition, as Tijuana scholar and activist Victor Clark-Alfaro puts it, "The [deported] gang members know how to use weapons, speak English, have contact with gangs in the U.S., and show no fear."[23] Cartels are especially interested in recruiting men with U.S. military training, for their insider knowledge of tactics of violence.

Most respondents said that on their release at the border, cartels immediately offered them guns and invited or forced them to join, especially if they'd been in prison. Cartel scouts know the U.S. release points and how to find new arrivals: disoriented, speaking English or "Chicano" accented Spanish, with certain tattoos and prison-issued or gang-affiliated clothing. These lookouts often pick men up on the street, strip searched them for tattoos, and interrogate them about their crimes, gang activity, and ties to other organizations.[24] Both military agents and cartel members also sit at the border bus stations, to trap men who look like they're lost. If cartels think men are "suspicious," they may torture them or offer a choice: join the local criminal rings or be killed.[25]

All this was common knowledge among our respondents. For instance, 28-year-old Gaspar, from chapter 2, had lived in the U.S. since he was six, joined a gang, and eventually served time in prison. When he got out in Mexico, he remembered:

> We arrived in Tamaulipas, well, and you [deportees] are talking all in English. From only hearing my mom [speak Spanish], you lose the accent. You lose all the idioms and the way you had with words. So, when we arrived in Tamaulipas, there were two or three people waiting for us to see if we wanted to work with them. They were from Mexican cartels. [They asked], "Were you in prison (*la cárcel*)?" "Yes." "Do you know how to do this and that?" "Yes." And about 50 percent of the people from where we were [in prison] went with them, because it's, "Either you come with me or—." Because here [in Mexico], no one is going to notice. They would threaten you with death. "Either you come with me to work, or what will we do?" . . . These people approached me, too, and they said, "Well, we're offering you work, to go work in Tampico, Sinaloa, and Tijuana," doing the same things, right? Selling drugs, selling drugs.

Once cartels confirmed that men had the desired experience, they gave a stark choice: join or die. By luck, a friend pulled Gaspar into his father's car, and they sped off to Mexico City. Had Gaspar not had such luck, he might have been recruited or murdered. By his estimation, half of men coming out of prison end up in cartels.

Other respondents described arriving at *la línea* (the border) as the start of a hunt in which they were the prey. Edgardo, a 35-year-old man from Oaxaca, told us that the day after his release in Nogales, Sonora (bordering Arizona):

> They [cartels] were picking up people to get them to carry drugs to the United States, and I told the guys [I got out with], "Dude, hide, because those guys are picking people up, and if they get you, they're going to use you as a mule, and you can't get out of that. There, they kill you because they kill you." So, when I passed them, we hid under a friggin' bus (*urbano*), and we were hiding there until those guys left. But they did get various people, and they took them as mules. In fact, most of them were the people who were trying to get back into the United States.

Men's desperation to get back to the U.S. compelled some to choose work as mules. Cartels exploited despair, then threatened torture or death if men did not comply.

Amid few, bad choices, some deportees did join cartels. The organizations offered one means to reclaim masculinity and refuse state control. At times, cartel abuse could seem like an invitation to reestablish their power as men. As one participant put it, "Get beaten down or join to reclaim your manhood." Several accepted this challenge. In chapter 6, I say more about how criminal organizations can give men a tenuous path into agency. Here, I address their role as constraint.

By targeting and integrating deported men, cartels extended the criminalization and violence of U.S. police and border enforcement. Reinforcing men's criminal histories enabled such organizations to use them as foot soldiers and fall guys. Men's histories in U.S. prison—and resulting isolation—made them exploitable and expendable.

Mexican Police and Military Abuse

U.S. politicians often frame Mexican state brutality as a sign of corruption, ineffectual government, or failed rule of law. Yet the fortification of the U.S. side of the border has pushed a parallel Mexican border militarization.[26] For one, the U.S. Criminal History Information System (CHIS) enables the U.S. government to share information on "criminal aliens" (deportees) with the Mexican state.[27] The U.S. government also pours vast funding into the Mexican military to keep migration and drug trafficking down.[28] For instance, the Merida Initiative, begun in 2008, provided more than $3 billion in military equipment and training for Mexican police and military agents.[29] U.S. funding and demand have encouraged Mexico to deploy tens of thousands of army, marines, national guard, and local and federal police to the border, to stop organized crime, drug trafficking, and migrants who "threaten" to enter the United States. In some border states, soldiers have replaced local police, driving a radical increase in violence.[30]

Stigma and isolation make deportees easy targets for these officials. As long as the government marks repatriated men as criminals and narcos, it can beat and kill them with little scrutiny from the public.[31] Furthermore, many Mexican police and military agents are secretly in the pay of cartels, up to the highest ranks of the state. Cartels often bribe or coerce police and soldiers to arrest and assault deportees or serve them up to criminal organizations. Often, the narcos dictate rules, patterns of migration, and targets of abuse.

Human rights reports show that Mexican soldiers and municipal police officers are among the primary perpetrators of violence against deportees.[32] Like U.S. police, Mexican police regularly stop migrants arbitrarily, ask for identification, take their money, beat them, arrest them, or throw them in jail without a clear charge.[33] Since deported men rarely have access to their Mexican birth certificates or IDs, such arrests are frequently made on the pretext of "no identification." "Undocumented" in their country of their birth, deported men cannot access jobs, housing, or safety. Scholars and journalists have also reported kidnapping, torture, theft, verbal abuse, and other assaults by public officials in Tijuana and across the Mexican side of the border.[34]

Border politicians also deploy police to "clean up" their cities for tourists and investors from the United States. Blaming deportees for crime, economic burdens, and undermining Baja California's relations with the United States, the state government pressures repatriated Mexicans to return to their places of origin. Sometimes, they do this via "soft" information campaigns at places like shelters. Other times, they literally beat them out of there. In one exemplary show of force in the 2010s, Tijuana's municipal police "cleaned out" thousands of homeless men living in encampments in the canal near the U.S. Mexico border, most of them deportees.[35] The cops arrested 90 people, destroyed thousands of dwellings, and brutally beat up the residents—leading to several deaths. Branding deportees as criminals and outsiders gives border states a convenient scapegoat for urban problems.

Like cartels, state agents take advantage of deportees' disorientation and single them out by their accents, haircuts, or U.S.-style clothing. One interviewee explained that coming from the U.S., you might be wearing a baseball cap, but to Mexican cops, "Oh, *es cholo* (he's an Americanized gangster) . . . it is like gang affiliated, or you're a *malandro* (a crook) or whatever, but *nada qué ver* (it has nothing to do with that), so you always have to give them something [a pay-off]." In other words, Mexican police sometimes *claimed* to see men as criminals, in order to make arrests and get bribes. Most people we interviewed had endured such shakedowns, which typically involved stops for minor offenses like improper driving, lack of identification, or being in the "wrong area" or a "conflict zone." As one man put it, "They'll pull you over for any tiny little reason; they don't even try to give you a ticket, they just straight up ask you, 'Give me a hundred pesos, and

I'll let you go.'" Tijuana police also planted drugs on several respondents or falsely claimed they had drugs on them. If the deportee had no money to give, he could expect to get beaten, harassed, or thrown into jail, echoing U.S.-side traumas.

In many cases, interviewees described Mexican police as more violent than their U.S. counterparts. Diego, for instance, said in Spanglish, "They'll throw you to the ground. They kick you. *Te dan con esa madre que* (they give you those beatings that)—they grab you, they handcuff you, and they throw you in the truck like that. They throw pure iron at you—it's ugly." Rogelio, likewise, remembered a series of incidents with police in Ciudad Juárez, including watching them shoot and kill a young girl and her dad on a bus in broad daylight. He recalled:

> The marines and the army had arrived [at the border], and if you haven't experienced the checkpoints or stops by the marines, you haven't seen anything. They're really ugly, *bien gachos* (really messed up), and they also take you out and they violate your rights. They pull you out of your car, they start to open everything, and they don't care . . . I don't have any respect for the police around here or the federal [police] because they don't help us. They come to rob us, to beat us, to violate our rights.

In some cases, police even kidnapped respondents. Stefano recalled that when ICE let him out in Tijuana, police grabbed him, stole his telephone and identification, threw him into a local prison, and then used his cell phone to call his family in the United States and ask for $5,000 dollars. The cops were clear: they were holding Stefano for ransom.

To prove they were fighting "drug traffickers," Mexican soldiers frequently beat up deportees whom they said "appeared" to have ties to prisons or gangs. Men's prior dehumanization and dislocation facilitated such assaults. Upon his release in Tijuana, for instance, Milton remembered:

> They [Mexican border guards] sent me to the soldiers, the marines, and they beat the crap out of me for a little bit. Because they thought I was with the bad guys, so I was like, "Look, I don't do drugs, I don't sell drugs, I just did something over there," but they beat me for a bit, about fifteen, twenty minutes . . . Two soldiers were waiting for me at the gate [from the U.S.], and they just escorted me, they stripped me naked, searched my property, my shoes, my socks, everything, and then they put the handcuffs on me. They took me to a room, but there were no cameras, no lights, no nothing. It was just a little light in there, and they got this yellow phone book, and they started beating the crap out of me . . . They just told me, "You got an hour to get to the airport or to go to the bus station and get the fuck out of here."

In such incidents, Mexican officials echoed the abuse and expulsions of U.S. police and prisons.

Mexican personnel also prefigured U.S. border agents' brutality. In several cases, they physically stopped men approaching the border to recross or smuggle drugs.[36] Brayan, who worked as a mule, told Ana of one such experience. Now 27, Brayan was born in Veracruz and moved to Arizona at age 15. Shortly thereafter, he landed in prison for trafficking drugs. Not only was Brayan incarcerated in the United States; he was also beaten by the *Mexican* army. One time, as he approached the border carrying a load, he described:

> We got to the desert, we got everything ready, and we had to walk some. Let's say a day or two days still inside Mexico to be able to get to the border, and all that time we had to hide from the [Mexican] soldiers, so they wouldn't catch us, because *nos pegan unas chingas bien feo* (they give you horrible beatings). Yes, they leave our whole body bruised, black eyes, bruised ribs, everything, everything, and then they send us back . . . There are some that aren't corrupt (*manchados*), if they get you with all of that, they let you go. But there are others that if they catch you like that— that you're walking like that in the desert and you have things hidden in there, they beat you until they have taken it all out—and they keep it for themselves.

When Ana, confused between U.S. and Mexican agents, checked *who* Brayan was talking about, he repeated, "That's the *Mexican* army."

Thus, Mexican state agents extended the logic, tactics, and targets of U.S. border enforcement. In the process, they added to U.S. banishment.

LIVING THROUGH SOCIAL DEATH

What did it feel like to live under such conditions—and try not to disappear?

At the border, deported men felt banished. That is, they felt pushed out of four, key things that made them both humans and men: (1) love, (2) place, (3) mind, and (4) hope. Isolated and afraid to connect with other people, they were, as they put it, *solos* (alone/lonely): alienated from love. Their minds still on the United States, with little welcome from folks at the Mexican border, they also felt *desubicados* (disoriented): alienated from place. Some also suffered from mental illness and felt out of their minds, alienated from a sense of themselves. Finally, several spoke of the threat of death, capturing the *desesperación* (despair) of the Casa's wall of the missing. That is, they felt alienated from hope. Many considered themselves in limbo not only between the U.S. and Mexico but also between life and death.

Out of Love

At the border, interviewees often felt *solos*: expelled from the relationships that make people human. U.S. prisons and border enforcement had stripped them of their loved ones in *both* the U.S. and Mexico. Some hid from family, ashamed by the stigma of prison or deportation. Scared of police and cartels, others hid from the world. To protect themselves from more grief, some avoided making friends or rebuilding families. Others were uncertain whether they *could* ever start a family anew. Aching, the men we met in Baja believed they belonged to no one.

Rafael, a 33-year-old at the Casa, said that in Tijuana, he lived "like a dog." Born in Guadalajara, Jalisco, Rafael was brought to California at two and raised in Fresno, a "son of the system." Though he finished middle school in the U.S. and spoke fluent English, he never learned how to read or write. For a while, he drove a forklift and worked in the fields. The first time Rafael went to prison, he was 18, a new father and a reluctant new husband. He got locked up for eight months for domestic abuse. After his 2004 deportation, Rafael returned to the U.S. within a week. He fathered three more children, and though he never stayed with the moms, his second son became, as he said, "my pride and joy."

The next time, the U.S. deported Rafael for selling drugs. He paid thousands of dollars to crawl back through a sewer to Arizona, but "as soon as we walked out, the [U.S.] border patrol was there—like just smacked us down. Literally, they like, hit us and tazed us and everything." He got six months in federal prison. When Fátima met Rafael at the Casa, he had just been deported a third time.

Now, Rafael was alone. He no longer spoke with his four "baby moms." Raised in the U.S., he had no family in Mexico. He didn't plan to build a family there, either. After prison, he said, he could "only handle" taking care of himself. Nevertheless, he longed for his son: "Fuck, you know, it hurts. I ain't have nobody out here. *Aquí estoy como un perro, estoy solo aquí* (Here, I'm like a dog. I'm alone here). I go through that like weekly. I'mma put a smile on there, but it's not really a smile."

Rafael struggled to like Tijuana and stay out of harm. He remembered that when he was in U.S. prison, inmates called Tijuana "the worst place in the world" and described it as filled with murder and decapitation. To live there, he learned, you needed to keep your head down and stay out of people's business. Though Rafael considered restarting his "hussle" (selling drugs) in Tijuana, he felt too afraid. After trying to do the same, a friend deported with Rafael got shot six times in the face. Cartels knew at a glance, he said, that you hadn't lived here for long. So, Rafael concluded, "You gotta be streetwise . . . You gotta walk with your head up high out here. You can't let your guard down for nothing because people will step all over you." To survive, he kept to himself. A friendship with someone "stupid," he figured, might get him killed.

Rafael had also been arrested by local police, whom he described as "assholes" who "treat you stupid." One night, after washing dishes at the Casa, he put on his uniform and left for his job as a security guard. Outside the shelter, a cop pulled him over, handcuffed him, and threw him into the car. When Rafael asked, "Why are you treating me like a criminal, you fools?," they said they were just doing random searches. Rafael argued back, "Yeah but you shouldn't be handcuffing me before anything. I got my security outfit on . . . let me see your badge number." Rafael began taking photos, only to have his phone snatched away. The cop snapped, "You're not supposed to be here, 'cause this is like real drug heavy right here, real risky." Rafael got 36 hours in jail. Then, he realized he had to bribe his way out: "Everything has a price. Out here, the law will sell theirselves [*sic*]." After that, he tried to blend in.

In prison and on the streets, Rafael had learned that he could trust no one. Suspicious and scared all the time, he avoided making new friends. When Fátima asked what it felt like to try to make friends in Tijuana, he simply said, "I don't have friends. It's hard to make friends here cause it's really hard to trust people. Just me, myself—it's hard for me to trust nobody . . . There's really nobody out here to trust. There's a lot of people burned out here. From my background [in prison], it's hard to trust [mumbles] . . . It's been me, myself, and I here. I think everybody's like that . . . it's everyone to themselves." His fears ranged from fellow migrants stealing his cigarettes at the shelter to someone gunning him down in the streets.

In Tijuana, Rafael admitted, he was "doing bad." Often, he could hardly function at all. He went on in mixed Spanish and English:

> Sometimes I stay in bed for like two or three days. I don't wanna work, I don't wanna do nothing . . . Here no one is going to give you [tell you], "Hey, dude, get up, *ánimo* (cheer up)." No one! . . . Two or three days being a bum. Just no shaving or nothing, just like, fuck. It's like—I don't know, *como una depresión o algo* (like a depression or something). I think about it, is this depression? What the hell is this? I don't know what it is, but . . . it happens to me a lot. And it never happened to me out there. It's hard out here. Super hard.

Compared with this life at the border, Rafael felt, U.S. prison looked almost good. He went on, "Sometimes, I feel like, 'Fu- I'mma just go.' And if I get caught, I'll be better off in jail than here [in Tijuana], you know. I ain't gonna have to worry about my rent, I ain't have to worry about nothing. I just eat, rest, and eat, you know. 'Cause I've been institutionalized like all my life." Rafael felt he was losing his mind—so much that returning to prison sounded like respite.

Facing similar fear and distrust, almost two-thirds of men we met in Tijuana said they were lonely. Occasionally, they, too, wondered if life might be better if they got locked up in the U.S. again.

For Gaspar, the experience of losing family and getting attacked in prison made it hard to engage with people. He felt socially awkward. When he got deported, he explained:

> It was starting all over from zero, because I had to get used to [people saying], "Well, what do you . . . feel like doing?" [I'd answer], "I don't know. Stay in this room because I'm afraid to be outside. I don't know what to do." . . . It was really hard for me to incorporate into society. I didn't know what to do. I didn't know where to go, and I felt discriminated against here in Mexico because even though I was Mexican I didn't speak Spanish, or it was *pocho* (Americanized) Spanish . . . All those friends I had, it was all gone.

Gaspar wasn't alone. Men routinely told us that U.S. prison made them isolated, insecure, and shy, leaving them "alone in this world." One explained that after removal, "my life was a cage. I didn't want to see anyone. I felt like everyone looked at me with contempt." The feeling of being locked up traveled with them, embodied in their mindsets of self-protection.

Assaults, beatings, and theft in Mexico reinforced such men's instincts to keep to themselves. A respondent who'd been beaten within an inch of his life by cartels said bluntly, "I like to keep my distance because they can do things to you. They can kill you. They can kidnap you. There are a lot of crazy people—and more in the community [of deportees] I belong to." After a pause, he corrected himself: he "had no community." Crying, another man told me that in Tijuana, "friends don't exist."

Out of Place

Men in Tijuana also felt *desubicados* (disoriented, placeless), as if they belonged to nowhere. Almost no one we interviewed grew up in the border region, so they lacked the social ties of earlier migrants returning to loved ones back "home." Many also stayed at the border "in waiting." Even when their U.S. spouses or children were long-since estranged, they fixated on getting back. Often, they thought of themselves as "American." Their focus on return kept them attuned to the U.S., making it hard to adapt in Mexico. Many felt like strangers in their own land.

Violence at the border reinforced their distaste for Mexico. Respondents often said that they thought Mexico was corrupt or that they "hated" the Mexican government. Others were cynical about the prospect of legitimate politics in either country—given the chains of debasement and violence they faced across place. They linked the racism and abuse they endured in the U.S. with the beatings, corruption, and disfunction they now faced south of the border.

Enrique, the father who'd lived 40 years in LA and tried to get back 12 times, said frankly, "To be sincere, my adaptation in Tijuana—no. I have not been able to adapt in Tijuana."

Enrique traced his unease to his multiple apprehensions by U.S. border patrol—and the abuse he faced at the border from both cartels and police. The twelfth time Enrique tried to rejoin his family, the U.S. government sent him to prison in Pecos, Texas. As Enrique's release date approached, he heard rumors the Gulf Cartel was killing people from his home state of Michoacán. He remembered, "The news there was crazy, running, that it was really dangerous out where they [ICE] were throwing people out, which was Reynosa and Matamoros . . . They were killing us mercilessly." A few days later ICE released Enrique in Tamaulipas, the most violent state on the border. As Enrique got into a Grupo Beta (government) van, armed men surrounded the car, asking the deportees for their "password" and shaking them down for dollars. Enrique remembered, "They put like three rifles in my chest. They stopped me, and they put rifles in my face. People were walking behind us, guarding us, and I told them not to hurt me, that I'd give them my money. I gave them my envelope of money, and they threw me over there and said,

'We don't want your money. We want to know where you're from and what you are doing here.'"

The van driver (who may have been in the pay of cartels, delivering migrants), eventually talked their way out. Enrique was spooked. He went on, "I'm a man, and I swear to you that I am not a fearful person, but there are moments we all get stuck. I couldn't even swallow my own saliva . . . They came with weapons, and a really young little guy [deportee] there started to yell, to cry, to double over because he thought they would gun us down." Later, Enrique heard that cartels had chopped others to death. Many people from Michoacán disappeared. The murders set the stage for Enrique's "reintegration." As soon as he could, Enrique left for Tijuana.

In Tijuana, Enrique was constantly harassed by police, making him feel even more out of place. Between recrossing attempts, he often slept or came for a meal at the Casa del Migrante. He explained to Fátima that though he found work in a lightbulb factory (*maquila*):

> It's really hard. Why is it so hard to adapt? A lot of things. For example, over there in the United States, the police respect people a little bit more. Here, no. Here the police from the moment you get out of the—from the time they tell you to stop, they get there and start disrespecting you, swearing . . . How I suffered! I want you to know that [when I arrived], I would go out of here from the Casa del Migrante. I would walk down those train tracks without knowing where I was, without a path or direction, crying my tears, just crying. It's really dangerous here—down below, they kill people on those stairs—and at that time I watched my first shootout on television [news] . . . 30, 40 dead appeared on all sides, with *narcomantas* (a message or threat left by a cartel) . . . [The Casa] would kick you out at 8:00 in the morning, and . . . the police would come and say, "Hey, at nine if you don't have work, get out of here, because at nine I'm coming back, and I'm going to take you all." There were times I thought it was better if they just took me. I'd sit there, the police would come, and [they'd say], "Hey, I told you, get in." And boom, I'd do 24 hours there [in jail], in the nothing, in the 20—20 de Noviembre [jail]—and it would be freezing in there . . . because you came out of here [the Casa] not knowing where to go, not knowing anything or knowing Tijuana. And there was a lot of danger from people who wanted to carve out tunnels, to plant *mota* (marijuana), to do this—*sicarios* (hitmen), they [cartels] went around hiring *sicarios*.

Enrique was not just lonely; he was also afraid. He knew that police would come looking for dollars—as well as for migrants they could arrest. He explained, "If they have a little reason to take you, they're going to take you—you're in a prohibited zone, they ask for your identification, or they don't care." Once, when Enrique tried to escape arrest by acting like he was mute, the officer told him, "I am going to make you talk by beating it out of you." Right in front of the Casa del Migrante, they beat him, breaking his ribs. Later, they loaded him into their truck and kept beating: "It was like two hours of beat me and beat me. They beat me with a bottle, until I finally started swearing." For Enrique it all felt senseless: "I wasn't doing anything wrong. I don't take drugs. I was going to look for work." At one point, police harassment got so bad that Enrique chose to risk more time in U.S. detention, rather than stay in Tijuana.

Enrique was not alone. Bernardo, another Michoacano, had no family left in Mexico and missed his loved ones in California. Targeted by Tijuana police, he struggled to feel at home. In Spanglish, he told Zianía:

> All my family is back there, all of it. I'm out here solo, I'm ridin' solo. I'm just trying to be optimistic. Getting used to (*acostumbrando*) something is very hard. Here, the Latino that comes from up there, we are money, we are easy prey (*una presa fácil*). We don't know the streets. We don't know a lot of people. If they see me talking in English, that's money right there . . . I try my best. But sometimes just—I just go to my room, hide, and stay there, think about it, and cry alone you know? 'Cause I got family over there, you know? *Esta vida no era mi vida, esta vida* (this was not my life, this life) is different, a different life . . . I imagine that I'm over there [in California], but it's hard. It's complicated because I just want to run and scream and kick and do stuff. The point is I just want to run, go home, and tell my daughter, "I love you, *m'ija*. Daddy is back." I wish I could get that opportunity, but I don't see it . . . I'm crying, I'm crying in the inside. I just gotta be a man.

In Tijuana, Bernardo felt he was "prey." Depressed and longing for California, he hid in his room, just wishing to be somewhere else. Though he had no choice but to "be a man," he continued crying inside.

Out of Mind

Deported men often felt they had lost not just families and homes but also their minds.[37] They spoke of struggling to stay sane, especially in Tijuana: of fighting depression, anxiety, post-traumatic stress disorder, dissociation, and psychosis (among other disorders). Without prompting, 51 of 171 men we interviewed described themselves as depressed, 25 talked about trauma, and 18 told us they'd tried to kill themselves (leaving aside those who spoke of their mental health in less searchable terms).[38] Some men we met were so disoriented that their stories were incoherent or unintelligible.[39]

These interviewees bore the embodied and affective scars of U.S. incarceration, the grief of losing their families and prior lives, and the terror of Mexican police and cartels. Depressed, psychotic, or agoraphobic after living in U.S. prisons, many found it hard to root in reality, let alone settle in Mexico. Some dissociated. Others self-medicated with drugs and alcohol. Several spoke of friends who took their own lives. In short, these men no longer trusted *themselves*. As one participant put it, they no longer "had an identity."

Roberto, who'd lived in Watts (LA) for four decades, had been in Tijuana for 23 months when he met Pamela at the Casa. In LA, Roberto sold drugs, got beaten by cops, and went to prison until his deportation in 2017. Roberto was one of three brothers, all three "sons of the system," and all three locked up and deported. Both of his brothers had died in Tijuana: one from drinking (he didn't specify how) and the other from choking on crystal meth. The specter hung over Roberto, who was beaten up by Tijuana police and often recruited by gangs. He admitted then when he arrived in Baja, "I wanted to take my life. I never told nobody this because I don't know nobody here. I don't have no family here. I don't have friends here, family, so you feel alone. I feel alone sometimes, and I get depressed, you know?" Having used "dope" since he was 14, Roberto relapsed on drugs.

Other men, too, said they barely had reason to live. Stuck in shelters, without work and struggling to stay sane since their deportations, numerous interviewees tried suicide (some more than once). Thus, when Nick (a student) asked 38-year-old Álvaro what kept him going, Álvaro told him, "For me? Nothing really. I don't have a reason. To be honest, I try to find a reason to live and keep going, but I really don't have one. So, my life is more like a real 'make it or break it.' All it takes is a couple bad thoughts and a drink." Alfredo, 32, felt hopeless as well. After foster care, gangs, and prison, Alfredo was deeply alone. In Tijuana, he shared, "I attempted once to commit suicide. I swallowed a razor blade. I guess I was very depressed."

Under such conditions, it was hard for men to take care of themselves. Several showed signs of physical degradation. Some were on crutches or used canes. Often, based on respondents' worn faces and unkempt appearance, students guessed they were decades older than their actual age.

For relief, some turned to drugs or alcohol. In his interview with Camila, Timoteo did not hide his addiction to crystal meth. A 33-year-old from Guadalajara, Timoteo rode up on a motorcycle to his interview, in black pants and dress shoes. His eyes were unusually red, but Camila persisted. Timoteo had moved to Santa Ana, California, when he was 15. A few years later, the U.S. sent him to prison for gang violence and armed robbery. In prison, Timoteo lost touch with his parents, his siblings, and his now 15-year-old daughter. Stigmatized back in his hometown, Timoteo had nowhere to go. In his mind, he was "like an American citizen . . . even though I'm Mexican, and I was born in Mexico." Though Timoteo had been in rehab in the U.S., his deportation triggered a relapse with drugs:

> I guess that's my way of like coping with things or, like, I wanna forget it. But then I start using, and then I start doing worse. And then I get this moral feeling like, "Oh my God, I shouldn't have done it. I'm fucking up again." So, it's a cycle . . . I would tell my parents, "It's because I don't like how I feel. I feel like everybody is attacking me. I feel like everybody is looking down on me, like they don't even know me, and they don't even—" They say, "Well, it's the drugs. If you don't like how you feel, then why do you do it?" But it's because . . . the feeling is like, "I don't wanna feel anything." And that's my way of coping . . . I guess I see it as: the opposite of addiction is—it would be like, *connection* [my italics]. If I don't feel connected to somebody or to someone or to something, I feel like I have no purpose, and I feel like I just go and get into drugs. . . . I feel like, *Ya valió verga todo* (It was all worth shit)—Everything's fucked up, so why am I even trying? Fuck it.

In Mexico, Timoteo felt like *everyone* saw him as less than human. Stripped of his family, his home and his sanity, he stopped wanting to feel at all. Drugs let him numb the pain.

In Tijuana, drugs and the drug trade permeated deported men's lives. Addiction then reinforced their vulnerability to cartels and the drug trade in general.[40] As one man put it, "In Tijuana, . . . there is drugs everywhere, everywhere you go there is drugs, there is alcohol, there is trouble." Indeed, 82 percent of the men we interviewed in Tijuana mentioned using, selling, or being around or threatened by drugs and addiction.[41] Some sold drugs to get out of financial problems. Others used or encountered drugs in the call centers where they worked.

Men often said they "took refuge" in alcohol, especially when they'd lost any sense of fairness—or even reality. During our interviews, some men drank; appeared to be high, fidgeting, or avoiding eye contact; or looked frantic or red in the eyes. By their own admission, once men began using drugs, a cascade of problems ensued. Landlords and shelters expelled them. Some ended up in rehab, Mexican jails, or the streets.[42] At Tijuana's main soup kitchen, we met deported men who'd started selling drugs in the U.S. at 13, gone in and out of U.S. prisons, and grown hooked on meth once again when they landed back in Tijuana. Such men ping-ponged between shelters and life on the streets. Few had contact with loved ones at all. Addicts were also more vulnerable to homicide and more likely to see addiction as their own fault. Some admitted that thanks to alcohol and/or drugs, they saw no future at all. One self-described alcoholic who'd been sent to a mental asylum after an abusive childhood, foster care, and then prison, said that the doctors told him he'd die before he reached 35. As for his plans, "I don't see any future. I really don't."

Out of Hope

When our team asked how men felt in Tijuana, more than half said "desesperados": hopeless, in despair. It was hard for men to contend with the degradation of their self-worth. They spoke of feeling they had fallen apart or reached the end of the world—as if they had no agency left. When asked of their plans, one said, "To tell you the truth, right now I don't have any dreams." Many grew jaded. Some felt like shells of their former selves, unable to reclaim their lives or their status as men. Struggling to stay sane, they found it hard to contest their criminalization.

Men's despair manifested itself in their stories of disappearance or death.[43] Many were haunted by friends who vanished from shelters or videos they'd seen of bodies rotting in the Sonoran desert or Tijuana ditches.

Teodoro, a chubby 26-year-old man with an earring and hair shaved close at the sides of his head, associated his two-year stay in Tijuana with loneliness and drug use so deep it started to "kill him." Teodoro had lived most of his life in Escondido, California (near San Diego), raised by his drug-addict mother and sometimes his grandma. He got into gangs and was deported at 21. In Tijuana, he found work at a taco shop. Police in Tijuana often harassed Teodoro for his tattoos, so he started to wear his apron to work—as a sign to leave him alone. Constantly anxious, he also began to use drugs. Then his friend Blacky was murdered.

Chatting in a disordered mix of English and Spanish, Teodoro remembered that one day Blacky asked to borrow his apron—to get through a zone the police marked off limits. A few days later, the cops found a body, bloody and beaten to death, wearing Teodoro's blue apron. Sitting in a coffee shop in Mexico City (where he'd moved to escape the border), Teodoro told Ana:

> I have a lot of friends here [in Mexico] who—they deport them, and they get into drugs, and they feel alone. And because of that—aside from the fact that they're already used to consuming drugs—they start to use more. They're alone, they feel worse, and think about it, loneliness and drugs is [*sic*] killing them little by little. That's the bad thing, I think—that when you get here you feel so alone and without support. And for many people, their relief is to say, "Let's go smoke." Or "Let's go use drugs to forget." . . . I've had friends that arrive here and get into drugs or get into things they shouldn't, and soon they wake up dead or things like that. Like my friend Blacky. He used to rob houses, and we'd always tell him to go get some work. I'd tell him, "Go work in the call center," and no. Then one day—because I worked in a *taquería* in Tijuana, too, and I would always keep my [work] aprons on so the police wouldn't stop me. You walk in Tijuana, they see you with a shaved head, and they stop you, [saying], "You're in a conflict zone; get in [the police car]." And that's why I said, "No," and I would keep my work aprons on. And Blacky said, "Lend me an apron." I lent him an apron, and then a girl they used to call *la guera* (the white girl) who's like the neighborhood reporter, you could say, she came one day and told me, "They found Blacky dead." And I said "What?" "In a wasteland (*baldío*), where they found him with a blue apron." And yes, it was the same apron . . . so he could go and walk, and if the police stopped him [he could say], "Well no, I'm going to work, I have my work apron." And they found him dead.

For Teodoro, the story portended his *own* death of drugs and loneliness, should he fail to get out of Tijuana. "It was like a wakeup call, you could say, . . . like 'get with it' or if not, you're going down."

Of course, we could not find "disappeared" men themselves. But their traces threaded through other men's stories of barely escaping death. As one man in Oaxaca remembered, when he got let out at the border, "I was hearing a lot of shit of people who go in the wrong spot or in the wrong taxi, and they make you disappear . . . I was actually going to stay in TJ [Tijuana] but then I was like, nah. I'm gonna wanna—temptation is going to be right there, I'm gonna wanna—I'm going to end up getting into shit over here for sure."

Disappearance loomed on the Casa's wall of the missing and in tales of friends who were killed, addicted, kidnapped, or working as low-level smugglers. Of men who landed back in U.S. or Mexican prison, found themselves on the street, or died in the borderland desert. Friends warned men that if they stayed at the border, "You're going to die here. You're not going to be able to do anything here. You're going to get into more of that stuff, and then you're going to have to pay. The Mexican police are going to put you in prison."

It's hard to estimate how many got so unlucky or to determine if these stories were "true." But clearly, disposability seeped into men's *emotions*, as a symbol of social death.

A SECOND CHANCE?

Sometimes, men in Tijuana hoped that return would give them a "second chance"—an opportunity to reinvent themselves not as "criminals" but as "good people" and "men."

When our team began interviewing deported men in Tijuana in 2019, students pointed out that several adopted this "reset" mentality. The men talked about wanting an "opportunity to be someone," "be good," get in shape, or find God. The students were often surprised that people seemed so optimistic amid lockup, isolation, and border assaults. But we realized that like the redemption narrative common in prison, this "second chance" framework gave some men meaning and hope—and a promise of release from gangs or addiction. It also helped deportees make sense of their "criminality," by framing arrest and prison as part of the "past."

Typically, men's "reset mentality" was tied to belief in God or rebirth. Most encountered such thinking in U.S. prisons. Sometimes, Catholic shelters or evangelical groups in Tijuana reinforced their Christian worldview. For example, Santino, mentioned in chapter 2, was sent to U.S. prison for selling meth. There, he started to read the Bible and turn to God. Now back in Tijuana, Santino claimed he was no longer looking for fun, booze, women, or money. Instead, he said, "I know that I can remake my life, and I know there are a lot of things I could do here . . . I hit rock bottom [in a disgusted tone]. The drug business is easy money . . . But in reality, that is not happiness. At my age right now . . . What I'm looking for and what I pray to God for is just to behave myself well and help my daughters." This mindset help Santino feel that all was not lost in Tijuana. Like others, he thanked God for setting him "free."

Deportees who believed in a "second chance" had more hope than their peers in Tijuana. For instance, Emilio remembered U.S. prison as the worst experience of his life. While locked up, he wanted to be deported just to escape the misery. When Emilio got to Tijuana, he felt he could start again "clean." Now, he was working and no longer using drugs. Alfredo, who grew up in U.S. foster care and had diagnosed PTSD, also tried to frame Tijuana as a new start. For the future, he said, "I have to be brave and stand tall and deal with the consequences instead of me just whining or just feeling bad about myself, that life hasn't treated me fair, that I never really had a family or a home. Instead of me just being—like feeling depressed . . . you have to forget about the past and move forward and start all over here and face reality, this place. Right now, I try to better myself, try to survive here in Mexico." Alfredo used the "reset mentality" to convince himself he could survive. He exercised, he played sports, and he tried to forget. It was his only alternative to getting lost in depression.

In practice, however, individual-level redemption was often an empty promise. For one, it emerged out of deprivation. Men who adopted this story tended to be the most isolated, traumatized deportees—the same men whose lives were so degraded by U.S. prison that they felt happy to just get "out." Thus, while Alfredo hoped to begin again, his chances were slim. In reality, he had diagnosed PTSD and no close family or friends. Likewise, Valentín was drunk when Camila entered his shop in Oaxaca. Covered in motor oil, he slunk out from under a faded Volkswagen to tell Camila his vision of starting anew. Despite his second chance story, he was widely known to be using drugs.

The redemption narrative also invited self-blame. While the idea of a second chance helped some deportees find hope, it also suggested that deportation—and the feeling of alienation afterward—were an individual's fault. Sometimes, men who adopted this mentality implied that when others died in Tijuana or crossing the desert, it was due to their "personal" choices. Others blamed themselves for their pain. As mentioned in chapter 2, men who had "found religion" in prison often deflected blame from the system onto themselves, taking the stance that "I was with the devil, and now I have come to God." Some even expressed appreciation for the United States. In turn, self-blame may have decreased men's interest in connecting with others who were also excluded or in challenging structural forces that reinforced violence against them.

CONCLUSION

The photos on the Casa del Migrante's "wall of shame" hint at how violence and isolation threaten men's lives in Tijuana. Interviewing people in shelters—often the most desperate and vulnerable after removal—our team saw the heavy emotional weight of such threats. Many men we met had nowhere to turn. Coming from prison, several had lost their families and homes. At the border, they faced cartels, police, and military personnel.[44] By extending the criminalization and erasure begun by U.S. police and prisons, cartels made money, drug customers, and recruits. Police proved their legitimacy, efficacy, and ability to meet monthly quotas. As they did, these institutions extended the impacts of U.S. prisons onto the Mexican side.

Because cartels and Mexican military and police were concentrated at the border—as were the most anomic of deportees—the feeling of banishment was especially acute in this site.[45] Interviewees in Oaxaca and Mexico City echoed some elements of these emotions, but few felt so close to death. Sometimes it was a matter of timing: men arrived in Tijuana alienated then left to find friendlier settings as they settled back into Mexico. Those in other sites had often been in Mexico longer (a median of 24 months, versus 3 at the border), giving them time to adjust. The men who stayed at the border the longest were often people in waiting. Instead of *reintegrating* to Mexico, they felt *disintegrated* as people: cut off from their families, homes, sanity, and sense of hope. They had not just been exiled from a nation (the U.S.) but from human value. For them, the border was a hot spot of alienation.

Publicly, such alienation has often stoked fear that "angry young men" (of color) are poised to become the foot soldiers of terror and organized crime (see, e.g., work by *New York Times* columnist Thomas Friedman). On the Mexican side, politicians have also blamed deportees for destabilizing local political life. Thus, such figures pander to—and reinforce—the U.S. story of a Latino male "threat."[46] While some deportees, indeed, turn to violence (as addressed in the coming chapter), these media and political stories frame men *themselves* as sources of violence—a looming crisis in need of still deeper control.

In contrast, I highlight how in both the U.S. and Mexico, police, ICE, prisons, and cartels create the conditions that leave men emasculated, scared, and untethered. Combining imprisonment and deportation not only dehumanizes men and weaponizes family separation; it also enables violence by Mexican police and cartels. This radioactive combination has left some parts of the U.S.-Mexico border so wracked by violence that NGOs and state agents no longer dare to help, especially in the east. In turn, their fears feed demand for even *more* punishment and exclusion.

Rather than stemming violence, adding more U.S. or Mexican military, police, or prisons would likely intensify deportees' alienation.[47] The resulting conditions could also fuel more migration. At its extreme, the binational carceral system may push deported men to return to the U.S. despite the risk to their lives or the threat of prison. Indeed, in our work, some men felt such despair at the border (thanks to aftereffects of U.S. imprisonment and ongoing threats of policing) that they *preferred* going back into U.S. prison. This system is also unjust.

Instead, U.S. and Mexican institutions must open space for migrant men to belong. This is not a fool's errand. Displacement, suffering, and disengagement coexist with *agency*. In our research, deported men's sense of alienation varied with urban context, as well as with time. In some border sites, where cartel violence was most intense, men felt subject to imminent death. But with less acute policing and cartel recruitment, and lighter U.S. prison or detention, deported men faced fewer abuses, especially in Mexico's interior.[48] In places like Mexico City, they challenged erasure by moving away from the border, building community, and enlivening new, binational ways of being. Examining the alternatives that *already exist*—as I do in chapter 6—can light the path toward more humane support.

6

Reclaiming Removal

Acknowledgment: Fátima Khayar Cámara, Ana López Ricoy, and Abi Thornton's volunteer and organizing work with deportees greatly informed this chapter. In particular, Ana spent summer 2019 volunteering at Otros Dreams en Acción and interviewing more than 50 men and women in Mexico City, giving on-the-ground context to the stories men told us. I am also grateful to the leaders described for their candor.

In 2018, when this study started, newspapers in Mexico, the U.S., and Europe were abuzz over deportee-led movements in Mexico City. From the ashes of deportation, they announced, migrants were building new ways of being. For instance, *El País*, the most-read Spanish newspaper online, described an area in Mexico City called "Little LA." There, the article touted, more than 2,000 repatriated Mexicans had started food stalls, barbershops, and mutual aid organizations: "The neighborhood, in the center of Mexico's capital, has become a refuge for Mexican Americans, attracted first by the call centers that capitalized on their bilingual talents, and later by a community that is no longer scandalized by Spanglish, baggy pants, or tattoos."[1]

Deportados Unidos en la Lucha (Deportees United in Struggle, or DUL)—a grassroots organization that arose around the same time—exemplifies the fight to flip deportation from a source of shame to an object of pride. In summer 2019, on a visit to Mexico City, I met Jonathon, Patricio, and Itzel, who cofounded DUL. Each wore an emblem of the fight to restore their status as human. Jonathon had a ragged gray beard and stretched lobes from old earrings, but he also sported a bright red T-shirt emblazoned "Deportados Brand: 100% Mexicano." Patricio's black tee declared him freshly deported—merging the word *deportado* with the phrase *aguas frescas* (fresh juice) into a playful portmanteau: "Deportaguas frescas." Meanwhile, Itzel's forearm was tattooed, in English, "Believe!" Each time she raised her fist, the big, blue letters proclaimed her defiant hope. Her shirt bore the word "Chingona" (badass), in cursive like the old logo for the Chicago White Sox, recalling the city where she once lived. Below, it read "aquí y allá:" here and there.[2] The trio designed and printed the shirts themselves. With each clever turn of phrase, they reclaimed the label "deported."

Three years after removal, these activists still bore scars from their deportations. Patricio had lost his wife and 4-year-old daughter the day ICE detained him in Vegas. His teeth were cracked and crooked, and when we spoke, he hinted at how detention had damaged his mental well-being. In Mexico City, he said, it was hard to find work, to hold up his head. He longed for the days he used to play with his daughter back "home" in Nevada. Likewise, Itzel cried when she spoke of the years spent away from her two teenage sons. Deportation felt—as she said in a video later—like "living without living" (*un vivir sin vivir*).[3]

Still, DUL's creativity diverged starkly from the border-town alienation I looked at in chapter 5. Itzel and her comrades twisted the words that had been used to degrade them and wore them, instead, with pride. Together, their clothes, words, and tattoos pronounced that instead of belonging to no one and nowhere, deportees could create new space to belong.

Naming who they were (*deportados*/deported) and what they were doing (*unidos en la lucha*/united in struggle) helped Itzel, Jonathon, Patricio, and their comrades form the collective that became DUL. At the group's early meetings, they took time to *desahogarse* (unload) and build solidarity. Later, the group realized they could make money off their binational identities and their refusal to be erased. With help from a government program (and Itzel's Chicago contacts), they bought a printing press, adopted the name Deportados Brand, and began selling T-shirts in Mexico and the United States. The sales brought in income. They also raised awareness of the pain inflicted by deportation. As Patricio put it later, "Organizing gives you community. *Es como sanar un corazón roto.* (It's like healing a broken heart)."[4]

DUL makes clear that even in a system of banishment, there are alternatives to alienation. Though carceral deportation leaves most people traumatized, isolated, and displaced, some refuse to accept social death. They do this *not* by reintegrating or becoming Mexican again, per theories of return migration, but by parlaying their status into radical new identities.

How do deported men (and women) exercise agency, rebuild community, and reclaim their dignity? And what conditions or past experiences help them refuse to simply be "banished"?

Theories of social death suggest that carceral institutions (including deportation) reduce people to "bare life."[5] That is, such systems strip people of their identities and social relations, leaving them barely alive, let alone able to advocate for themselves. Yet even under state violence, some people refuse erasure. Postcolonial scholars and Black feminists have long questioned the idea that people subjected to social death end up abject or outside the law. Even those who endure profound dehumanization continue to exercise agency, through embodied survival, joy, and collective care.[6] Despite the violence of carceral deportation, deportees go to great lengths to affirm their humanity.[7]

Alongside heartbreaking stories of loss, our team also heard something different. Deportees were finding ways to reclaim masculinity, forge community, and seek rights and resources, inside or outside the law. Some of their strategies took shape in the limbo of border sites like Tijuana. Others relied on the resources of bigger, interior cities (and on the know-how of younger, more educated, computer-savvy deportees). Respondents adopted multiple, different modes of refusal, three of which I trace here: (1) they flipped stigma on its head, to build organizations around migrant pride; (2) they brokered and sold their skills to "earn dollars;" and (3) they embraced the criminality others imputed to them, plugging into cartels and breaking state-imposed rules.

Deportees' new subjectivities had four things in common. First, they claimed a place for themselves between (or beyond) "here" and "there."[8] Second, they used these frames to forge community among deportees and migrants who felt "in between." Third, they upended the terms of banishment. Instead of feeling disgraced, they reclaimed their status as forced returnees. Fourth, they leveraged these reframes to make money or claim political entitlements. In the process they also built hope.

Much of this reclamation was driven by charismatic individuals who brought toolkits from the U.S. into institutional contexts that enabled their innovation. Founders of deportee organizations all had relevant training from the United States: know-how in English, activism, business, or with violence and gangs.[9] In addition, they were not *completely* worn down by incarceration.

Depending on deportees' histories in the U.S. and the conditions around them in Mexico, they had access to varying strategies of refusal. If men came out of carceral deportation still able to see and choose for themselves, they fought dehumanization. Mexico City also enabled them to leverage their experiences in the U.S.[10] A metropolis of more than 22 million people, Mexico City is one of the largest cities in the world, on par with Delhi, Shanghai, and São Paolo. Given its concentration of political, economic, and civic power, deportees in the capital had more access to government money and civil organizations than those in other locales. Mexico City was also a hub of call centers, coding, and other computer-based jobs. It drew deportees who were already politicized. Then, it made others political, too.[11]

While advocacy centered in Mexico City, the border context fostered a different kind of refusal: joining criminal organizations. Men with histories in prison or gangs often found themselves stuck at the border, where one of the only ways out of alienation was to (continue to) participate in organized crime. Some scholars argue that border zones embody the *mestizaje* (cultural mixing) and duality that deportee organizations embrace.[12] The liminality of the border and its distance from national structures of power may facilitate cultural transformations, including identities that seek to escape from federal government confines.[13] That is, the region housed organizations already refusing state laws, borders, and norms.[14]

In what follows, I trace how deportees came to these different approaches. I also consider the limitations of each for full "liberation." First, I show, women and those least exposed to U.S. prison often *built grassroots organizations.* Second, young men with moderate carceral histories were drawn to a work-based approach, in which they *brokered binational skills.* Third, for those who'd spent time in prison, *breaking laws and borders* could feel like the only way to re-prove they were men. While I trace the emergence of these strategies one by one, they can (and do) overlap. At times, people moved between them, as they fought against alienation and sought a place in the world.

BUILDING GRASSROOTS ORGANIZATIONS

In Mexico City, DUL and grassroots groups like Otros Dreams en Acción (ODA) and Deportado no Agotado (deported not exhausted) organized to reframe deportees as multicultural, multitalented people. Often led by women who had been activists in the U.S., these organizations leveraged their binationality to build community, earn money, and demand recognition from Mexico and the U.S. They also forged new, physical spaces in which to belong, such as ODA's Poch@ House (loosely, House of U.S.-based Mexicans), in the center of Mexico City. Men who took up this strategy had often been activists in the U.S., as well, and few spent more than a year in U.S. detention or prison. Yet such men also felt tension, especially when "pure" activism conflicted with pressure to reestablish their status as breadwinning men.

Advocacy post-deportation had its seeds in U.S. immigrants' rights. Most of the leaders of DUL, ODA, and other organizations had been activists in the U.S. When they returned, they applied skills, slogans, strategies, and networks from U.S. immigrant movements to fight the stigma of deportation. Though deportation was painful for them (as for anyone), they had rarely spent much time in prison. Their sense of a "right to have rights" was intact. They had frequently *chosen* Mexico City, where proximity to the state helped them access funding and sometimes spur policy change. Organizing at the grassroots was a "maternal" strategy. That is, not only did women lead most such organizations but these groups also emphasized mutual care, "nesting" (creating spaces of belonging), and cultivating public compassion. Through talk of emotions, the members restored their own worth.

Itzel García, the founder of Deportados Unidos en la Lucha, exemplifies the conditions that helped such groups bloom. A dynamic, passionate mom in her early forties, Itzel had thick black hair with a white streak in the front. In 2000, Itzel moved to Chicago to support her young family in Mexico. She learned English, got a GED, and took classes in leadership. She sent for her son and had one more child. She worked in a wide range of jobs: at a secondhand store, a sweets factory, and ultimately at Arise Chicago, an immigrant advocacy organization. In 2016, Arise offered to sponsor Itzel for a work visa, and she prepared to return to Mexico to finish the papers. She only got to the airport. There, ICE detained and deported her, imposing a 20-year ban on return. Itzel was shocked: "I was not on the list of 'deportables.' I never had so much as a traffic violation." Though ICE denies targeting activists (and doing so is illegal), Itzel insisted, "The deportation was due to my activism in the United States." In an instant, "Everything my life had been up to that point ended . . . My life was there: my children, my house, my work, my friendships." Itzel was 41.

Itzel grew up in a *rancho* (village) in Jalisco, Mexico. After 16 years in Chicago, she did not feel like she could go back. So, when the U.S. flew Itzel to Mexico City, she stayed. Still feeling shell-shocked, she faced stigma and public hostility. As Itzel put it, "The truth is that we continue being undocumented" post-deportation. In Mexico, "It's really difficult to reclaim your identity—or an ID document, a place to live." Without a Mexican birth certificate or work record, Itzel could not get an ID card, rent an apartment, or find a job. Her friends from Arise Chicago pitched in, contacting the Mexican Secretariat of Labor to help Itzel get unemployment.

When Itzel arrived to claim her support, the secretary of labor invited her to an event where she—gregarious—met other deportees. That, Itzel said, was how Deportados Unidos en la Lucha was born:

> It was to talk, more than anything, it was to chat. It started like that at first, as a self-help group . . . We would get together every Tuesday outside the Franz Mayer Museum, and the first thing we did was to talk, vent, vent, vent (*desahogarnos*). And a symptom of deportees is always complaining. We would complain about everything, everything. There is a lot of rejection on the part of your family here—or other people, even if they were your friends. [They'd tell us], "Ay, get *with* it. You're here; this is Mexico." But yes, that's part of the process of healing, complaining about Mexico. So, we represented this space where we could complain all the time about what we wished for from Mexico, and you didn't feel rejected. You didn't feel bad.

Building community helped members heal from losing their families and U.S.-based homes. The group, one member said, made him feel "comfortable, protected, like a family." As DUL grew, it turned its focus to new deportees. Members began going to Mexico City's airport to meet repatriation flights and offer support like phone calls, or advice on government benefits.

Energized, Itzel quit her job to work full-time on DUL. The men in the group had trouble finding good jobs, due to their lack of education and the stigma they faced after deportation. But Itzel had saved money and contacts from her advocacy work in the United States. So, she said, "I took charge of the campaign to help people make a living." Itzel had seen people selling candy on the streets in Mexico City and decided that DUL could sell sweets as well.

As DUL's members went out to sell treats, their visibility brought new scrutiny. People denigrated the deportees as criminals and dependents on the Mexican state.

Itzel went on, "I started to get texts from people, that 'You migrant thieves, you want to come live off the government . . . Go work, you traitors. You left and now you want to return.'" On the streets, people constantly asked Itzel and her friends, "What [crime] did you do?" Rather than hide, Itzel decided, "No, you know what? We're going to do something. We're going to start working . . . to make visible the people the system had forgotten." She would stand outside conferences, do interviews with the media. To break down myths about deportation, she told critics her story: "Look, I'm this person. I have kids. I have a family just like you. I *had* a family, and my only crime was not having papers." Echoing the "undocumented but unafraid" language of U.S.-based immigrants' rights, Itzel maintained that she and her friends were "Deportado pero no derrotado" (deported but not defeated).

Embracing the word "deported" was a crucial step to empowerment. Itzel went on, "For me there is no problem if people use the word deportee. That's why we call ourselves Deportees United in Struggle. It's the first step to [help them] see what is going on underneath and what we are living through." Over time, DUL integrated the word into all they did. To survive, Itzel felt, they had to reclaim deportation, make new, binational space, and earn money. In the process, they also started marketing deportation itself as creative or trendy.

To do this, DUL built on U.S. approaches and slogans. When the group ordered labels to put on their sweets, they also got T-shirts and flyers. The first, which they made "just to blow off steam," used the logo of handcuffed fists from the U.S. anti-deportation campaign "Ni Uno Más" (Not one more):

> We would go out to sell T-shirts, and we would talk to people. I started talking to people, and I would tell them, "We're not criminals. We're this, we do this." . . . I'd say, "You know what, if you can't buy sweets no problem, just hit 'Like' on our [Facebook] page." And that's how we also got a lot of followers, and we were able to expand the work of Deportados Unidos a lot, because it wasn't just my family that had liked it, it was people we talked to in the street.

Woven throughout DUL and Itzel's reinvention of deportation were strategies and even phrasing from the United States.

In the capital, migrants could also access state funds. Itzel's Chicago contacts connected her with the Mexican Secretariat of Labor, which offered DUL credit to establish a print shop: Deportados Brand. Soon, DUL sold T-shirts on both sides of the border. The team knew English, and they had a sense for which styles appealed to Latinos in the United States. Their slogans were inventive, direct, and popular. Their "Fuck Trump" shirt was a notable hit. While the employees could not return to the U.S. themselves, they sold their products through friends, family, and eventually formal distributors.

Such tactics were most accessible to women. For one, women predominate in immigration protests and advocacy in the United States. In addition, while U.S.

police frame undocumented men as criminals, their female counterparts some-times get state or NGO support by playing the role of "good immigrants" or empowered women.[15] In a Chicago program called Empresarias del Futuro (Busi-nesswomen of the Future), Itzel was trained in this mold. She also learned, in her words, "to develop and empower the community through knowing their rights." She recalled:

> That's what I learned in Empresarias del Futuro, that I should give it another turn . . . something different. So, I thought of the idea, "OK, let's call it Deportados Brand, 100% Mexican," since we were deportees. And also, for me it was really important to say the word like that, "deportees." . . . On a personal level, the world deported, it made me feel shame. It made me embarrassed . . . it was important to give the word new meaning, to take out that side of criminalization, of failure, of frustration, of shame, like, to be able to notice that the word "deported" also meant rising up again.

Itzel used her training, charisma, and contacts to reclaim deportation and start DUL. Organizing post-deportation was easier with experience.

The men who joined DUL were, perhaps, more "typical" deportees. Few had been activists in the U.S. Most left their children up north, and they rarely felt welcome in Mexico. At the same time, these men had been spared the worst degradations of carceral deportation, spending less time detained or in prison than other interviewees. A few also had U.S. business or other acumen that helped land them in Mexico City and drive them to seek community. Only later did they get politicized.

Jonathon, the mild-mannered cofounder of Deportados Brand, provides an example. When Jonathon was 25, he moved to Washington State. He built a construction business that supported him and his two U.S.-citizen daughters for nearly two decades. In 2016, ICE detained and deported him, breaking his family as well as his heart. Jonathon spent two years trying to fight his case, with a lot of grief in the process. Ultimately, he lost. Though Jonathon was born in Oaxaca, ICE flew him to Mexico City. When he landed, he told Fátima:

> I felt alone. Despite the fact that I was with my [Mexican] friends, with my brother, I couldn't find myself (*no me ubiqué*). Once I got to the Secretariat of Labor . . . Itzel arrived, and a couple of other *compañeros* who came with her. And we started to talk about the things that were happening to us . . . I was building solidarity with the *compañeros*. Why? Because they're living the same pain, and they're facing the same situation, right? And I went to be with them because they were as lost as I was. And there, we started caring for each other. And from there we started building this union.
>
> It was, more than anything, listening to each other, because you get back and you're thinking to yourself, "What do I do? How can I talk to my brother, my friends who don't understand me?" And there were moments in which the sadness got the best of us, and it was just to care for each other that we were together. And that's how we started building unity. It was a group to listen to each other (*de autoescucha*).

Itzel, with everything she knows about community organizing and activism, guided us and taught us. And I started realizing how important it was to serve the community, and we started going to the airport and offering help . . . I didn't know it was activism; I didn't know it was a community organization. I didn't have a clue. But I think, in the process, I started learning it here with Itzel. And I'm still learning from her to this day.

Unlike Itzel, Jonathon did not set out to reclaim deportation. But he had the initiative and resources to seek state benefits. By luck, he found Itzel and the support of others like them.

Jonathon could never forget the United States; he had U.S. citizen daughters. In Mexico City, it was also hard for him to find well-paying jobs. In his desperate moments, Jonathon thought, "Fuck it all. I'm going [back]. I'm going because I can't—I've been here three years, it's going to be three years, and I can't—I don't have *una vida digna* (a dignified life). I don't have stable work. I arrived to a country that wasn't mine [the U.S.], without knowing the language, and in eight months I had a car and I could buy a house, and I could buy things and have credit and have access to medical services. And I can't do that here—right?" Though Jonathon still lived in limbo, especially as a breadwinning dad, he found roots in DUL.

Patricio, 47, was a new activist, too. When ICE stopped Patricio on the street near his Las Vegas home, he had already applied for U.S. citizenship. Instead, he was ripped from his Salvadorian wife and their 3-year-old daughter. When I met Patricio, he told me they called the group Deportees United in Struggle because it *was* a struggle, and the organization gave members unity. In DUL, Patricio gained a voice that he'd never imagined. He spoke at the United Nations, the Global Pact on Migration, and the National Palace (Mexico's White House). He helped write and act in a play on YouTube called *Visa Fronteriza* (Border Visa). He learned "how to value yourself and make your voice be something—so they know that you're here as a deportee, not as a delinquent, but from a deportation. So that people see that deportation is something sad because it leaves families [broken] like this." In such statements, he reframed deportation for the state and the public as well.

ODA also drew on U.S. organizing to invent ways for deportees to "florecer aquí y allá" (flourish here and there). Like DUL, ODA's key leaders were women with political experience in the United States. One of them was U.S.-born graduate student Jane Taylor. As part of her PhD dissertation, Jane organized young deportees and returnees who had feared deportation. Again, ODA emerged from a need for mutual support and then began to take action.

As its name suggests, ODA built on the DREAM movement in the U.S.[16] ODA also focused on claiming more legal rights. To do this, the group used three key strategies: (1) They built a physical space they called Poch@ House; (2) They used members' U.S. education to make demands of the Mexican state; and (3) They built an NGO network to honor binational culture.

First, ODA rented a space. In a bright corner office in Mexico City, members put up murals of liberation. They offered tea to all who came in the door. Together, they chose a name that played on words used to denigrate Mexican Americans. Clad in a long, knitted sweater and sporting blue-rimmed glasses, the founder Jane Taylor recalled:

> In some ways the naming of the place as Poch@ House has been about saying, you know, "I'm *pocho*—or *pocha*—so what?" That used to be a very—it had a very negative connotation, particularly for a lot of Chicano and Chicana-identifying Mexicans in the U.S. who have come back and suddenly they're *pocho* or *pocha* in a derogatory sense. I feel like this return and deportation—where you're in exile in Mexico. You feel all that stigma. You're faced with it, sometimes by your own family members. But . . . there's healing in saying, "So what? I'm proud, I can't undo 20 years of my life. I also can't necessarily go back right now, even though-." This sense of, "I'm not from here *or* from there, *no soy de aquí ni de allá*, but I'm claiming my identity and my rights to be *de aquí y de allá* (from here *and* from there)—something that doesn't exist, something that is not really valued culturally or politically in either country, but I'm creating the space and this identity."

At Poch@ House, ODA members centered the hybrid culture of Spanglish. Claiming belonging despite the pain of return, they made their own "really healing and empowering and amazing" transnational space.

Second, ODA's young, bilingual members pressured the Mexican state. While DUL's participants skewed toward middle age, those in ODA tended to be in their twenties, with U.S. high school or college degrees. In the early 2000s, as U.S. immigration reform faltered, the Mexican government actively opened its arms to DREAMers from the U.S. ODA used such talk for leverage. They insisted that the state ease documentation requirements for returned migrants and validate their identities and educational histories, so they could get jobs. ODA also pushed to reduce documentation hurdles to school enrollment. It convinced Mexico City to eliminate barriers to employment such as requiring official (notary) seals from the U.S. and copies of high school diplomas. In addition, its members connected with U.S. universities and nonprofits (including UCSD) to train students about deportation and advocate against ICE.

Third, ODA built a network to celebrate binational culture, holding festivals that used arts, music, and poetry to foster public support for the group's demands. They called for reunification of families, guaranteed safety for migrants and deportees, and recognition of diverse communities.

ODA took public pride in its ecosystem of advocates that included DUL, Deported Veterans, DREAMers Moms, and several other organizations.[17] They also aligned with the DREAM movement in the U.S. by working with immigrant youth who returned to Mexico on their own.[18] Their website declared, "We are a part of a dynamic and ongoing process to build the convergence of voices and experiences in the aftermath of return, and to connect with other movements for justice, such as gender rights. In collaboration with our partners, we support concrete projects to benefit our community, join with other movements to denounce discrimination and violence, and amplify the artistic and cultural voices of those in exile."[19]

Organizations like DUL and ODA inspired other deportees to find ways to reject U.S. banishment. Elías, a 38-year-old self-identified punk with a long beard and glasses, was deported from North Carolina after working 17 years in chicken processing plants. He lost his children. In Mexico, he felt, remaining family did not understand him. So, he joined DUL and turned other deported migrants into his "chosen family." After learning to print bags and T-shirts, Elías decided to start his own shop. He called it "F*ck la Migra" (a nickname for ICE) to both criticize the U.S. deportation system and appeal to U.S.-based activists. Though at first he thought the name sounded "a little much," he grew to identify with the slogan: "It's like an attitude of *coraje* (anger/courage), but at the same time it's funny."

Likewise, Ramón, deported after serving time for reentry, established a group he called Deportado no Agotado (Deported, Not Exhausted), with a logo mixing the U.S. and Mexican flags. He hoped, one day, to open a home for deportees emerging from prison. Similarly, Mercedes, who had been an organizer and the first Latina and undocumented student body president of Cal State Northridge, started a blog and an organization to fight against ICE after her deportation. Many others simply turned to the web to share stories, documenting Mexico City's flourishing, bilingual, bicultural population of deportees.

Through grassroots organizing, these individuals and groups converted binational experience into a source of creativity and pride—and, in some cases, a lever to pressure the Mexican state or make money. In those cases, they created a "struggle brand," intersecting with entrepreneurial modes of refusal.

BROKERING BINATIONAL WORK

In other cases, deportees adopted a strategy I call brokering. That is, they strove to reclaim deportation through entrepreneurship and work. Expelled from U.S. jobs and threatened with social death, they showed agency by embracing a neoliberal breadwinner identity. Like DUL, these groups leveraged binationalism for pride and connection, benefiting from Mexico City's resources and appeal for young workers. Yet for them, capitalizing on deportation was not just a tool of resistance. Instead, their end game was to get deeper into American business. Via work, they explicitly sought to restore deportees' standing as *men*.

Typically, brokering organizations were led by men who had business experience in the United States and embraced the idea of "earning dollars in Mexico" by doing business north of the border. These men recruited deported workers to call centers and other U.S.-focused companies. They enticed recruits to remake themselves as status-worthy entrepreneurs. Men who adopted such strategies tended to have moved to the U.S. as kids and been deported after limited time in detention and/or in prison. Work gave them a path forward, helped them establish community, and offered a Mexican variation of the American dream. As good capitalists, the leaders both gave their peers opportunities and exploited them.

César Quiroz, the founder of an organization called New Comienzos (New Beginnings), had lived in the U.S. on-and-off since he was a toddler. He earned a BA in business in Texas and started a taxi company. When police detained César for a traffic violation, he had just learned his partner was pregnant. For two years, he fought his case from detention. He lost. When César arrived at the border for his removal, cartels kidnapped him. He moved to Mexico City in search of safety.

There, César saw a labor market thirsty for U.S.-trained, bilingual workers. He'd made cash in the U.S. and wanted to prove he could "do it again" in Mexico. Fluent in English, he got a job at a call center. Then, he learned he could earn commissions if he referred others to work there as well. He described, "So, I would start referring to this call center—over 200 people a week. I was making so much money, you know? . . . This is where I started, just by myself, in one of these spots, on the computer helping people find jobs." Soon, César became a full-time labor broker, earning commissions for connecting English-speaking deportees to Mexican jobs. Thus began New Comienzos (a tellingly blended name), an organization that served returned and deported migrants. As of 2019, César bragged to the press, New Comienzos had helped thousands of deported DREAMers find work.

New Comienzos was headquartered at Homework, a swanky coworking space in the middle of Mexico City. Modeled on the incubators of Silicon Valley, Homework had glass walls and wood trim, an expensive espresso machine, and U.S. music playing over the speakers. The space itself seemed to frame deportation as trendy, pronouncing its inhabitants' pride in being "American in Mexico" (albeit on capital's terms). Surrounding the office were five- and six-story call centers, plastered with photos of well-dressed, attractive young workers, inviting other "cosmopolitan" young people to join them.[20] Such jobs were not just for deportees; in fact, Ana López Ricoy, one of the RAs who helped to research this book, grew up in Mexico City and worked for one of the centers before she came to UCSD. Yet in presenting deported men as ideal employees, organizations like New Comienzos portrayed removal as a source of useful bicultural skills.

When I visited New Comienzos in September 2019, César greeted me with his hair slicked back and a crisp white T-shirt stretched across his muscular, barrel chest. (He said he often worked out, as if cultivating the physique to match his manly persona). His greeting echoed the grandeur he showed to the press. In one You-Tube video, for instance, César wears a full suit and tours reporters through Homework and the neighborhood of "Little LA." "Welcome!" he boasts, "The American Dream can be achieved in Mexico, too! . . . Now millions of people can turn toward Mexico and see that there is life after deportation, there is a light at the end of the tunnel."[21] It was the first time I saw someone proactively *sell* deportation.

In 2018, César also founded a business of his own, an internet service called EG Logistics. There, he hired recently deported, English-speaking workers to connect producers with shippers around the United States and transport their goods. We toured the company that same day. Near Homework, the office contained a series of rooms filled with dual monitor workstations, each equipped with a clean-cut and muscular man, most of them under 40. In the hallway, with César's prompting, the men traded weightlifting stories. As if on purpose, these workers presented a striking contrast to deportees we'd met in Tijuana. They were young, optimistic, and smartly dressed in U.S.-brand clothing. César made the comparison explicit: "The idea here is that if you're not doing well, if you're depressed, [deportation to Mexico] is gonna be horrible . . . But if you're able to come here and get an opportunity . . . [You're] recently deported and now you're creating your own opportunities, you're gonna see things different."

César considered New Comienzos a direct but friendly competitor to organizations like DUL and ODA. He used a comparison to highlight his own flashy, masculine approach:

> Imagine a family. The older sister, you know, the rocker, the one that likes motorcycles, maybe in a motorcycle gang, that's Itzel, Deportados Unidos, you know? She's a little bit of a feminist perhaps, but an activist. She's a fighter. Then we have the younger sister. She's all about love and peace; maybe she's a little bit of a hippie. I see ODA that way, you know? And they're feminist—I never understood that, how can you be a feminist and help migrants? . . . According to them it's not about men, it's about women sticking together, but also about helping migrants . . . And then we have the little brother. He's the favorite, you know, he's the youngest, the favorite brother. But guess what? He's also charismatic, so all the attention is going toward the little brother. But at the same time, he's kind of smart and beginning to help so many people and think outside the box always . . . that's New Comienzos.

Beyond a cute metaphor, César's description captured the tensions among different methods of organizing. He also linked his approach to *men*. All three groups were trying to use Mexico City's resources to forge new identities and communities. But in César's mind, DUL was an activist, ODA a feminist, and New Comienzos an innovative, intentionally masculine businessman.

César leaned into U.S. capitalism. He held up becoming "American" in Mexico as *the* path to overcoming the story that deportees were subhuman, criminals, or no longer men. When I asked what the "American Dream in Mexico" meant, he simply said "dollars." To avoid being erased, he concertedly strove for a place inside U.S. capitalism.

At the same time, by hiring deportees for *lower* wages than they had earned as unauthorized migrants in the U.S., César (and the corporations he worked for) profited off their displacement. Tanya Golash-Boza calls such exploitation the "neoliberal cycle" of deportation.[22] Several of his workers complained of hours-long bus commutes. It was hard to ignore that the structure of New Comienzos looked, from some angles, like a pyramid scheme. César also made money off academics, including me and my graduate RAs, whom he charged a fee for the privilege of meeting the people who worked at his company.[23] Near the end of our fieldwork, ex-employees accused Cesar of exploitation and worker mistreatment. In short, neoliberal masculinity (and the strategy of working for betterment) could not be divorced from labor abuse. Indeed, neoliberalism itself relies on the illusion of becoming a self-made man, rather than encouraging concrete, coalition-based flourishing.

Either way, neoliberal masculinity offered a powerful alternative to erasure. Like DUL, New Comienzos and its peers became spaces of belonging.[24] Despite César's mixed reputation, his businesses attracted thousands of deportees (far more than DUL membership). Among them was Ángel, the young man described in this book's opening pages.

When I asked César why people moved to Mexico City to work with him, he speculated:

> The media has grown tremendously, also our social media, also all the groups we're in. Besides the Facebook page, we're in many groups. We're connected with many people, especially in the U.S., many universities, especially DREAMer groups, which is the group that's, like us, better organized. So, a lot of people know about us . . . [They think,] "Hey, there's an area where people can have opportunity." . . . People from our community that were deported, they may be suffering from substance abuse, maybe from—how would you say it? Psychological issues, depression. So instead of living in some other part of Mexico, guess what? They want to live here in this area because here they feel safe or at least understood by some people . . . people from our community that are fully bilingual, and they're here for a reason, so it's now, you know, a group of people, is not one person, it's something that's happening.

New Comienzos especially appealed to deportees aged 18–39, who saw the office as a place to be "cool." Many people we met there had moved to the U.S. as kids and grew up speaking English. Some—like Ángel—used the Internet to find New Comienzos or similar organizations, then moved to Mexico City to join. Others attached working there to a fantasy of "earning" a U.S. visa, and with it the respect of their family in the United States. If they worked hard enough, they hoped, they could earn back their manhood.

For these respondents, combining community with a job was very appealing. Christopher, a 29-year-old from Puerto Vallarta, recalled how it had been hard to fit in or find work at home after his 2019 deportation. He "felt useless" when he could not make enough money to send to his kids in the United States. When Christopher read about New Comienzos in the news, he started saving up bus fare. He stepped off that bus one Sunday night, and Monday morning he was shaking hands with César, accepting a job at EG Logistics. Christopher had been there a month when we met. He felt a small thrill on earning commissions, and he was grateful that César had taken him on. Like others at New Comienzos and EG Logistics, he finally felt he was "home."

When Fátima, Ana, and I interviewed people at New Comienzos, most said the organization promised a path out of suffering post-deportation. After detention and often short stints in prison, they said, work felt like one of few areas left for agency. Some had learned this entrepreneurial mentality in the U.S. Others echoed the narratives of redemption from prison, in which "getting pumped" (physically fit), cleaning up their style, hiding their tattoos, and joining a business became almost like a religion. Often, they appeared to be making a physical effort to "look the part": dressing in button-up shirts, neatly combing their hair, working out, and thus claiming their newfound roles.

Aldo, who ran an organization similar to New Comienzos, proclaimed himself an enemy of César Quiroz, though his approach was strikingly similar. A handsome man in his early thirties with gelled hair, glasses, and a carefully trimmed beard, Aldo met me for breakfast south of downtown Mexico City. Before his deportation, Aldo had run a small landscaping business in North Carolina. Then, police caught him selling marijuana. Aldo spent two years in prison, missing his three-year-old daughter, whose name and birthdate he had tattooed along his arm. He tried to defend himself, begging $20,000 from his parents to pay a lawyer. When the judge said he'd lost the case, he cried. Eight months before we met, he was removed from the United States.

When Aldo got to Mexico City, he saw César Quiroz making money by linking recently repatriated people to jobs. So, he set up a Facebook group to do something similar: build community, lift deportees' spirits, and offer to find them work. He, too, earned commissions for worker recruitment. Some of his "members" became virtual assistants. Others were paid to call homeowners in California or Florida to ask if they wanted to sell their houses. Aldo also used people's Facebook profiles to vet potential workers for businesses: "I got all my groups, I got the skaters, I got the druggies . . . So, if I get a job, I'm gonna look through someone's Facebook [scroll motion]." Like César, Aldo constantly spoke of community, boasting of his group's huge membership and insisting that God had "called" him to do this work. "I'm here for a reason," he said with conviction. He, too, nurtured a clean-cut, businesslike image, admitting he'd changed from a T-shirt into a starched gingham button-down to make a better impression on me. After losing his family and business and then spending time degraded in prison, Aldo said, brokering labor *was* his route back to manhood.

An organization called Hola Code offers a third example of this entrepreneurial model. In its own description, Hola Code was "an immersive, five-month software engineering bootcamp that fosters social mobility through accessing high-demand jobs in the tech sector for youth." Founded in 2017 with support from Hack Reactor, a well-known U.S. coding bootcamp, Hola Code worked with employers to create a new tech sector in Mexico City and hire deported youth. With an eye to reintegration, Hola Code's leaders put in a great deal of effort to building community, helping returnees empower themselves and find ways to be "both here and there." Its average worker was 18–35 years old and had lived in the U.S. a decade or more. The organization's appeal was obvious: it promised to convert deportees into twenty-first-century tech workers, who could echo the masculinity (and money) of Silicon Valley men.

Perhaps organizations like New Comienzos and Hola Code "sold people to the system," making money off their bilingual skills and familiarity with the U.S., while the men themselves were unable to travel north. Yet, in the face of banishment and limbo, neoliberal masculinity gave men identity, belonging, and a sense of importance. In this sense, brokering sometimes overlapped with organizing, bringing deportees together to advocate for their standing in Mexican (and U.S.) society. In other moments, its logic intersected with the strategies of criminal organizations, which offered an alternate—extralegal—means to make money and claim a place in the world.

BREAKING LAWS AND BORDERS

A third group of people rejected state violence by breaking the laws of the states that sought to erase them. They smuggled narcotics or migrants, sold drugs, worked for cartels, or engaged in other prohibited actions. After enduring abuses in U.S. prisons, these men echoed the same tactics to earn money, pride, and ties to a social group. Under border conditions, crime was one of the only ways to reclaim the story of their criminality. For men, in particular, cartels, violence, and illegal markets pitched a tantalizing path "back" into masculinity.

As classic studies reveal, men join gangs for money and pride, particularly in contexts of degradation.[25] In his ethnography *Selling Crack en El Barrio*, for instance, anthropologist Philippe Bourgois documents how, by selling drugs and practicing violence, men earn "respect."[26] Joining gangs gives people an identity, solidarity, and a sense of place,[27] the very things they lose under carceral deportation. At the U.S.-Mexico border, Shaylih Muehlmann adds, the *narcotraficante* (drug trafficker) offers an alluring and omnipresent symbol of dignity and income, contrasted with widespread economic and social limbo.[28]

But is engaging in organized crime a form of agency, or are men forced into it by deprivation? Trafficking industries reward men like ex-U.S. prisoners and gang members, who already have skills in violence but lack the education to work in most other places.[29] For some, embracing the "criminal" stigma bestowed by the state is the only choice left.

Despite these constraints and contradictions, I argue that organized crime is a form of "delinquent refusal."[30] Anthropologist Gilberto Rosas, who proposed this term in his book *Barrio Libre*, argues that by joining gangs, young people refuse the state's terms about who is fully human and who can legitimately exercise violence. That is, unable to escape the criminality thrust upon them, deportees *embrace* it instead. Many adopt the label "cholo" (Americanized gangster) as an identity of their own.[31] In the process, they resist being banished and claim a circumscribed self-renewal. Rather than staying broken, they break the law.

This kind of refusal was most common at the border. Border zones are rife with criminal groups that reward such actions. Men who stay there have frequently lost their families and even a sense of themselves. Those recently out of prison tend to lack the wherewithal or resources to relocate away from the border or seek other jobs.[32] Amid border limbo, smuggling also promises funds to get back to the United States or just buy a bus ticket home.

Like grassroots organizers and self-described businessmen, those who broke laws drew on toolkits from the U.S. In this case, they used skills both surviving and practicing violence, which might appear to outsiders as liabilities. Most of these men had spent time in U.S. prisons. Their incarceration disconnected them from friends and family, leaving them as "free agents." Having witnessed prison brutality, many no longer believed in state "justice" or the fairness of laws. In prison (if not before), many had been in gangs for community, identity, masculinity, and, indeed, survival. These gangs *trained* men to engage in violence. Alongside prison guards, gangs also instilled a particular kind of discipline.

It was not easy to trace the scope of men's participation in organized crime. I worried about students' safety and did not let them recruit on the street, let alone seek out current members of gangs or cartels. If we met such people by chance, they may not have disclosed their criminal actions to students from the U.S.— most of whom were young women. (Though masculine preening *could* be a reason to boast or exaggerate violence or crime). Nevertheless, more than 20 of 171 male interviewees *volunteered* that they witnessed, were tempted into, or participated in such activities. We heard stories from deportees who had been recruited by cartels or seen their peers join or be killed. Several had worked for criminal groups in some way since their deportations, and many more knew other people who had. Occasionally, participants openly admitted to engaging in organized crime.

One such person was Cristos, a 32-year-old ex-gangster recently out of U.S. prison, who now helped traffic heroin for the Aztecas Cartel. When Cristos met Ana in 2019, he squeezed her hand so tightly it hurt. He spoke in a hyperactive jumble of Spanish and English that made Ana wonder if he was high. Cristos grew up in a neighborhood called Little Mexico, in Phoenix, Arizona. He had been in gangs since he was a teen, starting with Phoenix's 18th Street Gang. He had also been addicted to drugs. During the interview, he talked openly about stabbing people. He boasted that Mexican police were afraid of him and that he "liked" U.S. federal prison, "Because I got to know a lot of big narcos, a lot of powerful people. Like, literally, you get to meet the heavy leaders, you know. Motherfuckers that I saw when I was growing up, that you see them on the news and you're like 'Oh shit, I'm with *them*.' You know, like, 'Hey, with all due respect, can I take a picture with you, sir?' People of respect, literally who would kill you." For Cristos, being associated with such men was a source of pride.[33]

Cristos had also faced brutal abuse at Victorville and Riverside Federal Prisons, leading him to scorn the "justice" of U.S. incarceration. He saw friends killed behind bars. He was forced to kill others as well. He had lingering trauma from the time his gang made him murder another inmate. He recalled, "When they tapped me to kill a guy . . . It's hard when I look back at it. When I saw that person die, he was bleeding. He was right there on the fucking ground, you know. You just see him like—he just shook, and he just pissed in his pants. You just like see him take his last breath, I was like, 'Fuck!'" Prison guards also lied to Cristos repeatedly and beat him without remorse. Several times, they told him he was about to be released, only to extend his time or move him into another prison. At his trial, he decried, they presented evidence of *his* violence but nothing of the beatings he endured under prison guards.

After deportation, Cristos arrived in Mexico disillusioned, with a history of drug use and violence (and little else). Then, he met cartel scouts recruiting people like him. He remembered:

> Over there at the border is nothing but people like us. I mean, not like you [Ana] [laughs]. Just like myself. Or not *just* like myself but similar situations, where they go through the [U.S. prison] system. They've been put through it, you know. They've been to prison, but the one thing that we all have is that we're all hustlers, you know? If we're locked up or in the streets, we know how to make money *y andamos así en chinga* (and we work our asses off) . . . They [cartels] went to border towns, and from there it's just a requirement that you were locked up. After a while when I learned [how to do that, too], they told me that it's in the way they [deportees] dress. They look for people who were locked up or who were like that because they've already struggled (*batallado*) and they know how to get around, or they're going to find a way to survive. So, there's gonna be a way for them to go ahead and sell this [drugs].

Wrecked, hardened, and trained by U.S. prisons and gangs, Cristos saw the next step as a no-brainer. Moving heroin for the cartels gave him a way to be cool, to be "free."

In describing his criminal life in Mexico, Cristos presented a posture of invincibility, living large and outside the law. He showed off tattoos that linked him to the Barrio Azteca Cartel (formed in Texas prisons, the Aztecas aligned with the armed wing of the Juárez Cartel, whose primary source of income was smuggling drugs). Though Cristos was vague about his exact activities, he spoke of growing and managing heroin. He also talked at length about how much money he made, bragging:

> I lived in San Pedro. It's super cool, super fresh. It's like fucking Polanco [a swanky Mexico City neighborhood]. Really *mamalón* (awesome), really cool, and there the police—it's the opposite [of the border], they take care of you. Like if you live in San Pedro, it's because you're a thing, you know? And I was there because I made really good money. In just a year I made like 800,000 pesos on pure sales, and I was stupid that I didn't buy land. I didn't buy cattle, but I bought a shitload of drugs, a shitload of women, a shitload of watches . . . I really love this—I love Mexico. I feel safer here,

and free. And here, well, here is where I've become a big man (*me he puesto gordo*).
I don't have to work. I'm not working in construction . . . earning friggin' 200 pesos
[$10] a day . . . It's fucking awesome.

Cynical about anything "inside" the law, Cristos worked the drug trade as a way
out of police abuse and into (in his mind) riches, safety, and "freedom." Again, his
manhood was deeply embodied. Yet, where César got buff at the gym, Cristos got
fat and bought sex. In claiming this image, Cristos felt powerful—more powerful
than the state agents who had abused him on either side of the border. Now, he
said, police took care of *him*.

Cristos also gained pride and a community (of sorts). Compared to U.S. prison,
he said, "I think I'm doing fucking damn well. I mean, I'm living by myself, but
I have gorgeous women that surround me, that love me. I have people that are—
well, that support me." He did not feel alone. He also contrasted his swagger with
the shame he saw among most deportees. He insisted:

Being in California you have that sense of Mexican pride or Chicano pride, "Viva la
Raza!" . . . And then you get back here, and everyone's going around with their heads
down. They don't have any damn pride in their own people. Like literally, what the
fuck? Lift up your chest, son! Lift your head up high. You come from Aztec roots!
. . . And that's what we have—by "we" I mean the people that come from over there
[the U.S.]—because we're hustlers, and that's why we make it so good . . . I've seen
1.5 million pesos in cash they gave my manager. Like, who the fuck does that shit?

If deportation made men go around with their heads down, for Cristos, "hustling"
directly challenged that outcome.

Other respondents hinted at similar patterns—toying with the invincible
image that Cristos portrayed. They talked about how, when ICE released them in
Mexico, cartels picked them up based on their clothes or tattoos. For some past
gang members, it was harder to get *out* of cartels than *in*. During men's time at
border—whether a night or a decade—many tried or considered taking a cartel
job. Some said that while in Tijuana, Reynosa, or Ciudad Juárez, they "did nothing
good," "did nothing legal," or "were drawn into illegal things." At least 15 respondents considered or attempted smuggling, drug sales, or other illegal activities.[34]
Some trafficked money or drugs. Others guided people across the desert. Secondary contacts also told us that men we'd interviewed were currently stealing, selling, or trafficking drugs. Some men said that *everyone* leaving prison got asked to
work for cartels the moment they crossed, and that easily half accepted. If these
reports are anywhere near correct, embracing criminality may be the default path
for deported men after prison.

As anthropologist Shaylih Muehlmann points out, criminal organizations permeate life at the border, so it can be tough to separate who is "in" a cartel or "out,"
and who is involved *intentionally*, versus by force. The informal drug economy
involves a wide range of players, from sellers to stashers, smugglers to addicts,

and many others whose roles fly under the radar. Muehlmann argues, the "line between participant, *narco*, and someone who is simply dabbling around the edges of criminal activities is blurry and confusing." For some people, Muehlmann adds, it can be riskier *not* to participate in the drug market.[35] Deportees may already be part of this trade, whether they choose to or not. Under such circumstances, the victim/perpetrator and subject/object binaries are profoundly gray.[36]

Whatever the scope of participation, cartel activity hung over deportees as a threat and a constant option. Pancho, a 35-year-old veteran of LA gangs, had the teardrop tattoos to show for it. In fluent English, he explained that in Tijuana he almost "headed back to the homies" or took cartels' offers to work as a mule. By chance, a call from a cousin stopped him. He remembered:

> I was tempted to go back by Sonora, because I found out—this friend of mine, he's like, "Hey, we could come back [to the U.S.], and they're gonna pay us. All we have to do is just take 25 kilos of weed, and they're gonna pay us." And I was like, "Oh, hell yeah, I'm gonna go back, and then I'm gonna get paid." But then I was like, "You don't know if these people—once you do take that drug, they're gonna kill you there. You're in the middle of the desert. They don't know you; you don't know them. No, I ain't trying to take that risk." So, I didn't took [*sic*] it.

Transporting weed through the desert was a tempting way to get back to the U.S. and "get paid" in the process. Yet this alternative came with risks not just of prison but also of assassination or death. Eventually, Pancho "got out" and moved to Mexico City. Others were not so lucky.

Men who *did* admit to illegal activity post-deportation said it made them feel "above" the state whose threats they had long endured—and more like a man. Twenty-seven-year-old Brayan, whom Ana met in a shelter in Mexico City, worked for years as a drug mule, as mentioned in prior chapters. He was caught more than a dozen times and beaten at the border by the Mexican army. The last time, he spent two years in U.S. prison and seven months in detention. After that, he felt desensitized to the state and its threats: "You think they [U.S. prisons] are going to scare me now, by saying that 'I'm going to give you more time'?" Brayan waved a dismissive hand, calling the whole system arbitrary. Disillusioned and desensitized by U.S. prison, he no longer believed in the law. By breaking it, he claimed a precarious sense of self. As a mule, he could "make his own rules."

Similarly, Milton told Ana that getting brutalized by the Zetas cartel made him feel tempted to rejoin a gang. When Milton landed in Tamaulipas, at Mexico's northeastern border, he had just bought a car, and the Zetas stole it (along with his cell phone and money). They also beat him, leaving him bloody and stranded. Milton thought to himself, "You know? I can do the same thing they're doing. That's not a problem, I got what it takes to do it." Milton had been in gangs in the past. Maybe, he thought, he should "man up" and do it again. If you can't beat 'em, join 'em, right? Facing abuse from both the state and cartels, he figured that *joining* the violence might be one of the few ways to show them that he, too, was still a man.

Like Cristos, Pancho, and Milton, interviewees who admitted such thoughts were often young men who'd previously been in gangs. Like César Quiroz, they liked money. Many adopted neoliberal, U.S.-type mindsets about "success" or the American Dream. Yet they'd also grown up in U.S. cities and been criminalized as teens. They emerged deeply critical of the U.S. carceral system. Now, state-run "justice" felt like a farce. They thought of the government as a corrupt, abusive machine made to crush men like them. Often, these interviewees talked or acted like U.S. and Mexican laws were meaningless, or like they themselves were "above" the law. Policing and prison broke their trust in the state and left them feeling betrayed.

For some, crime was inescapable. They risked being killed if they did not comply with their previous masters or enemy groups. After prison, some had no alternative means of subsistence. As Gilberto Rosas puts it in his study of gangs at the U.S.-Mexico border, "It's a circumscribed agency, of those who face imminent death."[37] Other scholars emphasize that gangs offer a path to "respect" *in a context* of danger, constrained lives, and bad jobs (or no jobs at all). This context includes the alienation, addiction, and specter of death produced by carceral deportation and detailed in chapter 5.[38] As Rosas points out, most people are not criminals, but U.S. and Mexican security regimes "crystallize the haunting effects of more nightmares to bear."[39]

Criminal activity was also a double-edged sword. It gave men agency, but only by turning them into perpetrators of crime and/or violence. It also made them more vulnerable to addiction, brutality, and death. Caught in the game of the "big man," respondents like Cristos rarely presented a broader vision of social transformation or collective agency. As gang scholar David Brotherton writes, their actions were "opposition without the possibility of any political or cultural transcendence, any meaningful link to larger movements of the marginalized, or any indigenous self-renewal, innovation or discovery in which consciousness is changed, agency is redefined, and other worlds are imagined."[40] Nevertheless, scholars must take seriously the strategies men adopt to refuse the terms set by states that have marked them as less than human.

CONCLUSION

If banishment portends social death, deportees are never simply erased. Even in deeply adverse conditions, they fight the system that oppresses them and find new forms of love, hope, and home. Using their experiences in Mexico and the U.S., deportees have invented new, binational identities, created spaces beyond "here and there," built community, and reclaimed deportation. At best, such innovations enable deported men and women to build "chosen family" in Mexico, even after losing their families in the United States. They *name* new identities that challenge the stigma of deportation and reclaim the stories told of them by the U.S. All insist on recognition.

Some groups also make money from their new identities (whether by selling T-shirts, U.S.-based houses, or drugs) and market their binationalism to buyers in the United States, even if they cannot physically cross. Others' efforts also lead to policy change, ensuring better access to resources or formal acknowledgment of their educational and labor achievements in the U.S.

Different deportees also take varying strategies. Some organize at the grass-roots, others embrace a binational business masculinity, and still others refuse to play by the government's rules.[41] Each of these strategies is embodied and gendered. While grassroots organizing often takes the form of maternal care, many men turn to other approaches to demonstrate masculinity, sometimes even physically, through bodily strength or "bigness."

Whether deportees got involved in such organizations—and which approach they adopted—depended on the skills they brought from the U.S., their mobility within Mexico, their histories in prison (and related constraints), and the institutional landscapes they encountered in Mexico. While Mexico City was not the *only* place innovation could happen, it offered government funding and NGO networks unparalleled elsewhere. To get into that context, however, deportees needed emotional wherewithal, economic resources, and the capacity to find opportunities (often on the Internet) and make the move.

In practice, most deported men and women did *not* join such organizations. It was hard to find groups like ODA or New Comienzos unless one was young, bilingual, and capable with the Internet. Often, one had to be in Mexico City already, where most of the first two forms of organizing (flipping the script and brokering deportation) took place. Even if deportees made it into the capital, many continued to struggle with alienation. As a result, reclaiming deportation was limited to those with experience in organizing or business, the gumption to seek alternatives, or the luck to meet a charismatic organizer. For formerly incarcerated people, there were rarely viable paths to resisting erasure *except* to join gangs or cartels. At the border, where deportees often got stuck after prison, their chances were shaped by a different set of powerful institutions.

Deportees' strategies also contained contradictions, to the point that one might question whether they can truly be thought of as "agency." Their efforts were not always cohesive. They often fell short of transforming the system that kept them down. For one, virtually all the groups relied in some way on U.S. capitalism, hustling (out of necessity) to sell things to the United States. Deported workers were subject to transnational enterprises (legal or illegal) that profited off their binational capabilities *and* off their immobility. The capitalist "trap" was especially poignant in brokering, as men actively identified with U.S.-based masculinity but struggled to avoid exploitation in practice. Meanwhile, grassroots organizers were often stymied by infighting; indeed, Deportados Unidos itself splintered several times.

Cartels and gangs presented their own problems, defying "acceptable" form of refusal. Historically, scholars and advocates have hesitated to frame men's engagement in extra-state violence and or informal markets as "agency." Many fear that doing so would reinforce the "Latino threat" narrative or fuel further punishment, cruelty, and social control of Latino immigrant men. Yet, respondents' stories hint at the subjectivity involved in going to work for cartels. On one hand, gangs extend violence and rarely offer a broader vision for change. Given deportees' severely circumscribed lives, participating in gangs also walks a line between voluntary and forced, subjectivity and subjugation. On the other hand, as any observer of Mexico can attest, cartels are currently doing more to change Mexico (and the U.S.-Mexico border) than most "civil" modes of resistance. If states and advocates want to help men in the face of multisided state violence, they must take seriously the omnipresence of extralegal institutions and their compelling offers of dignity, manhood, community, or simply the ability to stay alive.

Conclusion

The Opposite of Banishment Is Care

Today, U.S. deportation has merged with ICE detention and prison. Together, they assault men's humanity. Consider Ángel Morales. U.S. police marked Ángel worthy of cages, like so many Latino men. He spent nearly two years in prison and ICE detention. The time behind bars left him "psychologically destroyed." When Ángel landed in Mexico, he struggled to live outside the walls of an institution, let alone build a new life. He fought for a place to call home.

While the U.S. government frames immigration detention and removal as administrative, this book shows how they punish men. As I underscore throughout, deportation is now a multi-institutional and multinational system. That system begins with policing and arrest, followed by ICE detention and sometimes prison. If deported men try to return to their families in the U.S., they are often caught by border patrol and punished again. In Mexico, cartels and police extend the brutality of the U.S. carceral state, especially near the border.[1]

This kind of system is new. For most of the twentieth century, U.S. enforcement worked like South African apartheid, using legal exclusion and deportation to make migrant workers exploitable. Banishment is different. In addition to using immigration control to cheapen the labor of Mexican men, banishment aims to erase them. Its targets are not would-be workers so much as people the U.S. economy no longer needs. It has rendered a civil violation—undocumented migration—worthy of social death.

Banishment takes effect not just by beating men into submission (quite literally) but also by assaulting their relationships, self-confidence, and masculine pride. By eroding men's social ties, contemporary immigration enforcement breaks the association between hometown and "home," and thus the binary here-there relationships often (mis)attributed to Mexican migrants. Instead, it shunts men into "elsewheres" in Mexico's cities or northern border, where many of them live in limbo. There, they are haunted by isolation and the specter of violence and death.

On one thing, Ángel and our other 185 interviewees were insistently clear: banishment is *emotional.* Arrests, prison cells, removal, border apprehensions, and Mexican state violence take their toll through the ways they make people *feel.* Banishment *feels* like getting told, from childhood, that you are a criminal. It *feels* like getting ripped from your children at night with no chance to say goodbye. It *feels* like being locked up and beaten, like a dog. It *feels* like losing your sense of time and your place in the world. It *feels* like scraping by in Mexico, while all you've ever worked for is in the United States. For many, it *feels* like losing your emotional core and your place as a man, even after your body is "free." For some, it feels like ending up dead.[2]

I would not have seen these feelings so clearly without the 31 students who did interviews for this book. As sociologist Victor Rios points out in his 2015 essay "Decolonizing White Space in Ethnography," scholars often default to framing research on oppressed groups as a project of "normalizing" an unfamiliar "other."[3] What Rios calls "white ethnography" depicts the subjects of research as strange—or somehow in need of "humanization." Here, in contrast, students spoke openly of their own grief. They drew our shared focus to respondents' trauma and loneliness. Often, participants felt to students like family. Sometimes they *were* family, as in the case of Camila and her brother Ever. As a result, students *already* saw men we spoke with as deeply human.

From this standpoint, students insisted that our work interrogate and *de*normalize the brutality of U.S. policing, incarceration, and immigration enforcement. They reminded me that, as Rios puts it, "Ethnography should not be about making the strange familiar; it should be about making the familiar strange."[4] I wish that students had been able to work on writing the book as well. By the time I started drafting its chapters, they had graduated, taken jobs, or gone on to their own dissertations. In putting together the research we gathered, I tried to honor their lead and unsettle a process that most Americans take for granted: the militarization and masculinization of deportation from the United States.

The stories men told us—and their examples of innovation—offer hints at how to advocate for deportees and change this inhumane system. Though carceral deportation is notably brutal, it also has variations. Men's ability to reclaim their masculinity, pride, and well-being differed depending on how badly their lives were eroded by U.S. prison and on where they resettled in Mexico. Getting stuck at the border often ensured more intense isolation, while moving to Mexico City opened options for building community and reframing the terms of exile.

Ángel, for instance, joined an innovative, binational organization in Mexico City, where he found purpose. Despite his disorientation, the group gave him community and a "place" in the world. Instead of punishment, it gave him care. Such care—like the compassion my students extended to Ángel and other men— offers a path beyond banishment.

BANISHMENT AS GLOBAL PROJECT

This book focused on Mexicans. What might the findings mean for other deported migrants and marginal men? On one hand, the people we interviewed are a tiny slice of humanity: Mexican-born men (and 15 women) who came to the U.S. in the 1990s and 2000s and endured a punitive deportation regime in the 2010s. One might argue that their stories overrepresent the experience and impacts of U.S. detention and prison. Yet, punishment and policing have grown increasingly integrated into migration control all over the world. Many rich countries now lock up and expel racialized, economically "redundant" migrants, especially men.

The removal of Mexican men from the United States is part of a global pattern. In addition to Mexicans, the U.S. detains, imprisons, and deports hundreds of thousands of migrants from all over the world each year, with astonishing brutality. Using violence to wipe out Latino, Muslim, Asian, and Afro-descendent men is not an idiosyncrasy of the open white supremacy of Donald Trump or others like him. Rather, scapegoating immigrants, branding them as racialized "outsiders" or "criminals" and violently confining and excluding them is a core and long-standing tactic of Western nationhood.[5] Barack Obama and Joe Biden, for instance, embraced similar caging to Trump, framing immigrant men as "felons" and deporting more people than any Republican president has to date.

Banishment also finds global precedent in the forced relocation of oppressed and racialized people to their ascribed homelands, as of Pakistanis after the partition of India, of Haitians from the Dominican Republic, or of the Irish from England after the border was drawn. Yet I argue that banishment has grown especially prominent in the present moment, as low-wage (masculine) jobs dwindle globally under late neoliberal capitalism. In recent years, not just the U.S. and European countries but also places like the Dominican Republic, Iran, Pakistan, Saudi Arabia, and Mexico itself have expelled hundreds of thousands of migrants, including recognized refugees, long-term residents, and workers.[6] Frequently, these countries lock people up and then send them back into contexts of violence and insecurity. For instance, Saudi Arabia's crackdowns on Yemeni workers "return" them to a brutal civil war. Angola has forced hundreds of thousands of migrants back to the Democratic Republic of Congo, where they face extortion, arbitrary detention, and severe deprivation.[7] Indeed, Mexico now has a vast, militarized immigration enforcement apparatus and a network of detention facilities, aimed primarily at Central Americans. While practices vary, most entail imprisonment and state violence.

Studying deportation can also shed light on the racial banishment occurring *inside* the United States and other rich nations. As scholars like Ananya Roy and Katherine Beckett and Steve Herbert reveal, the U.S. *also* "removes" its own citizens, zoning poor Black and Brown people out of public spaces, enhancing the power of police to monitor and arrest them, and thus "banishing" such people from public life.[8] While most scholars analyze deportation under the rubric of immigration enforcement, I consider it *part of* the system of mass incarceration and urban removal.[9] In practice, these "regimes of disappearance" work in parallel *and* in tandem to target racialized men and expel them from public space. Both internal and external banishment intensify policing and punishment against people of color in the name of "security" and public safety. They use racial othering to mark people physically and morally inferior, often through notions of "criminality."[10] For the people they target, both systems trigger protracted psychological, social, and economic struggles.[11] Ultimately, both subordinate people of color to premature death.[12]

My analysis highlights how the mechanism of banishment—whether external (as in deportation) or internal (as in urban removal)—is emotional, psychological, and social. By integrating multiple institutions of state violence, carceral deportation—and other modes of banishment—subject people not only to premature *physical* death but also to *social* death. They eat at men's ties to the world. Men return to their places of origin changed by the impacts of being locked up. One might assume that prisoners released in the United States face different hurdles. But this study reveals how incarceration undermines men's relationships and sense of themselves. Under internal racial banishment, U.S. ex-prisoners are likely to feel alienated as well.

The impacts of punishment also extend beyond the borders of deporting nations.[13] Today, the U.S. has converted much of Mexico into a "buffer" state, which aims to block people (and goods) from reaching the United States from the south and must absorb those forced to return from the north.[14] As Mexican cities and border regions grapple with flows of internally displaced people, asylum seekers from Central America (and elsewhere), and deportees from the U.S., the Mexican government has increasingly used police and military violence to regulate migrants. Deportees are also convenient scapegoats for police to legitimate their own, ongoing role. At the same time, U.S. border militarization fuels cartel violence, creating profit motives for moving people and drugs. While Mexico is paradigmatic of this buffering, similar patterns are playing out in countries like Turkey, Greece, Poland, and Belarus, among others, that also lie "in between" the Global North and the Global South. In such places, transnational deportation regimes leave displaced and racialized people vulnerable to violence.

THE STATE AND EXCLUDED MEN

Banishment is not just racialized; it is also deeply gendered. U.S. deportation exemplifies a trend in which states shunt racialized *men*—already cast off by capitalism—to the margins of human dignity. Feminist scholars have long examined the gendered power of states over *women*, especially the marginalized.[15] Likewise, studies of gender and migration have drawn attention to the feminization of migrant labor and the disadvantages facing immigrant women.[16] Yet, researchers and the public tend to presume that men benefit from capitalism, hegemonic masculinity, and state power.

A new wave of scholars has started to question the marginalization of men, especially in relation to capitalism. Following Raewyn Connell, most scholars define hegemonic masculinity as the normative, most honored way of being a man (currently conceived in most countries as a breadwinning family patriarch).[17] Sociologists like Jordanna Matlon, Lynne Haney, and Raka Ray note that this version of masculinity clashes with the reality of mass unemployment in many parts of the world.[18] As James Ferguson argues, full employment is no longer possible.[19] Men cannot realize the breadwinner ideal. The result is a "crisis" of masculinity, especially for Black and Brown men.[20] Disconnected from productive labor in the formal economy and struggling to build families, these men must redefine and reclaim their manhood in relation to capitalism, women, and other men.[21]

In this book, I turn this lens to the state, to ask how governments *use* ideas about masculinity to control certain men. To legitimate state violence against migrants, institutions like police, ICE, prisons, and border enforcement leverage multiple, controlling images of masculinity. On one hand, these institutions hold men to an unattainable ideal of a breadwinning patriarch.[22] On the other hand, states lean heavily on an opposing image for exculpation: the "Latino threat." That is, they depict deportees—and other racially and economically marginalized men—as potential terrorists, gangsters, and violent criminal threats, worthy of spectacular state force.[23] U.S. politicians frame such men as "hardened criminals" and threats to the "good order," who are too "lazy" to work in the formal economy and in need of swift, corrective control.[24] After deportation, the Mexican state and criminal organizations target the very same men, based on their supposedly "ingrained" criminal character.

Across nations, powerful men (and women) also frame Black, Brown, and other racialized men as threats. States scapegoat such men for social ills, lock them up, and throw them out. After the jobs are gone, the state comes to punish—indeed, erase—those who cannot find work. That is, as historian and feminist theorist Joan Scott argues, politics "gets enacted on the field of gender." States manipulate public "common sense" about gender difference to construct and consolidate power and "to articulate the rules of social relationships or construct the meaning of experience."[25]

Scholars have also begun to consider how men *respond* to emasculation. Many studies show that they find novel ways to reassert masculinity.[26] For instance, exclusion can lead men to violence, weapons, sex, or sexual violence as markers of manhood (some of which echo here in this book).[27] In other cases, scholars argue, men become complicit in neoliberal capitalism. That is, they respond to the inaccessibility of the breadwinning ideal through consumption and entrepreneurial aspirations—though the latter may never fully be realized.[28] Here, to refuse the emasculation of being deported, some respondents adopted business/worker identities, and others were drawn to hypermasculine drug cartels. At times, however, men also redefined masculinity as emotional and fraternal, defying the terms of the institutions that oppressed them.[29] Indeed, subordinated men have long valued expressing feelings and love in ways that defy the "macho" stereotypes cast upon them by academics and other elites.[30] For instance, men like the members of Deportados Unidos en la Lucha found new masculinities in mutual aid, humor, and solidarity toward one another. As one member put it, "organizing . . . is like healing a broken heart."

For men, state violence is powerful partly *because* it degrades their manhood—their ability to be breadwinners and patriarchs, as well as (less visibly) their ability to give love and care. Banishment leaves men in a social vacuum. In the process, it renders them even more disposable.

THE GEOGRAPHY OF IMMIGRANT LIMBO

Contemporary deportation also challenges the frameworks that scholars typically use to understand immigrants. For one, this system is multi-institutional. It combines removal with incarceration and detention.[31] Therefore, understanding deportation requires examining prisons and policing as fundamental parts of the U.S. immigration and border enforcement regimes.[32]

Geographically, banishment also severs the dualism often ascribed to migration: between sending and receiving sites, home and away. For most deportees, one's birthplace is no longer "home." Rather, returned migrants are often excluded from their places of origin or labeled "delinquents." As scholars like Shahram Khosravi and Lisa Malkki point out, the assumption that returning to Mexico entails "reintegration" naturalizes the idea that deported men were "integrated" in rural Mexico to begin with—or can be again.[33] A focus on reintegration also individualizes the process of return, obscuring the painful impacts of U.S. institutions. By imposing trauma and severing relationships, contemporary deportation leaves men disconnected. Many are uncertain whether to risk death or arrest by crossing the U.S. border again. Thus, banishment extends the limbo of living without papers in the United States.[34] By leaving people existentially displaced, it makes reintegration almost impossible.

Instead, men tend to end up in places and among people they do not know. Unable to return to either the U.S. or their hometowns, deportees get stuck in liminal spaces, such as unfamiliar cities and/or border regions. At the border especially, the U.S. funds both its own enforcement and Mexican military violence against would-be crossers or criminals. The Mexican state and cartels extend the stigma and brutality of U.S. policing and prisons across the border, creating a transnational landscape of violent regulation.

Imprisonment also "sorts" men into different spaces in Mexico. Where they go varies with time and the tenor of their histories in the U.S. Those most debased by U.S. prison tend to feel most precarious back in Mexico. Upon release at the border, they often seem emotionally "broken." They have fewer social contacts than other deportees. They may not know where else to go. Their histories in U.S. prisons and gangs makes them prime targets for both police and cartels. Some end up using drugs or just "disappear." Others reclaim standing and manhood by joining in organized crime.

By contrast, men who endure less brutality in U.S. prison or detention emerge with more self-esteem and often more tools to seek out favorable urban locations (especially Mexico City). While they, too, are released at the border, they use English, personal contacts, and internet fluency to find jobs and peers in safer locales. There, they slowly build community and new senses of self—drawing on their binational experiences and bilingual skills. In big cities, they are more likely to forge transformative new groups and organizations that opt out of the damaging loop—indeed, the prison—of punishment and crime.

THE LEGACIES OF DEPORTATION

The geopolitical impacts of banishment do not end with removal. From a U.S. government standpoint, deportation allows the United States to wash its hands of "criminal" men. On the surface, they become "Mexico's problem." In practice, however, deportees do not disappear. Nor do their impacts on the United States.

On the contrary, U.S. policing, incarceration, deportation, and border militarization fuel the very crises they claim to be solving.[35] After spending time in U.S. prisons and detention facilities, deportees feel devastated. They grow accustomed to violence. They lose emotional support. Then, they get released in places where they are vulnerable to attacks by Mexican cartels and police—caught between the iron fists of Mexico and the United States.

For some, participating in organized crime can fill the financial gap left by exclusion from wage-earning jobs. Gangs and cartels can also assuage the emotional and psychological pain of family loss and U.S. and Mexican state abuse. Engaging in violence offers one way to claim power. Yet it also feeds the public stereotypes that legitimate such men's imprisonment and deportation—the media and political stories about the "risks" of "violent Brown men." In these stories, violence comes *from* Mexican men, instead of from U.S. (and Mexican) institutions. Blaming violence on Mexico or Mexicans obscures the role of the U.S. state and the ways it subjects men to abuses and leaves them at the border to join cartels— and sometimes to die.[36]

U.S. imprisonment and deportation may also fuel more migration. For one, most deportees hope to return to their families north of the border. In addition, the growth of Mexican cartels—partially spurred by the integration of deport-ees—is driving ever more people to flee Mexico and seek asylum in the U.S.[37] Most seek escape from organized crime. Echoing a process that has been occur-ring in Central America for more than two decades, the U.S. "war on drugs" has combined with deportation and the militarization of Mexico to drive Mexican refugees north.

In the U.S. today, both organized crime and migration are objects of moral panic: exaggerated fears that a person or group threatens the values and interests of the United States.[38] The more cartels expand, and the more desperate people seek to enter the U.S., the more intense the U.S. obsession with walls and border "security."[39] In the name of suppressing "Latino male violence," the U.S. and Mex-ico intensify the same policing, border enforcement, prison sentences, and violent repression that fuel insecurity in Mexico.

Deportation also harms family members who stay in the United States. Most deported men leave wives, children, parents, or siblings north of the border. Stud-ies of immigrant families make clear that men's removal imposes incredible costs on those who remain—including economic struggles, heartbreak, and fear. As detailed in chapter 1, the impacts can span generations, leaving deportees' chil-dren vulnerable to policing and criminalization themselves. Deporting one "bad hombre" may thus be the start of a multigenerational cycle that leaves U.S. citizen children and loved ones vulnerable *inside* the U.S. as well.[40]

STEPS TOWARD TRANSFORMATION

Policymakers often accept deportation as a necessary practice of governance. When criticized, they call for tweaks to U.S. enforcement. Some even suggest *harsher* treatment, as a tool to deter reentry or more migration. Others insist that *Mexico* must do better at reintegrating deportees. For instance, some advocates argue that the Mexican government should take more responsibility for protecting and providing aid to repatriated migrants—a role currently played primarily by NGOs and the Catholic Church.[41] Rarely do policymakers consider how difficult reintegration can be when a person has been stripped of his family, home, man-hood, and even his sense of self. Nor do they think about reforming the underly-ing, institutional causes of this sense of loss.

Scholars and journalists propose more immediate measures to lighten the pain of removal. These calls begin with disentangling, reforming, and even dismantling the five arms of carceral deportation: policing, detention, incarceration, border militarization, and Mexican state abuse. These are critical steps toward change. For instance, sensible reformers demand an end to the arbitrary and pretextual arrests of Latino men and boys, especially minors under 18. They also call for eliminating cooperation between police departments and ICE, which funnel men from arrest into deportation.[42] They propose simple pathways to legalization, especially for childhood arrivals to the U.S. Advocates have also fought for constraints on ICE detention, including time limits and greater sanctions against verbal and physical abuse. They push for universal legal representation for migrants—as has begun to take place in cities like Santa Ana, California—and judicial discretion to halt deportation.[43]

Going further, reformers demand the U.S. end excessive sentencing, especially for drug crimes and reentry, and reduce the list of offenses that trigger a deportation. They argue that people who have served full sentences or completed community service should not be removed.[44] There are also proposals to extend sentencing reforms to immigration cases, end the time-bound bans on deportee visits to the U.S., and reduce the penalties for reentry, which disproportionately affect parents due to their high propensity for recrossing the border.[45]

These proposals offer important, concrete alternatives. They would keep more men with their families and significantly lessen deportees' pain. But they are not enough. They leave intact much of the emotional debasement and dehumanization that are fundamental to banishment. Instead, as deported men insisted to me and my students, confinement itself must be brought to an end. It is time to eliminate immigration detention and overhaul U.S. imprisonment. Men's stories also hint at a much-needed shift in the terms of institutional change: not only must the U.S. end the violence of banishment, but also, the U.S. and Mexico must increasingly practice care. The case for abolition is both moral and geopolitical.

CARE IN A WORLD OF DISPLACEMENT

Migration is not going away. By all accounts, the twenty-first century will be an era of mass displacement. Climate devastation and the economic and political crises that follow portend the uprooting of unprecedented numbers of people. The concentration of refugees at the U.S.-Mexico border is a harbinger of the systemic destabilization and forced migration to come.

As economic insecurity, climate crisis, and conflict drive up migration, rich-country policymakers have used removals to cast out unwanted "others" whom they frame as threats.[46] Think of the anti-immigrant fervor and hypermilitarization happening in the United States. These trends suggest that the rich world is headed into a dystopian future, in which wealthy nations respond to the uncertainties of climate change and large-scale migration with racial animosity and state-sponsored violence. Indeed, the U.S. Department of Defense has been on the cutting edge of anticipating—and arming the United States against—widespread migration driven by climate disaster. To insulate rich countries from insecurity, it is plausible that governments like the United States will further scapegoat marginalized groups (especially men) and even seek their extermination. The U.S. may also export its punitive stance into other places, funding and orchestrating the expansion of U.S. techniques of control. "Buffer" countries like Mexico will play a key role in this process—extending U.S. militarization to even more vulnerable people. As Achille Mbembe writes, it seems to be "a time when the sword, now again, resolves all."[47]

In the face of global displacement, state violence, and gestures toward outright erasure, how might one imagine flourishing for all people, especially men like Ángel? What might it mean to ground immigration policies in migrants' lived experiences—including their strategies of agency and struggles to build community? The migrants we interviewed hint at profound transformations—through their feelings, their strivings, their nascent organizations, and, indeed, their words to me and my students.

The stories they told us make it clear that the U.S. must end imprisonment and removal for minor crimes. Laws that punish small violations—and tie them to deportation—strip otherwise regular people from their loved ones, their homes, their jobs, and their well-being. The system is also biased by the racial and gendered stereotypes the government uses to legitimate violence. Deportees are generally not the "bad hombres" they are made out to be. Ending criminalization is also key to halting abuses against communities (and men) of color more broadly.

Decarceration must also extend to immigrants. Calls to abolish ICE and prisons may appear to be leftist slogans. In the face of the open white supremacy of many people in the U.S., they can also feel hopeless. But these ends only sound radical because imprisonment and removal have been so naturalized. In fact, this system is new—just a few decades old, at most. Thirty years ago, crossing the U.S.-Mexico border was not a crime. There were many more legal ways to migrate, and policing, detention, and prison were almost entirely separate from deportation. The U.S. rarely repatriated people who already lived in the United States.

That recent memory offers a model to begin walking back the current dehumanization. So does the movement for decarceration. Already, thanks largely to abolitionist movements, the U.S. has moved to reform its system of mass incarceration. Yet, the country continues to *increase* the imprisonment and detention of immigrants.[48] As Angela Davis puts it, prisons are obsolete. So is their role in immigration control.[49]

Decriminalization and decarceration must also go hand in hand with demilitarizing the U.S.-Mexico border and reforming policing in Mexico. Legalizing drugs and allowing freer cross-border movement would remove much of the incentive for intensifying criminal activity, especially trafficking. Meanwhile, the Mexican military and police—and their U.S. supporters—must stop adding to the abuses meted out against deportees. Given the part that Mexico plays in extending U.S. state violence, reintegration cannot succeed without demilitarization there.

Change requires the action of regular people as well. As long as the public refuses to see men's heartbreak, as long as our silence sanctions violence against them, it will go on. Those who suffer under this system cannot transform it alone. Citizens of the United States must speak out against their country's practices of banishment. Those in Mexico, too, must question police abuse. When we asked men what they'd like to tell readers, they implored people in the U.S. (and Mexico) to take a part in ending their suffering.

Abolition is not just about ending systems of violence; it is also about inventing alternatives and investing in real community and belonging. If the pain of banishment is emotional, so, too, are its solutions. Men heal when they feel included and find spaces of love. In this, their *own* actions signal the changes they need.

Migrants' *existing* practices, feelings, and strivings illustrate what they are seeking. Regardless of their level of isolation or their strategies for survival, men we spoke with sought to reclaim connection and care. Losing loved ones was a critical source of their pain. While their options were constrained in varying ways, their efforts at agency all grasped at belonging and home. Deportados Unidos en la Lucha and ODA offer powerful examples. Such deportee-led organizations redefined the meaning of home outside of—and against—the confines of nation-states. They created multivalent public spaces and "crossed borders" within and across countries and identities. They were creative. In the face of systems that tried to destroy their feelings and ties to the people they loved, they relentlessly sought out care.

Sometimes, as detailed in chapter 6, migrants also sought to reclaim their masculinity, breadwinner status, physical power, and even control over violence. Some did this by aspirational entrepreneurship. Others did it by refusing to follow laws, or by working under cartels. These *reactive* versions of masculinity can be twisted against deportees and even feed further abuse. Instead, it is important to heed men's reactions as calls for change. Even if "polite" publics find such projects unpalatable, they reveal men's need for belonging and dignity.

What would an immigration system that refuses banishment look like? As a first step, the U.S. government would end detention, imprisonment, and removal, building on the ongoing movement against mass incarceration. It would reduce deportation to (or below) 1980s levels. Above all, it would keep men with their families—their irreplaceable sources of love. The government would also invest in the projects deported men and women are already building—just as Mexico invested in Deportados Unidos en La Lucha, enabling migrants to claim community and a sense of themselves. Such a system would give marginalized men recognition and cultural space, including for gangs. Indeed, as David Brotherton notes, some countries in Europe have succeeded in legally recognizing gangs as cultural associations, in lieu of punishing them.[50] A transformed system would also let men retell the stories of their exclusion, on their own terms. In this book, in our own tiny way, my students and I hoped to give men such a space. They often responded with gratitude and with pride.

Ending banishment is a herculean task, but it is not impossible. A new system begins with replacing each institution of punishment with spaces of recognition and rights. In lieu of carceral deportation, both Mexico and the U.S. must invest in support for men. Governments must treat them as whole, emotional human beings. If we start from care instead of erasure, we might begin to see a triumph of love over social death.

Interviewee Demographics

The following table summarizes the demographics of the 186 deportees interviewed for this study. It includes a separate column for the 158 men who had lived in the U.S. a year or more, on whom we focus in this book.

We interviewed all respondents between January 2018 and March 2020. All were born in Mexico. All were at least 18. Though we aimed to recruit people who had lived in the U.S. at least a year, 14 of the people we interviewed (13 women and one man) had not yet lived in the U.S. Rather, they were apprehended while crossing the border and deported by U.S. Customs and Border Patrol.

	All respondents (n=186)	Men in the U.S. ≥1 year (n=158)
Gender*		
Men	171 (92%)	158 (100%)
Women	15 (8%)	0 (0%)
Age at Interview"	**median = 35**	**median = 35**
18–19	1 (1%)	0 (0%)
20–29	54 (29%)	44 (28%)
30–39	64 (34%)	56 (35%)
40–49	47 (25%)	40 (25%)
50+	20 (11%)	18 (11%)
Mexican State of Origin"		
Guerrero	18 (10%)	15 (9%)
Michoacán	21 (11%)	21 (13%)
Oaxaca	30 (16%)	22 (14%)
Mexico City	31 (17%)	26 (16%)
Mexico State	14 (8%)	13 (8%)
18 other states	72 (39%)	61 (39%)
Education completed"		
Primary school or less	37 (20%)	33 (21%)
Middle school	51 (27%)	41 (26%)
High school	71 (38%)	61 (39%)
University or more	24 (13%)	20 (13%)
Unknown	3 (2%)	3 (2%)
Years in U.S.	**median = 18.5**	**median = 20**
Age at First Migration	**median = 15**	**median = 15**
<12	72 (39%)	66 (42%)
13–17 (brought by parents)	19 (10%)	18 (11%)
13–17 (unaccompanied minors)	25 (13%)	22 (14%)
18+	70 (38%)	52 (33%)
Preferred Language		
Spanish	141 (76%)	113 (72%)
English	45 (24%)	45 (28%)
Civil Status		
Single	83 (45%)	69 (44%)
Married / Partnered	53 (28%)	45 (28%)
Separated / Divorced	50 (27%)	44 (28%)
Widowed	0 (0%)	0 (0%)

	All respondents (n=186)	Men in the U.S. ≥1 year (n=158)
Had Children		
Yes	121 (65%)	105 (66%)
No	65 (35%)	53 (34%)
U.S. Prison or Jail[**]		
Yes	107 (58%)	100 (63%)
No	74 (40%)	54 (34%)
Unknown	5 (3%)	4 (3%)
U.S. Immigration Detention[**]		
Yes	155 (83%)	130 (82%)
No	8 (4%)	6 (4%)
Deported directly from prison	23 (12%)	22 (14%)
Next Destination[**]		
United States	32 (17%)	30 (19%)
Tijuana (stay)	46 (25%)	43 (27%)
Mexico City	50 (27%)	44 (28%)
Oaxaca / Home state	42 (23%)	30 (19%)
Undecided	15 (8%)	10 (6%)
Other	1 (1%)	1 (1%)
Location of Interview		
Tijuana	107 (58%)	90 (57%)
Mexico City	54 (29%)	49 (31%)
Oaxaca	25 (13%)	19 (12%)

[*] All participants identified as women or men, and none as "other."

[**] Total percentages may not add exactly to 100 percent due to rounding in each category to the nearest whole percent.

PREFACE

1. A list of MMFRP publications under Dr. Cornelius appears at https://ccis.ucsd.edu /publications/books.html.

2. We worked with the Casa del Migrante, Madre Assunta, Padre Chava, YMCA, Ejército de Salvación, and Templo Embajadores de Jesús. In the wake of this book, MMFRP students and I have designed additional, community-led research projects with several advocacy organizations working for migrants' rights. See https://mmfrp.org for more on these projects.

3. A pseudonym at the student's request.

4. Jack (2019).

5. De Lira (2020).

6. Of particular help: van Dernoot Lipsky and Burk (2009), Weller (2015), and van der Kolk (2014). I am also grateful to Taylor Winfield (2022) for her piece on teaching competencies for trauma- and justice-informed ethnography; to Leticia Saucedo at UC Davis; and to the staff of Al Otro Lado for sharing their curricula on secondary trauma.

7. Robert Smith (2005) and others describe an "immigrant bargain," in which children from immigrant families seek academic success to validate their parents' sacrifices.

8. Andrea Flores (2021) also writes about how people expect DREAMers to be exceptional and how that characterization enables the demonization of certain men.

9. Chavez (2008).

10. See also Anderson and Solis (2014).

INTRODUCTION

1. COLEF et al. (2020).

2. Here, I build on Michel Foucault's (1977) book *Discipline and Punish*, whose final chapter describes a "carceral system" that extends disciplinary techniques from the prison into other institutions and society as a whole.

3. Chavez (2008); Golash-Boza (2012); Ngai (2004).

4. Farrell-Bryan and Peacock (2022); TRAC (2014).

5. Alarcón and Becerra (2012); Boehm (2016); Slack (2019).

6. Shams (2020).

7. Goodman (2020).

8. García Hernández (2017); Simon (1998); Stumpf (2006).

9. While prison refers to state-run penitentiaries, jail refers to local facilities run by county sheriffs or police, typically housing less violent offenders. See Cantor, Noferi, and Martínez (2015); Macías Rojas (2016).

10. Cantor, Noferi, and Martínez (2015); Cardoso et al. (2016).

11. Ngai (2004).

12. Hagan, Eschbach, and Rodriguez (2008).

13. Cantor, Noferi, and Martínez (2015).

14. Ewing, Martínez, and Rumbaut (2015).

15. Ngai (2004).

16. Andreas (2000); De León (2015); Dunn (2010); Nevins (2002).

17. See Slack (2019).

18. Cardoso et al. (2016). As of 2014, about half of all people sentenced in U.S. federal courts were noncitizens. Undocumented immigrants were more likely to be incarcerated pretrial and received longer sentences than U.S. citizens (Light, Massoglia, and King 2014).

19. Federal Bureau of Prisons (2015).

20. Calva Sánchez and Alarcón Acosta (2018).

21. Department of Homeland Security (2020); TRAC (2017).

22. Cardoso et al. (2016); COLEF et al. (2018).

23. Light, He, and Robey (2020).

24. Ewing, Martínez, and Rumbaut (2015).

25. Armenta (2017).

26. Cantor, Noferi, and Martínez (2015).

27. Estimates are rough. The Department of Homeland Security releases very limited data, and numbers vary over time as to how many deportees have been convicted of crimes and of which crimes. For more details see TRAC (2019a; 2019b). ICE claims that more than 86 percent of the people it arrests have "criminal convictions or *pending* charges" (my italics) (U.S. Immigration and Customs Enforcement 2019).

28. Ewing, Martínez, and Rumbaut (2015).

29. García Hernández (2019).

30. TRAC (2022).

31. See Nevins and Aizeki (2008).

32. Burawoy (1976); Wolpe (1972). Scholars refer to this arrangement as the "articulation" (or connection, joining) of capitalist exploitation and rural subsistence farming via the expression of racial and gendered difference (Hall 1980; Hart 2002). See Levenson (2022) for discussion.

33. Burawoy (1976); Hart (2002).

34. Burawoy (1976).

35. Ngai (2004).

36. Since the 1980s, women from Mexico and Central America have also migrated to the U.S., perpetuating a modified gendered care chain by leaving their children behind (Golash-Boza and Hondagneu-Sotelo 2014).

37. Golash-Boza (2015)

38. Beckett and Herbert (2009; 2010).

39. Roy (2019, 228).

40. Patterson (1982).

41. Cacho (2012).

42. Agamben (1998).

43. García Hernández (2019); Gurusami (2019); Loyd, Mitchelson, and Burridge (2012). As Susan Coutin (2015) and others point out, deportation is a *process* or "corridor" that includes arrest, imprisonment, detention, removal, and return and crosses numerous institutions, places, and actors (Drotbohm and Hasselberg 2014).

44. Gilmore (2008); Mbembe (2019).

45. Beckett and Herbert (2009; 2010); Roy (2019).

46. Comfort (2008); Haney (2018); Harding, Morenoff, and Wyse (2019); Miller (2021); Western (2018).

47. Other forms of banishment, such as eviction, focus on women (Desmond 2016).

48. Golash-Boza and Hondagneu-Sotelo (2013).

49. Farrell-Bryan (2021). Parallel tropes about Latina women as submissive and caring help cultivate a feminized workforce in the service sector (Salzinger 2003).

50. In the late 1990s, as men's deportations skyrocketed, U.S. deportations of women remained roughly stable (Golash-Boza and Hondagneu-Sotelo 2013).

51. For instance, under President Trump, there was immense outcry about mothers being separated from children while attempting to seek asylum at the U.S.-Mexico border (e.g., Dickerson 2022).

52. Ferguson (2015); Ray (2021). The growth sectors of many labor markets are in health care and social services, areas long dominated by women (Golash-Boza and Hondagneu-Sotelo 2013).

53. Carlson (2015); Connell (1995).

54. Matlon (2016).

55. Connell (1995). With a notable exception of scholars like Matthew Guttman (1996).

56. MacKinnon (1982); Brown (1995).

57. Hochschild (1983). See Mahmood (2005) for a review.

58. Haney (2018; 2022).

59. Randles (2020).

60. Between 1965 and 2015, more than 16 million Mexicans migrated to the United States, becoming the country's largest immigrant group. This trend began to reverse after the Great Recession in 2009, with fewer Mexicans coming north and more returning to Mexico, both forcibly and voluntarily. While net migration from Mexico is presently close to zero, scholars have yet to redefine their categories to understand flows in both directions (Gonzalez-Barrera 2021).

61. Andrews (2018b); Duquette-Rury (2020); Smith (2005).

62. Masferrer (2021); Masferrer and Roberts (2016).

63. Masferrer and Roberts (2016).

64. Golash-Boza (2015); Alarcón and Becerra (2012).

65. Boehm (2016); Khosravi (2017); Ybarra and Peña (2017).

66. See Levitt and Lamba-Nieves (2011); Duquette-Rury (2020).

67. Weber ([1919] 1946).

68. Turner (1967).

69. Gonzales (2015); Menjívar (2006).

70. In 2015, about 60 percent of refugees lived in cities, up from 42 percent in 2008 (UNHCR 2017). In Latin America especially, cities are the key nexus of forced displacement; there are no refugee camps and deported men often live among and share problems with the urban poor (Jacobsen and Medina Castellanos 2017).

71. Chávez (2016).

72. Muehlmann (2013); Slack (2019).

73. Butler and Mancillas Bazán (2011); Golash-Boza (2015); Morris and Palazuelos (2017); Slack (2019).

74. Chávez (2016).

75. Burawoy (1976).

76. Coutin (2015). As Nicholas de Genova (2002; 2007) points out, the U.S. uses the threat of deportation to induce fear among immigrant workers, reducing their capacity to challenge labor conditions.

77. Alarcón and Becerra (2012); Boehm (2016); Schuster and Majidi (2013).

78. Morris and Palazuelos (2017); París Pombo, Buenrostro Mercado, and Pérez Duperou (2017).

79. Roy (2019, 229).

80. Bayat (2013); Chatterjee (2004).

81. Matlon (2016; 2022).

82. These service providers helped us understand the demographics of deportees in their cities, the services available and organizing occurring, and the (mis)treatment of returning migrants. While the text homes in on *deportees'* stories, the stakeholder interviews helped triangulate our conversations with deportees and map out variations by place.

83. Since the 2010s, the U.S. has released 98 percent of Mexican deportees at the border, about a quarter into Tijuana (SEGOB 2019). Though 97 percent of unauthorized Mexican men come from the South and West of Mexico, roughly a third are released in Baja California and a third in Tamaulipas, with the others scattered between. There are only two repatriation sites in Mexico's interior, Mexico City and Guadalajara, which together receive fewer than 4 percent of deportees.

84. While Tijuana echoes the violence and precarity of much of the U.S.-Mexico border, at the time of our research it was not as besieged by drug cartels as places like Tamaulipas and Juárez. Compared to other border cities, Tijuana also had more humanitarian organizations supporting migrants and a better labor market. As a result, even though few deported migrants grew up in Tijuana, about 25 to 35 percent resettle in that city, compared with 10 percent elsewhere along the border (Calva Sánchez and Alarcón Acosta 2018; París Pombo, Buenrostro Mercado, and Pérez Duperou 2017).

85. Established in the mid-1990s to support labor migrants heading north, by 2017 the Casa del Migrante served 90 percent deportees.

86. Most found the program through their classes or majors, or by word of mouth.

87. All travel, lodging, and food was paid for by a University of California grant.

88. SEGOB (2019).

89. My UCSD research funds paid these RAs' summer salary, airfare, and per diem for travel.

90. See Slack, Martinez, and Whiteford (2018) for a description of violent incursions into shelters in Sonora and the security rationale for working there.

91. These agents do not represent a threat to Mexican returnees in the way they might to non-Mexicans since their role in this case is to support reentry.

92. We sought people who'd lived in the U.S. at least a year, because we wanted to study exile, rather than border crossing. To capture the experience of *carceral* deportation, we stuck to individuals deported after 2015. We included anyone who self-defined as deported, even if they had signed a "voluntary" removal order while in ICE detention. Initially, we offered compensation of $200 pesos (about U.S. $10) in cash, roughly half a day's wage. Subsequently, these payments sparked conflict, and staff requested we terminate them.

93. In these sites, we also offered participants $200 pesos, plus $50 pesos for each referral.

94. In Oaxaca, we recruited four interviewees via ads (on the street, radio, and Internet), two through community referrals, two on the street, ten through family contacts, and ten through "snowball" referrals from respondents. In Mexico City, we recruited nine participants via a local shelter (and a snowball from there), 22 through deportee advocacy organizations, 11 by talking to people outside of call centers, 12 through ads on the street and online, and one through a family contact.

95. See Casa del Migrante (2017).

96. Doering-White (2018); Fitzgerald (2019).

97. To compensate for this imbalance, the team watched and read interviews that other scholars conducted with deportees in Tijuana (notably, UC Davis's Humanizing Deportation video database). In general, the stories resembled our interviews.

98. See Weiss (1994).

99. Students and a professional transcriptionist transcribed all interviews in the original language. Students transcribed their own interviews, and the transcriptionist did mine and the ones from Oaxaca and Mexico City.

100. Boehm (2016).

101. While I instructed students to screen for people who had lived in the U.S. at least a year, they ended up interviewing one woman and 13 men who had not lived in the U.S. but instead got apprehended while crossing the U.S.-Mexico border.

102. COLEF et al. (2018). EMIF samples deportees upon reentry at all but the two or three least trafficked repatriation points. It can be considered representative. For these estimates, we refer to EMIF 2018 (our median year of removal).

103. COLE et al. (2018).

104. We followed the coding process described by Deterding and Waters (2018), beginning with processing all the data for general themes, then revisiting to analyze emergent trends in more depth.

105. U.S. government rhetoric often separates "felons" from families, rather than framing both as members of families severed by U.S. enforcement (Sarabia 2018).

106. *Merriam-Webster* (2022), s.v. "limbo."

107. Massey, Durand, and Pren (2016).

108. See Boehm (2016).

109. While in 2006 about 80 percent of Mexican deportees planned to recross the border within a week of being removed, by 2016 only 19 percent said the same (Calva Sánchez and Alarcón Acosta 2018).

110. The U.S. intentionally lets many migrants out in areas of the border they've never been to before. See De León (2015) or Slack (2019) for more on this practice of lateral deportation.

1. POLICED

1. Camila later wrote me, "I don't hold any grudge against the officers, not then and not the several other times they searched my house and cars, but oftentimes I find myself wondering how things would've been different if I would've been older and able to stop them from abusing their power."

2. Chavez (2008).

3. As Amada Armenta (2017) and William López (2019) underscore, racial profiling of Latinos is embedded in everyday policing, particularly in traffic enforcement.

4. Zilberg (2011).

5. Phillips (2012).

6. Rendón (2019).

7. Sociologist Tanya Golash-Boza (2015) describes a "neoliberal cycle" of deportation. This chapter links that broader, structural cycle to the life course of individual men.

8. Rios (2011). As Michel Foucault (1977) suggests, a wide range of institutions use prison techniques in a "carceral archipelago," well beyond prison walls (see also Simon 1998). These techniques are not just disciplinary. Rather, as Loïc Wacquant (2009) notes, many penal institutions have replaced welfare and discipline with force. Instead of enticing people to self-regulate through rewards (and punishment), they engage men primarily through violence.

9. Roberts (2022).

10. Consider, for instance, "broken windows" policing that punishes people for minor disorderly conduct or three-strikes policies that intensify punishments for people simply because they have repeated arrests (Howell 2016).

11. See also Duck (2015); Goffman (2014); Lopez-Aguado (2016); Martínez (2016).

12. Fader (2013); Rios (2011).

13. Cerdeña, Rivera, and Spak (2021).

14. Gonzales (2015).

15. Dreby (2012a); Enriquez (2015; 2016); Patler and Gonzalez (2021). The patterns among children of deportees resemble the patterns found among children with parents in prison (Foster and Hagan 2009; Wakefield and Wildeman 2013).

16. Abrego and Negrón-Gonzales (2020).

17. We did not explore the effects on immigrant girls. While they surely face impacts as well, police disproportionately target young boys.

18. Scholars use the term "1.5-generation" for people brought to the U.S. as children. If first-generation immigrants move to the U.S. as adults and second-generation immigrants are born and raised here, 1.5-generation immigrants' experiences fall somewhere in between.

19. While the mechanisms of gendering are not entirely clear, this pipeline almost exclusively targets men. In representative surveys, women tend to face deportation only after going to prison (COLEF et al. 2018; 2019).

20. COLEF et al. (2018; 2019).

21. In most states, unauthorized migrants are not permitted to have drivers' licenses, and a DUI while driving without a license is an automatic felony. In others, like California, DUI penalties rise with blood alcohol content, DUIs involving accident or injury, and/or refusal of a blood, urine, or breath test. However, sentences are up to judicial discretion, so a single DUI can result in anything from a fine to six months in jail, while a felony DUI (DUI without a license, resulting in death or injury, or repeat DUI) leads to one to five years in state prison.

22. Secure Communities and the 287(g) program, which allow for police-ICE collaboration, have been rolled out in distinct ways across the United States, depending on the local political climate (Andrews 2018b; García 2019). Thus, deportation risk varies by place (Coleman 2012; Coleman and Kocher 2011; Varsanyi 2010).

23. Armenta (2017).

24. ICE can stop people as they enter the country, at borders, or in airports. They can also track down immigrants if they apply for an adjustment of legal status or if ICE seeks to enforce a prior removal order.

25. Technically, such searches require a warrant, but few undocumented immigrants are well-informed about this requirement or willing to stand up for their rights in this situation.

26. Macías-Rojas (2016).

27. A green card holder can be removed for theft, failing to appear in court, repeated immigration violations, falsely claiming to be a U.S. citizen, or offenses that most states consider a misdemeanor or do not criminalize at all, such as consensual sex between a 21-year-old and a 17-year-old. For a list of eligible offenses, see Teresa Wiltz, "What Crimes Are Eligible for Deportation?" Pew, https://www.pewtrusts.org/en/research-and-analysis /blogs/stateline/2016/12/21/what-crimes-are-eligible-for-deportation.

28. See Abrego et al. (2017). Note: Data are hard to come by, and the percentage of people deported with violent crimes varies with local policies and police collaboration with ICE (TRAC 2019a).

29. Ewing, Martínez, and Rumbaut (2015).

30. Such treatment is more common in certain states and cities. Since everyone we interviewed had already been deported, our analysis may miss those arrested in relatively lenient locales and later released.

31. Other scholars have also documented verbal harassment, procedural failings, and use of excessive force during arrest and detention pre-deportation (Phillips, Hagan, and Rodríguez 2006).

32. Andrews (2018a).

33. Intergenerational trauma (sometimes referred to as trans- or multigenerational trauma) refers to emotional and psychological wounding that is transmitted across generations (Cerdeña, Rivera, and Spak 2021).

34. At the same time, many children in the U.S.—especially Black and Latino children—lost their parents to the prison boom. Children of deportees and of prisoners both grew up without parents and continue to endure the deprivation and trauma that result (Wakefield and Wildeman 2013).

35. Gleeson (2016); Patler, Gleeson, and Schonlau (2020).

36. Rendón (2019).

37. The "protective" removal of immigrant children from their parents to foster care also recalls histories in which the U.S. state has violently removed children of color from their families, such as under slavery and in Native American boarding schools (Roberts 2022).

38. Dreby (2012b).

39. Gonzales (2015).

40. As Maria Rendón (2019), Elana Zilberg (2011), and others show, boys who join gangs tend to be disconnected from family.

41. Contreras (2013).

42. As Leisy Abrego (2011) notes, life stage mediates migrants' interactions with police as well as their legal consciousness (understandings of the law). While first-generation migrants find their lives overturned when they're unfairly branded as criminals, 1.5-generation youngsters get policed piece by piece, until some begin to act out the very crimes the U.S. state feared.

43. Goodman (2020).

44. Foucault (1977); Wacquant (2009).

2. LOCKED UP AND BROKEN DOWN

1. Golash-Boza (2016).

2. Reiter and Coutin (2017).

3. Reiter (2016); Walker (2022); Woodfox (2019).

4. Miller (2021).

5. Patterson (1982); Price (2015). Giorgio Agamben (1998) calls this status "bare life," and Achille Mbembe (2019) "the edge of life."

6. See Mbembe (2019).

7. Insofar as carceral institutions treat people as beasts, they echo the logic of genocide. Nazis likened Jews to rats; Hutus called Tutsis cockroaches; and colonizers represented dark-skinned people around the globe as beasts (Stanton 1998). This denial of humanity can mark a pivot from "othering" to murder (Haslam 2006; Jackson 2020) or be used as an exculpatory rationale after killing (Luft 2019).

8. Guenther (2013).

9. Reiter and Coutin (2017, 570).

10. Reiter and Coutin (2017).

11. Hiemstra (2019).

12. Ryo (2018).

13. As of 2021, about 70 percent of immigrant detainees were held in private prisons run by corporations such as GEO Group and CoreCivic (up from about 49 percent in 2009). In 2014 the National Immigration Forum estimated the cost at about $161 per person per day or $2 billion per year (National Immigration Forum 2014; Simanski 2014). Private detention facilities are notorious for their mismanagement and mistreatment, such that private prisons run by the same corporations were shut down by both the Obama and Biden administrations (Bauer 2019).

14. Wong, Bonilla, and Coleman (2019); also see Cho, Cullen, and Long (2020); Wessler (2016).

15. In the 2018 EMIF survey of Mexican deportees, more than 55 percent of respondents reported inadequate medical care in U.S. detention (COLEF et al. 2018). The ACLU also shows that detention facilities are grossly unprepared for medical emergencies (Cho, Cullen, and Long 2020).

16. Sweet (2019, 851).

17. Only 14 percent of people in detention have access to counsel, and those with attorneys are 15 times more likely to get relief from removal (Eagly and Shafer 2015).

18. While federal law allows the Department of Homeland Security (DHS) to release people on bond, it leaves bond decisions up to judicial discretion and mandates detention for any migrant released from criminal custody.

19. Cho, Cullen, and Long (2020).

20. This process begins with a master calendar hearing in which detainees are asked to admit or deny the charges against them and decide whether to "fight" deportation (i.e., await a hearing). It can then proceed to various individual hearings in which detainees (and their lawyers, if they have them) provide reasons they should not be deported. Often, the entire process occurs by video conference.

21. TRAC (2021).

22. Slack (2019).

23. See Khosravi (2014); Turnbull (2016). As Victor Ray (2019) notes, time is racialized, and individuals' locations within racialized organizations shape their control over time and ability to plan for the future.

24. COLEF et al. (2018; 2019; 2020).

25. Beckett and Evans (2015).

26. As Macías-Rojas (2016) demonstrates, the U.S. increased deportation partly as a means to free up prison bed space.

27. Bloch and Schuster (2005); Conlon, Hiemstra, and Mountz (2017); Mountz and Loyd (2014).

28. Nancy Hiemstra (2013) shows how transfers move inmates through space in circuitous, unpredictable patterns that seem to defy all reason.

29. Price (2015).

30. Conlon (2011); Conlon and Gill (2013); Gill (2013).

31. Sweet (2019).

32. Ellis (2023).

33. Miller (2021, 226).

34. Miller (2021); Snyder (2016).

35. Cho, Cullen, and Long (2020); Franco, Patler, and Reiter (2022); Patler, Sacha, and Branic (2018).

36. Reiter (2016).

37. See Walker (2022) for a detailed description.

38. Reiter (2016); Walker (2022).

39. Studies of both U.S. detention and U.S. prisons show systematic abuses of inmates. For instance, Martínez, Slack, and Heyman (2013) found that 11 percent of deportees surveyed reported experiencing physical abuse in immigration detention and 23 percent reported verbal abuse. In Wong, Bonilla, and Coleman's (2019) study of immigration detention, more than 50 percent of respondents reported verbal abuse and 7 percent reported physical abuse.

40. A 2020 ACLU report likewise documents officers using physical force, tear gas, pepper spray, and threats (Cho, Cullen, and Long 2020).

41. Price (2015).

42. Skarbek (2014).

43. Reiter and Coutin (2017).

44. Miller (2021, 226).

45. Ellis (2023).

46. Miller (2021).

47. Davis (2003).

48. Gurusami (2019); Price (2015).

3. FORCED OUT OF FAMILIES

1. Andrews and Khayar-Cámara (2022).

2. Filmmakers Christina Clusiau and Shaul Schwarz got access to the inner operations of ICE to produce *Immigration Nation* in 2020 on Netflix, sparking threats and lawsuits from the Trump administration.

3. Capps et al. (2020). Though U.S. laws allow immigrants to apply for green cards for family reunification, family ties to a U.S.-born child are not enough to fight deportation. When families request a stay of removal, many find it difficult to prove "hardship above the expected" or to break the myth that separation can be surmounted (Rabin 2011).

4. Abrego (2014); Chaudry et al. (2010); Dreby (2012a); Enriquez (2020).

5. Cardoso et al. (2016); Dreby (2015); Enriquez (2015); Ybarra and Peña (2017). For a good example of attention to men's lives as caregivers and another expression of this critique, see Haney (2018).

6. Western (2018).

7. Comfort (2008); Haney (2022); Turney (2015).

8. Comfort (2008); Edin and Nelson (2013); Turney (2015).

9. Arditti (2012); Kirk and Wakefield (2018).

10. Haney (2018).

11. Chaudry et al. (2010).

12. After World War II, the U.S. state actively cultivated a link between Mexican manhood and migrant labor as it recruited Mexican laborers known as *braceros* to work on U.S. farms (see Massey et al. 1987).

13. Imprisonment is associated with debt and a diminished ability to find work (even *without* deportation), which can derail men from their "masculine" place in the family (Haney 2018; 2022).

14. Dreby (2012a).

15. See Dreby (2012a; 2015); Golash-Boza (2014); Lewis (2007).

16. De Leon (2015); Massey, Durand, and Pren (2016).

17. Fazel-Zarandi, Feinstein, and Kaplan (2018).

18. Patler and Branic (2017).

19. Mexican Migration Field Research Program and Innovation Law Lab (2021).

20. Imprisonment fosters dependence on institutional structures, interpersonal distrust, alienation, psychological distancing, social withdrawal, and other post-traumatic

stress reactions, inhibiting intimacy and leaving men ambivalent about their roles as fathers (Miller 2018; Travis and Waul 2003).

21. Massey, Durand, and Pren (2016).

22. See also Butler and Mancillas Bazán (2011); Caldwell (2019); Golash-Boza (2014).

23. This process was specific to men; the 15 women we interviewed almost all stayed together with family, with six bringing their spouses, children, or parents to Mexico and the rest remaining very close with their families. Women were also less affected by the strictures of masculine breadwinning.

24. Randles (2020); Sarabia (2018). As McKay et al. (2019) point out, denial about men's roles as fathers and partners helps justify a system that takes them away from their families.

4. NO PLACE CALLED HOME

1. The U.S. has fourteen repatriation points along the U.S.-Mexico border. Roughly a third of deported Mexicans land in Baja California, at the western end of the border and a third in Tamaulipas, at the eastern end, with the rest in between. There are only two interior repatriation sites: Mexico City and Guadalajara.

2. See Duane (2018).

3. Besserer (2002).

4. Boehm (2016); Cardoso et al. (2016); Schuster and Majidi (2013).

5. Khosravi (2017); Majidi (2017).

6. Alarcón and Becerra (2012). Deportees were far more likely than other Mexicans to enter the United States (Massey and Riosmena 2010; Schuster and Majidi 2013).

7. Cardoso et al. (2016); Hagan, Eschbach, and Rodríguez (2008); Martínez, Slack, and Martínez-Schuldt (2018).

8. Alarcón and Becerra (2012).

9. Rosales and Dingeman (2021).

10. Denier and Masferrer (2020); Masferrer and Roberts (2016); Majidi (2018).

11. As Claudia Masferrer (2021) and colleagues document, deportees are increasingly settling outside their original sending sites, disproportionately going to northern Mexico (Denier and Masferrer 2020; Masferrer and Roberts 2016).

12. Slack (2019).

13. Fazel-Zarandi, Feintstein, and Kaplan (2018).

14. Massey, Durand, and Pren (2016).

15. Cardoso et al. (2016).

16. Surveys suggest that even among those who do not attempt to remigrate, up to a third of deportees resettle at the border to be close to U.S.-based family (Calva Sánchez and Alarcón Acosta 2018).

17. The Mexican census says that up to 50 percent of deportees return to their states of origin (INEGI, 2020). Our research suggests that estimates of how many people return are inflated by deportees who visit their home states before settling elsewhere or return to *cities* in their home states, not the villages where they were born.

18. As past studies note, deported men are often dismissed as criminals or failed migrants even when they have not been convicted of crimes (Brotherton and Barrios 2011; Dingeman 2018).

19. Consejo Nacional de Evaluación de la Política de Desarrollo Social (2017); Riosmena (2004); Rivera Sánchez (2013).

20. Schuster and Majidi (2013).

21. Boehm (2016); Golash-Boza (2015).

22. París Pombo, Buenrostro Mercado, and Pérez Duperou (2017) suggest that 50 percent of women and 25 percent of men stay in Tijuana for connections to family or because Tijuana resembles the United States, versus 10 percent who resettle in other, more dangerous border cities.

23. Slack (2019).

24. As anthropologist Shahram Khosravi (2017) points out, deportation does not end migration but is part of a cycle in which people continuously weigh their options of where to move.

25. COLEF et al. (2018).

26. See Zilberg (2011) on the "boomerang effect" of U.S. deportation to El Salvador and the ways deportation leaves men in limbo, fueling both violence and further migration.

27. Menjívar (2006).

28. Gonzales (2015); Menjívar and Abrego (2012).

5. BANISHED

1. During our research, the shelter only accepted men. In 2020, after this study ended, the Casa's population shifted again to serve families seeking asylum.

2. Casa del Migrante (2017).

3. Slack (2019).

4. Alarcón and Becerra (2012); París Pombo, Buenrostro Mercado, and Pérez Duperou (2017).

5. Boehm (2016); Dingeman-Cerda and Bibler Coutin (2012); Ybarra and Peña (2017).

6. Patterson (1982). Others, like Lisa Marie Cacho (2012), have used this framework to understand the erasure of racialized populations in the contemporary United States.

7. Reiter and Coutin (2017).

8. Coutin (2010).

9. For instance, Reiter and Coutin (2017) separate deportation from incarceration analytically, calling the overlap an "eerie synchronicity" rather than a coordinated integration of removal and prison.

10. Elana Zilberg's (2011) book, *Space of Detention*, is a notable exception. Zilberg traces how zero tolerance policies in the United States and El Salvador helped *produce* a "gang crisis." Typically, media accounts fret that relocating "criminal types" between Los Angeles and Central America (including members of the Mara Salvatrucha and 18th Street gangs) creates a security threat to the United States, Latin America, and beyond. Yet, Zilberg reveals that, in fact, zero tolerance strategies enabled the transnational spread of these gangs. The violence attributed to such gangs became acute in the context of an all-out war against them.

11. While such patterns are not exclusive to the border, they are concentrated in that zone.

12. If drugs were legal and the border easy to cross, only corporations would profit from bringing them in.

13. Alienation is defined as isolation or separation from a group or activity to which one should belong. In psychology, alienation refers to a loss of identity in which the self seems unreal. *Oxford English Dictionary* online (2022), s.v. "alienation."

14. Duane (2018). The infrastructure of the border often uses technologies, surveillance tools, and materials from international U.S. wars: in the 1990s, much of the fence was made from Gulf War materials. Border technology was also adopted from Israel (Rosas 2012; Walia 2013).

15. Riosmena (2004); Rivera Sánchez (2013).

16. Moreno Mena and Niño Contreras (2013).

17. Killebrew (2011).

18. Slack (2019).

19. Muehlmann (2013).

20. Slack (2019).

21. Slack (2019); Slack, Martínez, and Whiteford (2018).

22. Slack (2019).

23. As quoted in Rivera (2022).

24. Slack (2019).

25. Slack (2019).

26. The Mexican state is ambivalent toward deportees. Formally, several state programs support repatriated Mexicans, offering medical checkups, financial support for food, phone calls, and health insurance; help finding jobs; certification of U.S. work experience, and until 2019, bus fare home. In reality, most such programs are nearly broke, and fewer than 20 percent of deportees know of them (IIPSOCULTA 2016).

27. Muñiz (2019).

28. Fitzgerald (2019).

29. Paley (2014). As of 2021, the Merida Initiative was under attack for a lack of accountability and was being rebranded as the "Bicentennial Framework for Security, Public Health, and Safe Communities" (Osborn 2021).

30. Beaubien (2011).

31. As geographer Jeremy Slack (2019) puts it, "The idea that it is completely natural for the government to kill drug traffickers has provided unique cover for . . . atrocities" (138).

32. Ángel et al. (2013).

33. Sarabia (2018).

34. Clark-Alfaro (2008); Chacón Castañón and Irwin (2022); Irwin (2020).

35. In the dried-out canal of El Bordo, thousands of men once lived in houses of cardboard, fabric, and trash. According to a survey, 96 percent of the people who lived there were men, 91 percent had lived in the U.S., and most of those had been in the U.S. a decade or more. They cleaned cars on the street for change, took out trash from the market, or scrounged food from charitable organizations (Velasco and Coubès 2013).

36. Rosas (2012) likewise describes watching Mexican authorities in Sonora arrest people who appeared intent on crossing the U.S. border—harass them, beat them, round them up, or pull them off the border fence.

37. Beth Caldwell (2019) also found that even deportees who were apparently "successful" in reintegrating into Mexico reported experiencing anxiety, depression, and post-traumatic stress disorders.

38. In Humanizing Deportation, a database of more than 250 deportees' life stories collected by scholars at UC Davis, mostly in the streets in Tijuana, vast numbers of deportees mention addiction, alcohol, drugs, anxiety, depression, and mental health issues—far more than any other health problems. In the project's index, mentions of negative feelings outweigh positive feelings five to one (Humanizando la Deportación 2022).

39. Ethically, we wanted to be sure respondents were leading the storytelling. If they seemed disoriented or mentally absent, we paused or ended the interviews.

40. See Muehlmann (2013) for details of how the drug trade at the border also fuels addiction.

41. Specifically, 31 mentioned crystal meth, 30 mentioned addiction, and 14 mentioned cocaine or heroin. Another 77 mentioned using alcohol or being drunk.

42. Slack (2019).

43. Similarly, Caldwell (2019) notes that many deportees she interviewed compared deportation to death.

44. To some extent, so did the institutions ostensibly designed to help them. Indeed, labels like those on the Casa del Migrante's wall can mark men as (inherently) addicts and thieves.

45. Other scholars document similar patterns on other parts of the border (Butler and Mancillas Bazán 2011; Slack 2019).

46. Chavez (2008).

47. Paley (2014); Zilberg (2011).

48. However, examples from the Humanizing Deportation database show that deported men can also be harassed in Mexico's interior, for their tattoos, accent, and style of dress (Humanizando la Deportación 2022).

6. RECLAIMING REMOVAL

1. Camhaji (2018), my translation.

2. For more examples of DUL creations, see https://deportadosunidosenlalucha.mx/.

3. López (2018).

4. After this research ended, DUL broke apart—in an evolution common to grassroots organizations. Yet their creativity and elements of the community still inspire spin-offs and other organizations.

5. Agamben (1998).

6. Jackson (2020). For instance, Alexander Weheliye (2014) argues that since Agamben based his theory of bare life on the Holocaust, he failed to recognize the ways colonial contexts provided a precedent for such erasure. To assume that colonial subjects lost all agency would be to deny the vast range of subjectivities of the colonized—not least, their overthrow of colonial powers. This argument also echoes a thriving scholarship on how people who are oppressed and formally "outside the law" exercise agency, often using different strategies than those typically imagined in literature on social movements and resistance (e.g., Bayat 2013; Chatterjee 2004; Scott 1985; Spivak 1988).

7. De Genova (2017). Some scholars worry that studies of deportation are a "porno of suffering," deflecting attention away from migrants' agency and joy (Hasselberg 2017).

8. In so doing, they transcended "traditional" immigrant transnationalism, in which migrants were said to exist both "here and there" and created new space *between* or *beyond* home and away (Levitt 2001; Portes, Guarnizo, and Landolt 1999; Smith 2005).

9. Thus, they affirm research showing that skills, relationships, and "soft capital" can be important to reintegration (Hagan, Hernández León, and Demonsant 2015).

10. Scholars have long shown that urban contexts play a key role in shaping opportunities for resistance and the kind of agency people, including migrants, adopt (Andrews 2018b; Nicholls 2008; Ray 1998).

11. As shown in chapter 4, relocating to Mexico City was most accessible for to younger, more educated, and more bilingual deportees who had not been overly beaten down by long stays in prison.

12. Anzaldúa (1987).

13. Brotherton (2008); Campbell (2015).

14. Rosas (2012).

15. Andrews (2018a).

16. Named for the proposed Development, Relief, and Education for Alien Minors (DREAM) Act.

17. Some of the organizations in ODA's network included spinoffs from DUL, such as F*ck la Migra and Estado 33 Aztlán, which separated from DUL to focus on politics (over the print shop).

18. Anderson (2019).

19. Otros Dreams en Acción (2021).

20. Anderson (2015); Golash-Boza (2015); Rodkey (2016).

21. See Israel Concha, "You're Not Alone No More, Come to Little L.A.," YouTube video, https://www.youtube.com/watch?v=k8cB4eUQdJM (retrieved May 14, 2022).

22. Golash-Boza (2015); Rodkey (2016); Walia (2013).

23. For us, this felt slimy. At the same time, we were unsure how to get "out" of the scheme. We later learned that many other U.S. scholars we knew in Mexico City had also paid New Comienzos to introduce them to interviewees.

24. As women scholars sympathetic to grassroots organizing, my RAs and I were personally drawn to the model offered by DUL or ODA. Still, we saw that César's model held strong appeal for deportees, especially men.

25. Bourgois (1995); Smith (2001).

26. Bourgois (1995). See also Contreras (2013); Brotherton (2008).

27. Smith (2001).

28. Muehlmann (2013).

29. Wolf (2021); Zilberg (2011). Notably, those who spoke English *did* sometimes appeal to call center employers, which profited off their lack of options and the discipline they learned behind bars. At the border, call centers were the main alternative employers for men coming out of prison.

30. In this, I follow scholars like David Brotherton (2008; 2015) and Gilberto Rosas (2012).

31. In Latin America, "cholo" originally signified racially mixed individuals, while in the U.S. it referred to rebellious Mexican American youth. Today, it is a widespread synonym for gang member or thug (Rosas 2012).

32. For many, the only alternative work was in call centers. See Rivera (2022).

33. Other scholars have noted how such hypermasculine "narcomasculinity" can be an answer to the emasculation of deportation (Chacón Castañón and Irwin 2022).

34. Since men are unlikely to report such activities unprompted, this may be a radical undercount.

35. Muehlmann (2013, 165–66).

36. Also see Paley (2014).

37. Rosas (2012, 130).

38. See Bourgois (1995); Contreras (2013).

39. Rosas (2012, 27).

40. Brotherton (2008, 61).

41. This list is exemplary but not exhaustive. For instance, some deportees, particularly U.S. military veterans, organized to demand rights from the United States.

CONCLUSION: THE OPPOSITE OF BANISHMENT IS CARE

1. As Walia (2013) and others have argued, deportation, the penal system, and border enforcement mutually shape one another and intertwine with each other in the lives of the men they target.

2. As Gilberto Rosas (2012) argues in his ethnography of gangs at the U.S.-Mexico border, part of the modus operandi of contemporary, late neoliberal sovereignty is to collapse punishment into death.

3. For a similar critique, see Linda Tuhiwai Smith's (1999) book *Decolonizing Methodologies*.

4. Rios (2015, 259).

5. Fitzgerald and Cook-Martín (2014); Goodman (2020); Kanstroom (2007).

6. Newland and Salant (2018).

7. Staedicke (2018).

8. Roy (2019); Beckett and Herbert (2009).

9. García Hernández (2019)

10. Bloch and Schuster (2005); García Hernández (2017); Kanstroom (2007).

11. Zarrugh (2018; 2020).

12. Ruth Wilson Gilmore (2008) argues that this is the very definition of racism (261). Also see Mbembe (2019).

13. While there is a growing literature on carceral geographies (Gilmore 2008; Moran 2016; Moran, Turner, and Schliehe 2018), much of this research focuses on space inside prisons, eviction, U.S. policing, and the location of prisons within the nation-state.

14. Fitzgerald (2019); Jacobsen and Medina Castellanos (2017).

15. MacKinnon (1982); Brown (1995).

16. Andrews (2018b); Boehm (2016); Donato and Gabaccia (2015); Hondagneu-Sotelo (1994).

17. Connell (1995) defines masculinity as "simultaneously a place in gender relations, the practices through which men and women engage that place in gender, and the effects of these practices in bodily experience, personality and culture" (71) and hegemonic masculinity as "the configuration of gender practice which embodies the currently accepted answer to the problem of the legitimacy of patriarchy, which guarantees (or is taken to guarantee) the dominant position of men and the subordination of women" (77).

18. Matlon (2016); Haney (2022); Ray (2021).

19. Ferguson's (2015) book offers a compelling account of the diminishing centrality of livelihoods based on stable waged labor worldwide, and the widespread loss of faith in the promise of the mythical "proper job."

20. A growing body of literature explores the gap between the head of household identity prized by global capitalism and the decline of conditions to support it (Edin and Nelson 2013; Jeffrey 2010; Ray 2021).

21. Matlon (2016).

22. Indeed, studies reveal that ICE actively targets those unable to work or conform to heteronormative prescriptions (Das Gupta 2014).

23. Radhakrishnan and Solari (2015).

24. These images work. Consider, for instance, how the Trump administration's separation of asylum-seeking mothers from their children sparked national furor. By contrast, ICE's annual removal of hundreds of thousands of immigrant fathers gets little mention in mainstream media. The public is angry about women's separation from children, but we often accept state violence against immigrant men.

25. Scott (1988, 49).

26. Carlson (2015); Radhakrishnan and Solari (2015); Ray (2021).

27. Bourgois (1996); Carlson (2015); Contreras (2013); Decoteau (2013); Hunter (2010); Lwambo (2013).

28. Matlon (2016).

29. See, e.g., Hansen (2019); McLean (2020).

30. Guttman (1996).

31. Zilberg (2011) calls this as an "assemblage."

32. García Hernández (2019).

33. Khosravi (2017); Malkki (1997).

34. Gonzales (2015); Menjívar (2006).

35. Paley (2014), Wolf (2010), and Zilberg (2011) emphasize how the deportation of gang members to El Salvador—and that country's adoption of U.S.-style "zero-tolerance" policing—fueled a deepening gang "crisis" as well as further migration.

36. Slack (2019).

37. These Mexican refugees now constitute more than half of the migrants stuck and seeking refuge at the U.S.-Mexico border (Leutert, Arvey, and Ezzell 2020).

38. Cohen (1972).

39. Rosas (2012).

40. This is not to say that the families are innocent while deportees are at fault. On the contrary, framing women and children as "innocent" can naturalize deportation and reinforce the image that immigrant men are "guilty" and must be removed.

41. See, e.g., Newland and Salant (2018).

42. For instance, this California bill would separate policing from ICE: https://www .levernews.com/ending-the-prison-to-deportation-pipeline/.

43. The City of Santa Ana, California, in a partnership with ImmDef, is piloting such a program. See Jean Guerrero, "Stop Dividing Immigrants into the 'Good' vs. the 'Bad,'" *Los Angeles Times*, March 10, 2022, www.latimes.com/opinion/story/2022-03-10/column-legal -counsel-immigration. Also see Slack (2019).

44. See Slack (2019).

45. See Cardoso et al. (2016).

46. Forced return was one of the most central and controversial items in the Global Compact for Safe, Regular and Orderly Migration, negotiated by 164 national governments

in 2018. See the text of that compact under the United Nations at https://refugeesmigrants
.un.org/sites/default/files/180713_agreed_outcome_global_compact_for_migration.pdf.

47. Mbembe (2019, 184).

48. For instance, even as the U.S. federal government has moved away from private
contracts for prisons, it has expanded private contracts for ICE detention.

49. Davis (2003).

50. Brotherton (2008).

Abrego, Leisy J. 2011. "Legal Consciousness of Undocumented Latinos: Fear and Stigma as Barriers to Claims-Making for First-and 1.5-Generation Immigrants." *Law & Society Review* 45 (2): 337–70.

———. 2014. *Sacrificing Families: Navigating Laws, Labor, and Love across Borders.* Palo Alto, CA: Stanford University Press.

Abrego, Leisy J., Mat Coleman, Daniel E. Martínez, Cecilia Menjívar, and Jeremy Slack. 2017. "Making Immigrants into Criminals: Legal Processes of Criminalization in the Post-IIRIRA Era." *Journal on Migration and Human Security* 5 (3): 694–715.

Abrego, Leisy J., and Genevieve Negrón-Gonzales, eds. 2020. *We Are Not Dreamers: Undocumented Scholars Theorize Undocumented Life in the United States.* Durham, NC: Duke University Press.

Agamben, Giorgio. 1998. *Homo Sacer: Sovereign Power and Bare Life.* Palo Alto, CA: Stanford University Press.

Alarcón, Rafael, and William Becerra. 2012. "Criminales o víctimas? La deportación de migrantes Mexicanos de Estados Unidos a Tijuana, Baja California." *Norteamérica* 7 (1): 125–48.

Anderson, Jill. 2015. "'Tagged as a Criminal': Narratives of Deportation and Return Migration in a Mexico City Call Center." *Latino Studies* 13 (1): 8–27.

———. 2019. "The Deportability Continuum as Activist Research." *Cultural Dynamics* 31 (1): 125–39.

Anderson, Jill, and Nin Solis. 2014. *Los Otros DREAMers.* Independently published.

Andreas, Peter. 2000. *Border Games: The Politics of Policing the U.S.-Mexico Divide.* Ithaca, NY: Cornell University Press.

Andrews, Abigail L. 2018a. "Moralizing Regulation: The Implications of Policing 'Good' versus 'Bad' Immigrants." *Ethnic and Racial Studies* 41 (14): 2485–503.

———. 2018b. *Undocumented Politics: Place, Gender and the Pathways of Mexican Migrants.* Oakland: University of California Press.

Andrews, Abigail L., and Fátima Khayar-Cámara. 2022. "Forced Out of Fatherhood: How Men Strive to Parent Post-Deportation." *Social Problems* 69 (3): 699–716.

Ángel, Perla del, Esmeralda Flores, Lizeth Martínez, José Moreno Mena, Blanca Navarrete, and Esmeralda Siu. 2013. "Violaciones a derechos humanos de personas migrantes Mexicanas detenidas en los Estados Unidos 2011–2012." Programa de Defensa e Incidencia Binacional de la Iniciativa Frontera Norte de México. https://corteidh.or.cr/tablas/29958.pdf.

Anzaldúa, Gloria. 1987. *Borderlands/La Frontera: The New Mestiza.* San Francisco, CA: Aunt Lute Books.

Arditti, Joyce A. 2012. *Parental Incarceration and the Family: Psychological and Social Effects of Imprisonment on Children, Parents, and Caregivers.* New York: New York University Press.

Armenta, Amada. 2017. *Protect, Serve, and Deport: The Rise of Policing as Immigration Enforcement.* Oakland: University of California Press.

Bauer, Shane. 2019. *American Prison: A Reporter's Undercover Journey into the Business of Punishment.* New York: Penguin.

Bayat, Asef. 2013. *Life as Politics: How Ordinary People Change the Middle East.* 2nd edition. Palo Alto, CA: Stanford University Press.

Beaubien, Jason. 2011. "Mexico Replaces Police with Soldiers in Border Area." NPR, *All Things Considered,* June 24, 2011. https://www.npr.org/2011/06/24/137393901/mexico-replaces-police-with-soldiers-in-border-area.

Beckett, Katherine. 2010. "Penal Boundaries: Banishment and the Expansion of Punishment." *Law & Social Inquiry* 35 (1): 1–38.

Beckett, Katherine, and Heather Evans. 2015. "Crimmigration at the Local Level: Criminal Justice Processes in the Shadow of Deportation." *Law & Society Review* 49 (1): 241–77.

Beckett, Katherine, and Steve Herbert. 2009. *Banished: The New Social Control in Urban America.* New York: Oxford University Press.

Besserer, Federico. 2002. *Topografías transnacionales: Hacia una geografía de la vida transnacional.* México, D.F: Plaza y Valdés: Universidad Autónoma Metropolitana, Unidad Iztapalapa.

Bloch, Alice, and Liza Schuster. 2005. "At the Extremes of Exclusion: Deportation, Detention, and Dispersal." *Ethnic and Racial Studies* 28 (3): 491–512.

Boehm, Deborah. 2016. *Returned: Going and Coming in an Age of Deportation.* Oakland: University of California Press.

Bourgois, Philippe. 1995. *In Search of Respect: Selling Crack in El Barrio.* New York: Cambridge University Press.

Brotherton, David C. 2008. "Beyond Social Reproduction: Bringing Resistance Back in Gang Theory." *Theoretical Criminology* 12 (1): 55–77.

———. 2015. *Youth Street Gangs: A Critical Appraisal.* New York: Routledge.

Brotherton, David C., and Luis Barrios. 2011. *Banished to the Homeland: Dominican Deportees and Their Stories of Exile.* New York: Columbia University Press.

Brown, Wendy. 1995. "Finding the Man in the State." In *States of Injury: Power and Freedom in Late Modernity,* 166–96. Princeton, NJ: Princeton University Press.

Burawoy, Michael. 1976. "The Functions and Reproduction of Migrant Labor: Comparative Material from Southern Africa and the United States." *American Journal of Sociology* 81 (5): 1050–87.

Butler, Edgar W., and Celia Mancillas Bazán. 2011. "Beyond National Borders: Family Frontiers and Expulsion from the US." *Journal of Borderland Studies* 26 (1): 53–63.

Cacho, Lisa Marie. 2012. *Social Death: Racialized Rightlessness and the Criminalization of the Unprotected*. New York: New York University Press.

Caldwell, Beth. 2019. *Deported Americans: Life after Deportation to Mexico*. Durham, NC: Duke University Press.

Calva Sánchez, Luis E., and Rafael Alarcón Acosta. 2018. "Migrantes Mexicanos deportados y sus planes para reingresar a Estados Unidos al inicio del gobierno de Donald Trump." *Revista Mexicana de Ciencias Políticas y Sociales* 233: 43–68.

Camhaji, Elías. 2018. "Little LA, el voto de los invisibles." *El País*, April 3, 2018. https://elpais.com/internacional/2018/04/03/mexico/1522731155_208882.html.

Campbell, Howard. 2015. "Escaping Identity: Border Zones as Places of Evasion and Cultural Reinvention." *Journal of the Royal Anthropological Institute* 21 (2): 296–312.

Cantor, Guillermo, Mark Noferi, and Daniel E. Martínez. 2015. *Enforcement Overdrive: A Comprehensive Assessment of ICE's Criminal Alien Program*. Washington, DC: American Immigration Council. https://www.americanimmigrationcouncil.org/research/enforcement-overdrive-comprehensive-assessment-ice%E2%80%99s-criminal-alien-program.

Capps, Randy, Julia Gelatt, Ariel Ruiz Soto, and Jennifer Van Hook. 2020. "Unauthorized Immigrants in the United States: Stable Numbers, Changing Origins." Migration Policy Institute. https://www.migrationpolicy.org/sites/default/files/publications/mpi-unauthorized-immigrants-stablenumbers-changingorigins_final.pdf.

Cardoso, Jodi B., Erin R. Hamilton, Néstor Rodríguez, Karl Eschbach, and Jacqueline Hagan. 2016. "Deporting Fathers: Involuntary Transnational Families and Intent to Remigrate among Salvadoran Deportees." *International Migration Review* 50 (1): 197–230.

Carlson, Jennifer. 2015. *Citizen-Protectors: The Everyday Politics of Guns in an Age of Decline*. New York: Oxford University Press.

Casa del Migrante. 2017. *Vidas en Vilo: Historias y Testimonios de Migrantes Internacionales*. Self-published.

Castañón, Arturo Chacón, and Robert McKee Irwin. 2022. *Listening to Sicarios: Narcoviolence in Ciudad Juárez, 2008-2012*. New York: Palgrave Macmillan.

Cerdeña, Jessica P., Luisa M. Rivera, and Judy M. Spak. 2021. "Intergenerational Trauma in Latinxs: A Scoping Review." *Social Science & Medicine* 270: 113662.

Chatterjee, Partha. 2004. *The Politics of the Governed: Reflections on Popular Politics in Most of the World*. New York: Columbia University Press.

Chaudry, Ajay, Randy Capps, Juan Manuel Pedroza, Rosa Maria Castañeda, Robert Santos, and Molly M. Scott. 2010. *Facing Our Future: Children in the Aftermath of Immigration Enforcement*. Washington, DC: Urban Institute.

Chavez, Leo R. 2008. *The Latino Threat: Constructing Immigrants, Citizens, and the Nation*. Palo Alto, CA: Stanford University Press.

Chávez, Sergio. 2016. *Border Lives: Fronterizos, Transnational Migrants, and Commuters in Tijuana*. New York: Oxford University Press.

Cho, Eunice Hyunhye, Tara Tidwell Cullen, and Clara Long. 2020 "Justice-Free Zones: U.S. Immigration Detention under the Trump Administration." American Civil Liberties Union, Human Rights Watch and National Immigrant Justice Center. https://immigrantjustice .org/sites/default/files/content-type/research-item/documents/2020-04/Justice-Free%20 Zones_Immigrant_Detention_Report_ACLU-HRW-NIJC_April-2020.pdf.

Clark-Alfaro, Víctor. 2008. "Migrantes repatriados: Arresto y detenciones arbitrarias. Derechos humanos: Derechos violados." Centro Binacional de Derechos Humanos.

Cohen, Stanley. 1972. *Folk Devils and Moral Panics: The Creation of the Mods and Rockers*. London: Paladin.

Colegio de la Frontera Norte (COLEF), Unidad de Política Migratoria, Registro e Identidad de Personas, Consejo Nacional de Población, Consejo Nacional para Prevenir la Discriminación, Secretaría del Trabajo y Previsión Social, Secretaría de Relaciones Exteriores, Secretaría de Bienestar (BIENESTAR). 2012. *Encuesta sobre Migración en la Frontera Norte de México* (EMIF). www.colef.mx/emif.

———. 2018. Encuesta sobre Migración en la Frontera Norte de México (EMIF). www.colef .mx/emif.

———. 2019. Encuesta sobre Migración en la Frontera Norte de México (EMIF). www.colef .mx/emif.

———. 2020. Encuesta sobre Migración en la Frontera Norte de México (EMIF). www.colef .mx/emif.

Coleman, Matthew. 2012. "The 'Local' Migration State: The Site-Specific Devolution of Immigration Enforcement in the US South." *Law & Policy* 34 (2): 159–90.

Coleman, Matthew, and Austin Kocher. 2011. "Detention, Deportation, Devolution and Immigrant Incapacitation in the U.S., Post 9/11." *Geographical Journal* 177 (3): 228–37.

Comfort, Megan. 2008. *Doing Time Together: Love and Family in the Shadow of the Prison*. Chicago: University of Chicago Press.

Conlon, Deirdre. 2011. "Waiting: Feminist Perspectives on the Spacings/Timings of Migrant (Im) mobility." *Gender, Place & Culture* 18 (3): 353–60.

Conlon, Deirdre, and Nick Gill. 2013. "Gagging Orders: Asylum Seekers and Paradoxes of Freedom and Protest in Liberal Society." *Citizenship Studies* 17 (2): 241–59.

Conlon, Deirdre, Nancy Hiemstra, and Alison Mountz. 2017. "Spatial Control: Geographical Approaches to the Study of Immigration Detention." Global Detention Project Working Paper 24. www.globaldetentionproject.org/wp-content/uploads/2017/09/Conlon -Hiemstra-Mountz-GDP-Paper-2017.pdf.

Connell, R. W. 1995. *Masculinities*. Berkeley: University of California Press.

Consejo Nacional de Evaluación de la Política de Desarrollo Social. 2017. *Medición de la pobreza 2008–2016*. https://coneval.org.mx/Medicion/PublishingImages/Pobreza _2008-2016/medicion-pobreza-entidades-federativas-2016.JPG.

Contreras, Randol. 2013. *The Stickup Kids: Race, Drugs, Violence, and the American Dream*. Oakland: University of California Press.

Coutin, Susan Bibler. 2010. "Exiled by Law: Deportation and the Inviability of Life." In de Genova and Peutz, *Deportation Regime*, 351–70.

———. 2015. "Deportation Studies: Origins, Themes and Directions." *Journal of Ethnic and Migration Studies* 41 (4): 671–81.

Das Gupta, Monisha. 2014. "'Don't Deport Our Daddies': Gendering State Deportation Practices and Immigrant Organizing." *Gender & Society* 28 (1): 83–109.

Davis, Angela. 2003. *Are Prisons Obsolete?* New York: Seven Stories Press.

Decoteau, Claire Laurier. 2013. "The Crisis of Liberation: Masculinity, Neoliberalism, and HIV/AIDS in Post-Apartheid South Africa." *Men and Masculinities* 16 (2): 139–59.

De Genova, Nicholas P. 2002. "Migrant 'Illegality' and Deportability in Everyday Life." *Annual Review of Anthropology* 31 (1): 419–47.

———. 2007. "The Production of Culprits: From Deportability to Detainability in the Aftermath of 'Homeland Security.'" *Citizenship Studies* 11 (5): 421–48.

———. 2016. "Detention, Deportation, and Waiting: Toward a Theory of Migrant Detainability." Global Detention Project Working Paper no. 18. https://www.globaldetention project.org/wp-content/uploads/2016/12/De-Genova-GDP-Paper-2016.pdf.

———. 2017. "Afterword: Deportation: The Last Word?" in Khosravi, *After Deportation*, 253–66.

De Genova, Nicholas P., and Nathalie Peutz. 2010. *The Deportation Regime: Sovereignty, Space, and the Freedom of Movement.* Durham, NC: Duke University Press.

De León, Jason. 2015. *The Land of Open Graves: Living and Dying on the Migrant Trail.* Oakland: University of California Press.

De Lira, Rubi. 2020. "Immigrant Students in the MMFRP." Mexican Migration Field Research Program. https://mmfrp.org/research/immigrant-students/.

Denier, Nicole, and Claudia Masferrer. 2020. "Returning to a New Mexican Labor Market? Regional Variation in the Economic Incorporation of Return Migrants from the U.S. to Mexico." *Population Research and Policy Review* 39 (4): 617–41.

Department of Homeland Security. 2020. *Yearbook of Immigration Statistics, 2020.* https://www.dhs.gov/immigration-statistics/yearbook/2020.

Desmond, Matthew. 2016. *Evicted: Poverty and Profit in the American City.* New York: Crown Publishers.

Deterding, Nicole M., and Mary C. Waters. 2018. "Flexible Coding of In-Depth Interviews: A Twenty-First Century Approach." *Sociological Methods & Research* 50 (2): 708–39.

Dickerson, Caitlin. 2022. "The Secret History of the U.S. Government's Family-Separation Policy." *Atlantic*, August 7, 2022. www.theatlantic.com/magazine/archive/2022/09/trump -administration-family-separation-policy-immigration/670604/.

Dingeman, Katie. 2018. "Segmented Re/integration: Divergent Post-Deportation Trajectories in El Salvador." *Social Problems* 65 (1): 116–34.

Dingeman-Cerda, Kathleen, and Susan Bibler Coutin. 2012. "The Ruptures of Return: Deportation's Confounding Effects." In *Punishing Immigrants: Policy, Politics and Injustice,* edited by Charles E. Kubrin, Marjorie S. Katz, and Ramiro Martínez, 113–37. New York: New York University Press.

Doering-White, John. 2018. "Evidencing Violence and Care along the Central American Migrant Trail through Mexico." *Social Service Review* 92 (3): 432–69.

Donato, Katharine M., and Donna Gabaccia. 2015. *Gender and International Migration: From the Slavery Era to the Global Age.* New York: Russell Sage.

Dreby, Joanna. 2012a. "The Burden of Deportation on Children in Mexican Immigrant Families." *Journal of Marriage and Family* 74 (4): 829–45.

———. 2012b. *Everyday Illegal: When Policies Undermine Immigrant Families.* Berkeley: University of California Press.

———. 2015. "U.S. Immigration Policy and Family Separation: The Consequences for Children's Well-Being." *Social Science & Medicine* 132: 245–51.

Drotbohm, Heike, and Ines Hasselberg. 2015. "Deportation, Anxiety, Justice: New Ethnographic Perspectives." *Journal of Ethnic and Migration Studies* 41 (4): 551–62.

Duane, Daniel. 2018. "City of Exiles." *California Sunday Magazine.* https://story.california sunday.com/tijuana-city-of-exiles/.

Duck, Waverly. 2015. *No Way Out: Precarious Living in the Shadow of Poverty and Drug Dealing.* Chicago: University of Chicago Press.

Dunn, Timothy J. 2010. *Blockading the Border and Human Rights: The El Paso Operation That Remade Immigration Enforcement.* Austin: University of Texas Press.

Duquette-Rury, Lauren. 2020. *Exit and Voice: The Paradox of Cross-Border Politics in Mexico.* Oakland: University of California Press.

Eagly, Ingrid V., and Steven Shafer. 2015. "A National Study of Access to Counsel in Immigration Court." *University of Pennsylvania Law Review* 164 (1): 1–91.

Edin, Katherine, and Timothy J. Nelson. 2013. *Doing the Best I Can: Fatherhood in the Inner City.* Oakland: University of California Press.

Ellis, Rachel. 2023. *In This Place Called Prison: Women's Religious Life in the Shadow of Punishment.* Oakland: University of California Press.

Enriquez, Laura E. 2015. "Multigenerational Punishment: Shared Experiences of Undocumented Immigration Status within Mixed-Status Families." *Journal of Marriage and Family* 77 (4): 939–53.

———. 2020. *Of Love and Papers: How Immigration Policy Affects Romance and Family.* Oakland: University of California Press.

Ewing, Walter, Daniel E. Martínez, and Rubén G. Rumbaut. 2015. "The Criminalization of Immigration in the United States." Washington, DC: American Immigration Council. www.americanimmigrationcouncil.org/sites/default/files/research/the_criminalization _of_immigration_in_the_united_states.pdf.

Fader, Jamie J. 2013. *Falling Back: Incarceration and Transitions to Adulthood among Urban Youth.* New York: Rutgers University Press.

Farrell-Bryan, Dylan. 2022. "Relief or Removal: State Logics of Deservingness and Masculinity for Immigrant Men in Removal Proceedings." *Law & Society Review* 56 (2): 167–87.

Farrell-Bryan, Dylan, and Ian Peacock. 2022. "Who Gets Deported? Immigrant Removal Rates by National Origin and Period, 1998 to 2021." *Socius* 8 (online first). https://journals .sagepub.com/doi/full/10.1177/23780231221091224.

Fazel-Zarandi, Mohammad M., Jonathan S. Feinstein, and Edward H. Kaplan. 2018. "The Number of Undocumented Immigrants in the United States: Estimates Based on Demographic Modeling with Data from 1990 to 2016." *PloS one* 13 (9): e0201193.

Federal Bureau of Prisons. 2015. "Offenses: Statistics Based on Prior Month's Data." *Inmate Statistics,* October 24. www.bop.gov/about/statistics/statistics_inmate_offenses.jsp.

Ferguson, James. 2015. *Give a Man a Fish: Reflections on the New Politics of Distribution.* Durham, NC: Duke University Press.

Fitzgerald, David. 2019. *Refuge beyond Reach: How Rich Democracies Repel Asylum Seekers.* New York: Oxford University Press.

Fitzgerald, David, and David Cook-Martín. 2014. *Culling the Masses: The Democratic Origins of Racist Immigration Policy in the Americas.* Cambridge, MA: Harvard University Press.

Flores, Andrea. 2021. *The Succeeders: How Immigrant Youth Are Transforming What It Means to Belong in America.* Oakland: University of California Press.

Foster, Holly, and John Hagan. 2009. "The Mass Incarceration of Parents in America: Issues of Race/Ethnicity, Collateral Damage to Children, and Prisoner Reentry." *ANNALS of the American Academy of Political and Social Science* 623 (1): 179–94.

Foucault, Michel. 1977. *Discipline and Punish: The Birth of the Prison.* New York: Pantheon Books.

Franco, Konrad, Caitlin Patler, and Keramet Reiter. 2022. "Punishing Status and the Punishment Status Quo: Solitary Confinement in U.S. Immigration Prisons, 2013–2017." *Punishment & Society* 24 (2): 170–95.

García, Angela S. 2019. *Legal Passing: Navigating Undocumented Life and Local Immigration Law.* Oakland: University of California Press.

García Hernández, César Cuauhtémoc. 2017. *Crimmigration Law.* Chicago: American Bar Association.

———. 2019. *Migrating to Prison: America's Obsession with Locking Up Immigrants.* New York: The New Press.

Gill, Nick. 2013. "Mobility Versus Liberty? The Punitive Uses of Movement Within and Outside Carceral Environments." In Gill and Moran, *Carceral Spaces*, 19–36.

Gill, Nick, and Dominique Moran, eds. 2013. *Carceral Spaces: Mobility and Agency in Imprisonment and Migrant Detention.* New York: Routledge.

Gilmore, Ruth Wilson. 2008. *Golden Gulag: Prisons, Surplus, Crisis, and Opposition in Globalizing California.* Berkeley: University of California Press.

Gleeson, Shannon. 2016. *Precarious Claims: The Promise and Failure of Workplace Protections in the United States.* Oakland: University of California Press.

Goffman, Alice. 2014. *On the Run: Fugitive Life in an American City.* Chicago: University of Chicago Press.

Golash-Boza, Tanya. 2012. *Due Process Denied: Detentions and Deportations in the United States.* New York: Routledge.

———. 2014. "Forced Transnationalism: Transnational Coping Strategies and Gendered Stigma among Jamaican Deportees." *Global Networks* 14 (1): 63–79.

———. 2015. *Deported: Immigrant Policing, Disposable Labor, and Global Capitalism.* New York: New York University Press.

———. 2016. "The Parallels between Mass Incarceration and Mass Deportation: An Intersectional Analysis of State Repression." *Journal of World-Systems Research* 22 (2): 484–509.

Golash-Boza, Tanya, and Pierrette Hondagneu-Sotelo. 2013. "Latino Immigrant Men and the Deportation Crisis: A Gendered Racial Removal Program." *Latino Studies* 11 (3): 271–92.

Gonzales, Roberto G. 2015. *Lives in Limbo: Undocumented and Coming of Age in America.* Oakland: University of California Press.

Gonzalez-Barrera, Ana. 2021. "Before COVID-19, More Mexicans Came to the U.S. than Left for Mexico for the First Time in Years." Pew Research Center, July 9, 2021. https://www.pewresearch.org/fact-tank/2021/07/09/before-covid-19-more-mexicans -came-to-the-u-s-than-left-for-mexico-for-the-first-time-in-years/.

Goodman, Adam. 2020. *The Deportation Machine: America's Long History of Expelling Immigrants.* Princeton, NJ: Princeton University Press.

Guenther, Lisa. 2013. *Solitary Confinement: Social Death and Its Afterlives.* Minneapolis: University of Minnesota Press.

Gurusami, Susila. 2019. "Motherwork under the State: The Maternal Labor of Formerly Incarcerated Black Women." *Social Problems* 66 (1): 128–43.

Guttman, Matthew. 1996. *The Meanings of Macho: Being a Man in Mexico City*. Berkeley: University of California Press.

Hagan, Jacqueline, Karl Eschbach, and Néstor Rodríguez. 2008. "U.S. Deportation Policy, Family Separation, and Circular Migration." *International Migration Review* 42 (2): 64–88.

Hagan, Jacqueline, Rubén Hernández-León, and Jean-Luc Demonsant. 2015. *Skills of the Unskilled: Work and Mobility among Mexican Migrants*. Oakland: University of California Press.

Hall, Stuart. 1980. "Race, Articulation, and Societies Structured in Dominance." In *Sociological Theories: Race and Colonialism*. Paris: UNESCO: 305–45.

Haney, Lynne. 2018. "Incarcerated Fatherhood: The Entanglements of Child Support Debt and Mass Imprisonment." *American Journal of Sociology* 124 (1): 1–48.

———. 2022. *Prisons of Debt: The Afterlives of Incarcerated Fathers*. Oakland: University of California Press.

Hansen, Tobin Michael. 2019. "Belonging: Place, Care, and Masculinities among 'Criminal Alien' Men Deported to Mexico." PhD diss., University of Oregon.

Harding, David, Jeffrey Morenoff, and Jessica Wyse. 2019. *On the Outside: Prisoner Reentry and Reintegration*. Chicago: University of Chicago Press.

Hart, Gillian P. 2002. *Disabling Globalization: Places of Power in Post-Apartheid South Africa*. Berkeley: University of California Press.

Haslam, Nick. 2006. "Dehumanization: An Integrative Review." *Personality and Social Psychology Review* 10 (3): 252–64.

Hasselberg, Ines. 2017. "Fieldnotes from Cape Verde: On Deported Youth, Research Methods, and Social Change." In Khosravi, *After Deportation*, 15–36.

Hernández, Kelly Lytle. 2017. *City of Inmates: Conquest, Rebellion, and the Rise of Human Caging in Los Angeles, 1771–1965*. Oakland: University of California Press.

Hiemstra, Nancy. 2013. "'You Don't Even Know Where You Are': Chaotic Geographies of US Migrant Detention and Deportation." In Gill and Moran, *Carceral Spaces*, 57–75.

———. 2019. *Detain and Deport: The Chaotic U.S. Immigration Enforcement Regime*. Athens: University of Georgia Press.

Hochschild, Arlie Russell. 1983. *The Managed Heart: Commercialization of Human Feeling*. Berkeley: University of California Press.

Hondagneu-Sotelo, Pierrette. 1994. *Gendered Transitions: Mexican Experiences of Immigration*. Berkeley: University of California Press.

Howell, K. Babe. 2016. "The Costs of Broken Windows Policing: Twenty Years and Counting." *Cardozo Law Review* 37: 1059–73.

Humanizando la Deportación. 2022. *Index*. University of California, Davis. http://humanizandoladeportacion.ucdavis.edu/en/index-j-m/.

Hunter, Mark. 2010. *Love in the Time of AIDS: Inequality, Gender, and Rights in South Africa*. Bloomington: Indiana University Press.

Instituto de Investigación y Práctica Social y Cultural (IIPSOCULTA). 2016. *Retorno con derechos: Acercamiento y atención a la población migrante de retorno en la Ciudad de México*. https://es.scribd.com/document/336493497/Retorno-con-Derechos-IIPSO CULTA.

Instituto Nacional de Estadística y Geografía (INEGI). 2020. *XIII Censo de población y vivienda.* www.inegi.org.mx/programas/ccpv/2020/.

Irwin, Robert. 2020. "Digital Resources: The Humanizing Deportation Archive." In *Oxford Research Encyclopedia of Latin American History.* Online. New York: Oxford University Press.

Jack, Anthony. 2019. *The Privileged Poor: How Elite Colleges Are Failing Disadvantaged Students.* Cambridge, MA: Harvard University Press.

Jackson, Zakiyyah Iman. 2020. *Becoming Human: Matter and Meaning in an Antiblack World.* New York: New York University Press.

Jacobsen, Karen, and Mariela Medina Castellanos. 2017. "Forced Displacement in Urban Settings: A Policy Brief, with examples from Tijuana." Policy brief, Tufts University Institute for Human Security. https://sites.tufts.edu/ihs/312-2/.

Jeffrey, Craig. 2010. *Timepass: Youth, Class, and the Politics of Waiting in India.* Palo Alto, CA: Stanford University Press.

Kandel, William, and Douglas S. Massey. 2002. "The Culture of Mexican Migration: A Theoretical and Empirical Analysis." *Social Forces* 80 (3): 981–1004.

Kanstroom, Daniel. 2007. *Deportation Nation: Outsiders in American History.* Cambridge, MA: Harvard University Press.

———. 2012. *Aftermath: Deportation Law and the New American Diaspora.* New York: Oxford University Press.

Killebrew, Robert. 2011. "Criminal Insurgency in the Americas and Beyond." *PRISM Security Studies Journal* 2 (3): 33–52.

Khosravi, Shahram. 2014. "Waiting." In *Migration: The COMPAS Anthology,* edited by Bridget Anderson and Michael Keith, 66–67. Centre on Migration, Policy and Society, Oxford University. https://www.compas.ox.ac.uk/2014/migration-the-compas-anthology/.

Khosravi, Shahram, ed. 2017. *After Deportation: Ethnographic Perspectives.* New York: Palgrave Macmillan.

Kirk, David, and Sara Wakefield. 2018. "Collateral Consequences of Punishment: A Critical Review and Path Forward." *Annual Review of Criminology* 1: 171–94.

Leutert, Stephanie, Savitri Arvey, and Ellie Ezzell. 2020. "Metering Update: February 2020." UT Austin Strauss Center for International Security and Law, and UCSD Center for U.S.-Mexican Studies. https://usmex.ucsd.edu/_files/metering-update_feb-2020.pdf.

Levenson, Zachary. 2022. "Make 'Articulation' Gramscian Again." In *Ethnographies of Power: Working Radical Concepts with Gillian Hart,* edited by Sharad Chari, Mark Hunter, and Melanie Samson, 187–216. Johannesburg: Wits University Press.

Levitt, Peggy. 2001. *The Transnational Villagers.* Berkeley: University of California Press.

Levitt, Peggy, and Deepak Lamba-Nieves. 2011. "Social Remittances Revisited." *Journal of Ethnic and Migration Studies* 37 (1): 1–22.

Lewis, Linden. 2007. "Man Talk, Masculinity, and a Changing Social Environment." *Caribbean Review of Gender Studies* 1 (1): 1–20.

Light, Michael T., Jingying He, and Jason P. Robey. 2020. "Comparing Crime Rates between Undocumented Immigrants, Legal Immigrants, and Native-Born U.S. Citizens in Texas." *PNAS* 117 (51): 32340–47.

Light, Michael T., Michael Massoglia, and Ryan D. King. 2014. "Citizenship and Punishment: The Salience of National Membership in U.S. Criminal Courts." *American Sociological Review* 79 (5): 825–47.

López, Ana Laura. 2018. "Deportation Is Like a Life without Living." Humanizando la Deportación, Narrative no. 48. http://humanizandoladeportacion.ucdavis.edu/en/2018/08/05/48-deportation-is-like-life-without-living/.

López, William D. 2019. *Separated: Family and Community in the Aftermath of an Immigration Raid*. Baltimore, MD: Johns Hopkins University Press.

Lopez-Aguado, Patrick. 2016. "The Collateral Consequences of Prisonization: Racial Sorting, Carceral Identity, and Community Criminalization." *Sociology Compass* 10 (1): 12–23.

Loyd, Jenna, Andrew Burridge, and Matthew Mitchelson. 2009. "Thinking (and Moving) beyond Walls and Cages: Bridging Immigrant Justice and Anti-Prison Organizing in the United States." *Social Justice* 36 (2): 85–103.

Loyd, Jenna, Matthew Mitchelson, and Andrew Burridge. 2012. *Beyond Walls and Cages: Prisons, Borders, and Global Crisis*. Athens: University of Georgia Press.

Luft, Aliza. 2019. "Dehumanization and the Normalization of Violence: It's Not What You Think." Social Science Research Council, Items: Insights from the Social Sciences. https://items.ssrc.org/insights/dehumanization-and-the-normalization-of-violence-its-not-what-you-think/.

Lwambo, Desiree. 2013. "'Before the War, I Was a Man': Men and Masculinities in the Eastern Democratic Republic of Congo." *Gender and Development* 21 (1): 47–66.

Macías-Rojas, Patrisia. 2016. *From Deportation to Prison: The Politics of Immigration Enforcement in Post-Civil Rights America*. New York: New York University Press.

MacKinnon, Catharine A. 1982. "Feminism, Marxism, Method and the State: An Agenda for Theory." *Signs: Journal of Women, Culture and Society* 7 (3): 515–44.

Mahmood, Saba. 2005. *Politics of Piety: The Islamic Revival and the Feminist Subject*. Princeton, NJ: Princeton University Press.

Majidi, Nassim. 2017. "Deportees Lost at 'Home': Post-Deportation Outcomes in Afghanistan." In Khosravi, *After Deportation*, 127–48.

Malkki, Lisa. 1997. "The Rooting of Peoples and the Territorialization of National Identity among Scholars of Refugees." In *Culture, Power and Place: Explorations in Critical Anthropology*, edited by Akhil Gupta and James Ferguson, 53–74. Durham, NC: Duke University Press.

Martínez, Cid. 2016. *The Neighborhood Has Its Own Rules: Latinos and African Americans in South Los Angeles*. New York: New York University Press.

Martínez, Daniel, Jeremy Slack, and Josiah Heyman. 2013. *Bordering on Criminal: The Routine Abuse of Migrants in the Removal System (Part 1: Migrant Mistreatment while in US Custody)*. Special report, American Immigration Council, Washington, DC.

Martínez, Daniel, Jeremy Slack, and Ricardo D. Martínez-Schuldt. 2018. "Repeat Migration in the Age of the 'Unauthorized Permanent Resident': A Quantitative Assessment of Migration Intentions Postdeportation." *International Migration Review* 52 (4): 1186–217.

Masferrer, Claudia. 2021. *Atlas de migración de retorno de Estados Unidos a México*. México, DF: El Colegio de México.

Masferrer, Claudia, and Bryan R. Roberts. 2016. "The Changing Patterns of Return Migration from the USA to Mexico and Their Policy Implications." In *Migration in an Era of Restriction and Recession*, edited by David L. Leal and Nestor P. Rodríguez, 235–58. New York: Springer.

Massey, Douglas S., Rafael Alarcón, Jorge Durand, and Humberto González. 1987. *Return to Aztlan: The Social Process of International Migration from Western Mexico*. Berkeley: University of California Press.

Massey, Douglas S., Jorge Durand, and Karen A. Pren. 2016. "Why Border Enforcement Backfired." *American Journal of Sociology* 121 (5): 1557–600.

Massey, Douglas S., and Fernando Riosmena. 2010. "Undocumented Migration from Latin America in an Era of Rising U.S. Enforcement." *Annals of the American Academy of Political and Social Science* 630 (1): 294–321.

Matlon, Jordanna. 2016. "Racial Capitalism and the Crisis of Black Masculinity." *American Sociological Review* 81 (5): 1014–38.

———. 2022. *A Man among Other Men: The Crisis of Black Masculinity in Racial Capitalism*. Ithaca, NY: Cornell University Press.

Mbembe, Achille. 2019. *Necropolitics*. Durham, NC: Duke University Press.

McKay, Tasseli, Christine Lindquist, Megan Comfort, and Anupa Bir. 2019. *Holding On: Family and Fatherhood during Incarceration and Reentry*. Oakland: University of California Press.

McLean, Kristen E. 2020. "Caregiving in Crisis: Fatherhood Refashioned by Sierra Leone's Ebola Epidemic." *Medical Anthropology Quarterly* 34 (2): 227–42.

Menjívar, Cecilia. 2006. "Liminal Legality: Salvadoran and Guatemalan Immigrants' Lives in the United States." *American Journal of Sociology* 111 (4): 999–1037.

Menjívar, Cecilia, and Leisy Abrego. 2012. "Legal Violence: Immigration Law and the Lives of Central American Migrants." *American Journal of Sociology* 117 (5): 1380–421.

Mexican Migration Field Research Program and Innovation Law Lab. 2021. *Cut Off: How ICE Detention Facilities Block Communication*. https://mmfrp.files.wordpress.com /2021/10/cutoff_howiceblockscommunication.pdf.

Miller, Reuben. 2021. *Halfway Home: Race, Punishment, and the Afterlife of Mass Incarceration*. New York: Little, Brown.

Miller, Robin. 2018. *Impacts of Incarceration on the African American Family*. New York: Routledge.

Moran, Dominique. 2016. *Carceral Geography: Spaces and Practices of Incarceration*. New York: Routledge.

Moran, Dominique, Jennifer Turner, and Anna K. Schliehe. 2018. "Conceptualizing the Carceral in Carceral Geography." *Progress in Human Geography* 42 (5): 666–86.

Moreno Mena, José Ascención, and Lya Niño Contreras. 2013. "Una mirada hacia las organizaciones civiles de apoyo al migrante en Baja California y Sonora." *Región y Sociedad* 57: 61–96.

Morris, Juliana E., and Daniel Palazuelos. 2017. "Displacing Lives and Closing Pathways to Hope: The Health Impacts of Deportation and Return Migration in El Progreso, Honduras." In Roberts, Menjívar, and Rodríguez, *Deportation and Return in a Border-Restricted World*, 149–66.

Mountz, Alison, and Jenna Loyd. 2014. "Transnational Productions of Remoteness: Building Onshore and Offshore Carceral Regimes across Borders." *Geographica and Helvetica* 69: 389–98.

Muehlmann, Shaylih. 2013. *When I Wear My Alligator Boots: Narco-Culture in the U.S.-Mexico Borderlands*. Oakland: University of California Press.

Muñiz, Ana. 2019. "Bordering Circuitry: Cross-Jurisdictional Immigration Surveillance." *UCLA Law Review* 66: 1636–80. www.uclalawreview.org/wp-content/uploads/securepdfs /2020/06/Muniz-66-6.pdf.

National Immigration Forum. 2014. "Detention Costs Still Don't Add Up to Good Policy." *Immigration Forum* (blog), September 24, 2014. https://immigrationforum.org/blog /detention-costs-still-dont-add-up-to-good-policy/.

Nevins, Joseph. 2002. *Operation Gatekeeper: The Rise of the "Illegal Alien" and the Making of the U.S.-Mexico Boundary*. New York: Routledge.

Nevins, Joseph, and Mizue Aizeki. 2008. *Dying to Live: A Story of U.S. Immigration in an Age of Global Apartheid*. San Francisco, CA: City Lights.

Newland, Kathleen, and Brian Salant. 2018. "Balancing Acts: Policy Frameworks for Migrant Return and Reintegration." Migration Policy Institute Brief. www.migrationpolicy.org /research/policy-frameworks-migrant-return-and-reintegration.

Ngai, Mae M. 2004. *Impossible Subjects: Illegal Aliens and the Making of Modern America*. Princeton, NJ: Princeton University Press.

Nicholls, Walter J. 2008. "The Urban Question Revisited: The Importance of Cities for Social Movements." *International Journal of Urban and Regional Research* 32 (4): 841–59.

Núñez, Guillermina, and Josiah Heyman. 2007. "Entrapment Processes and Immigrant Communities in a Time of Heightened Border Vigilance." *Human Organization* 66 (4): 354–65.

Osborn, Catherine. 2021. "The U.S.-Mexico Drug War Gets a Rebrand: Can the 'Bicentennial Framework' Be a Turning Point?" *Foreign Policy*, October 15, 2021. https://foreignpolicy .com/2021/10/15/mexico-united-states-drug-war-security-cooperation-merida -initiative-bicentennial-framework-biden-amlo/.

Otros Dreams en Acción. 2021. "Otros Dreams en Acción: About." http://www.odamexico .org/?fbclid=IwAR3cH3nwhiyVGGMHsLRoBI5BFGejMRjqMmv1Vl9XpD2fJjhNjRUF Pii9Owo.

Paley, Dawn. 2014. *Drug War Capitalism*. Chico, CA: AK Press.

Patler, Caitlin, and Nicholas Branic. 2017. "Patterns of Family Visitation during Immigration Detention." *Russell Sage Foundation Journal of the Social Sciences* 3 (4): 18–36.

Patler, Caitlin, Shannon Gleeson, and Matthias Schonlau. 2022. "Contesting Inequality: The Impact of Immigrant Legal Status and Education on Legal Knowledge and Claims-Making in Low-Wage Labor Markets." *Social Problems* 69 (2): 356–79.

Patler, Caitlin, and Gabriela Gonzalez. 2021. "Compounded Vulnerability: The Consequences of Immigration Detention for Institutional Attachment and System Avoidance in Mixed-Immigration-Status Families." *Social Problems* 68 (4): 886–902.

Patler, Caitlin, Jeffrey O. Sacha, and Nicholas Branic. 2018. "The Black Box within a Black Box: Solitary Confinement Practices in a Subset of U.S. Immigrant Detention Facilities." *Journal of Population Research* 35 (4): 435–65.

Patterson, Orlando. 1982. *Slavery and Social Death*. Cambridge, MA: Harvard University Press.

Phillips, Scott, Jacqueline Maria Hagan, and Néstor Rodríguez. 2006. "Brutal Borders? Examining the Treatment of Deportees During Arrest and Detention." *Social Forces* 85 (1): 93–109.

Phillips, Susan A. 2012. *Operation Fly Trap: L.A. Gangs, Drugs, and the Law*. Chicago: University of Chicago Press.

París Pombo, M. Dolores, Diana Buenrostro Mercado, and Gabriel Pérez Duperou. 2017. "Trapped at the Border: The Difficult Integration of Veterans, Families, and Christians in Tijuana." In Roberts, Menjívar, and Rodríguez, *Deportation and Return in a Border-Restricted World*, 131–48.

Portes, Alejandro, Luis E. Guarnizo, and Patricia Landolt. 1999. "The Study of Transnationalism: Pitfalls and Promise of an Emergent Research Field." *Ethnic and Racial Studies* 22 (2): 217–37.

Price, Joshua M. 2015. *Prison and Social Death*. New York: Rutgers University Press.

Rabin, Nina. 2011. "Disappearing Parents: Immigration Enforcement and the Child Welfare System." *Connecticut Law Review* 44 (1): 99–160.

Radhakrishnan, Smitha, and Cinzia Solari. 2015. "Empowered Women, Failed Patriarchs: Neoliberalism and Global Gender Anxieties." *Sociology Compass* 9 (9): 784–802.

Randles, Jennifer. 2020. *Essential Dads: The Inequalities and Politics of Fathering*. Oakland: University of California Press.

Ray, Raka. 1998. *Fields of Protest: Women's Movements in India*. Minneapolis: University of Minnesota Press.

———. 2021. "The Politics of Masculinity in the Absence of Work." *Oxford Development Studies* 49 (4): 311–23.

Ray, Victor. 2019. "A Theory of Racialized Organizations." *American Sociological Review* 84 (1): 26–53.

Reiter, Keramet. 2016. *23/7: Pelican Bay Prison and the Rise of Long-Term Solitary Confinement*. New Haven, CT: Yale University Press.

Reiter, Keramet, and Susan Bibler Coutin. 2017. "Crossing Borders and Criminalizing Identity: The Disintegrated Subjects of Administrative Sanctions." *Law & Society Review* 51 (3): 567–601.

Rendón, María G. 2019. *Stagnant Dreamers: How the Inner City Shapes the Integration of the Second Generation*. New York: Russell Sage.

Rios, Victor M. 2011. *Punished: Policing the Lives of Black and Latino Boys*. New York: New York University Press.

———. 2015. "Decolonizing the White Space in Urban Ethnography." *City & Community* 14 (3): 258–61.

———. 2017. *Human Targets: Schools, Police, and the Criminalization of Latino Youth*. Chicago: University of Chicago Press.

Riosmena, Fernando. 2004. "Return versus Settlement among Undocumented Mexican Migrants, 1980 to 1996." In *Crossing the Border: Research from the Mexican Migration Project*, edited by Jorge Durand and Douglas Massey, 265–80. New York: Russell Sage.

Rivera, Salvador. 2022. "Deported California Gang Members Are Prized Recruits for Drug Cartels." *Border Report*, April 25, 2022. https://www.abc27.com/border-report-tour /deported-california-gang-members-are-prized-recruits-for-drug-cartels/.

Rivera Sánchez, Luis. 2013. "Migración de retorno y experiencias de reinserción en la zona metropolitana de la Ciudad de México." *Revista Interdisciplinaria de Mobilidad Humana* 21 (41): 55–76.

Roberts, Bryan, Cecilia Menjívar, and Néstor P. Rodríguez, eds. 2017. *Deportation and Return in a Border-Restricted World*. Cham, Switzerland: Springer.

Roberts, Dorothy. 2022. *Torn Apart: How the Child Welfare System Destroys Black Families—And How Abolition Can Build a Safer World*. New York: Basic Books.

Rodkey, Evin. 2016. "Disposable Labor, Repurposed: Outsourcing Deportees in the Call Center Industry." *Anthropology of Work Review* 37 (1): 34–43.

Rosales, William Estuardo, and Katie Dingeman. 2021. "Deportation as Deterrence?: Social and Legal Predictors of Remigration after Deportation." In *Global Perspectives on People, Process, and Practice in Criminal Justice*, edited by Leonard Liam, 1–29. Hershey, PA: IGI Global.

Rosas, Gilberto. 2012. *Barrio Libre: Criminalizing States and Delinquent Refusals of the New Frontier*. Durham, NC: Duke University Press.

Roy, Ananya. 2019. "Racial Banishment." In *Keywords in Radical Geography: Antipode at 50*, edited by Antipode Editorial Collective, 227–30. Hoboken, NJ: Wiley and Sons.

Ryo, Emily. 2018. "Detention as Deterrence." *Stanford Law Review* 71: 237.

Salzinger, Leslie. 2003. *Genders in Production: Making Workers in Mexico's Global Factories*. Berkeley: University of California Press.

Sarabia, Heidy. 2018. "'Felons, Not Families': Criminalized Illegality, Stigma, and Membership of Deported 'Criminal Aliens.'" *Migration Letters* 15 (2): 284–300.

Schriro, Dora Bess. 2009. "Immigration Detention Overview and Recommendations." Vol. 6. Washington, DC: U.S. Department of Homeland Security, Immigration and Customs Enforcement. www.ice.gov/doclib/about/offices/odpp/pdf/ice-detention-rpt.pdf.

Schuster, Liza, and Nassim Majidi. 2015. "Deportation Stigma and Remigration." *Journal of Ethnic and Migration Studies* 41 (4): 635–52.

Scott, James C. 1985. *Weapons of the Weak: Everyday Forms of Resistance*. New Haven, CT: Yale University Press.

Scott, Joan. 1988. "Gender: A Useful Category of Historical Analysis." In *Gender and the Politics of History*, 28–52. New York: Columbia University Press.

Secretaría de Gobernación (SEGOB). 2019. "Repatriación de Mexicanos, 2019." www .politicamigratoria.gob.mx/es_mx/SEGOB/V_Repatriacion_de_mexicanos_de_EUA.

Shams, Tahseen. 2020. *Here, There, and Elsewhere: The Making of Immigrant Identities in a Globalized World*. Palo Alto, CA: Stanford University Press.

Simanski, John F. 2014. "Immigration Enforcement Actions: 2013." *Annual Report 2014*. Washington: U.S. Department of Homeland Security Office of Immigration Statistics. www.dhs.gov/sites/default/files/publications/ois_enforcement_ar_2013.pdf.

Simon, Jonathan. 1998. "Refugees in a Carceral Age: The Rebirth of Immigration Prisons in the United States." *Public Culture* 10 (3): 577–607.

Skarbek, David. 2014. *The Social Order of the Underworld: How Prison Gangs Govern the American Penal System*. New York: Oxford University Press.

Slack, Jeremy. 2019. *Deported to Death: How Drug Violence Is Changing Migration on the US-Mexico Border*. Oakland: University of California Press.

Slack, Jeremy, Daniel Martínez, and Scott Whiteford. 2018. *The Shadow of the Wall: Violence and Migration on the U.S.-Mexico Border*. Tucson: University of Arizona Press.

Smith, Linda Tuhiwai. 1999. *Decolonizing Methodologies: Research and Indigenous Peoples*. London: Zed Books.

Smith, Michael. 2001. *Transnational Urbanism: Locating Globalization*. Oxford: Blackwell.

Smith, Robert C. 2005. *Mexican New York: Transnational Lives of New Immigrants*. Berkeley: University of California Press.

Snyder, Susanna. 2016. "'La Mano Zurda with a Heart in Its Palm:' Mystical Activism as a Response to the Trauma of Immigration Detention." In *Post-Traumatic Public Theology*, edited by Stephanie Arel and Shelly Rambo, 217–40. New York: Palgrave Macmillan.

Spivak, Gayatri. 1988. "Can the Subaltern Speak?" In *Marxism and the Interpretation of Culture*, edited by Cary Nelson and Lawrence Grossbert, 271–313. Champaign: University of Illinois Press.

Staedicke, Sara. 2018. "'Silent' Refugee Crises Get Limited International Attention." Migration Policy Institute, December 10, 2018. www.migrationpolicy.org/article/top-10-2018-issue -10-silent-refugee-crises.

Stanton, Gregory. 1998. "The 8 Stages of Genocide." Yale Program in Genocide Studies Working Paper. www.genocide-watch.com/images/8StagesBriefingpaper.pdf.

Stumpf, Juliet P. 2006. "The Crimmigration Crisis: Immigrants, Crime, and Sovereign Power." *American University Law Review* 56 (2): 367–419.

Sweet, Paige. 2019. "The Sociology of Gaslighting." *American Sociological Review* 84 (5): 851–75.

Transactional Records Access Clearinghouse (TRAC). 2013. *Legal Noncitizens Receive Longest ICE Detention*. Syracuse University. https://trac.syr.edu/immigration/reports/321/.

———. 2014. *ICE Deportations: Gender, Age, and Country of Citizenship*. Syracuse University. https://trac.syr.edu/immigration/reports/350/.

———. 2017. *About the Data—All ICE Removals*. Syracuse University. https://trac.syr.edu /phptools/immigration/remove/about_data.html.

———. 2019a. *Growth in ICE Detention Fueled by Immigrants with No Criminal Conviction*. Syracuse University. https://trac.syr.edu/immigration/reports/583/.

———. 2019b. *ICE Detains Fewer Immigrants with Serious Criminal Convictions under Trump Administration*. Syracuse University. https://trac.syr.edu/immigration/reports/585/.

———. 2021. *A Mounting Asylum Backlog and Growing Wait Times*. Syracuse University. https://trac.syr.edu/immigration/reports/672/.

———. 2022. *Average Time Pending Cases Have Been Waiting in Immigration Courts as of Sep 2022*. Syracuse University. https://trac.syr.edu/phptools/immigration/court_backlog /apprep_backlog_avgdays.php.

Travis, Jeremy, and Michelle Waul. 2003. *Prisoners Once Removed: The Impact of Incarceration and Reentry on Children, Families, and Communities*. Washington, DC: Urban Institute.

Turnbull, Sarah. 2016. "'Stuck in the Middle': Waiting and Uncertainty in Immigration Detention." *Time & Society* 25 (1): 61–79.

Turner, Victor. 1967. *The Forest of Symbols: Aspects of Ndembu Ritual*. Ithaca, NY: Cornell University Press.

Turney, Kristen. 2015. "Liminal Men: Incarceration and Relationship Dissolution." *Social Problems* 62 (4): 499–528.

United Nations High Commissioner for Refugees (UNHCR). 2017. *Global Trends: Forced Displacement in 2016*. www.unhcr.org/5943e8a34.pdf.

United States Immigration and Customs Enforcement. 2019. *Fiscal Year 2019 Enforcement and Removal Operations Report*. www.ice.gov/sites/default/files/documents/Document /2019/eroReportFY2019.pdf.

van der Kolk, Bessel A. 2014. *The Body Keeps the Score: Brain, Mind, and Body in the Healing of Trauma*. New York: Penguin.

van Dernoot Lipsky, Laura, and Connie Burk. 2009. *Trauma Stewardship: An Everyday Guide to Caring for Self while Caring for Others*. Oakland, CA: Berrett-Koehler.

Varsanyi, Monica, ed. 2010. *Taking Local Control: Immigration Policy Activism in U.S. Cities and States*. Palo Alto, CA: Stanford University Press.

Velasco, Laura, and Marie-Laure Coubès. 2013. *Reporte sobre dimensión, caracterización, y áreas de atención a Mexicanos deportados desde Estados Unidos*. El Colegio de la Frontera Norte. https://imumi.org/uf/recursos/reporte-dimension-atecion-mexicanos -deportados.pdf.

Wacquant, Loic J. D. 2002. "Scrutinizing the Street: Poverty, Morality, and the Pitfalls of Urban Ethnography." *American Journal of Sociology* 107 (6): 1468–532.

———. 2009. *Punishing the Poor: The Neoliberal Government of Social Insecurity*. Durham, NC: Duke University Press.

Wakefield, Sara, and Christopher Wildeman. 2013. *Children of the Prison Boom: Mass Incarceration and the Future of American Inequality*. New York: Oxford University Press.

Walia, Harsha. 2013. *Undoing Border Imperialism*. Chico, CA: AK Press.

Walker, Michael L. 2016. "Race Making in a Penal Institution." *American Journal of Sociology* 121 (4): 1051–78.

———. 2022. *Indefinite: Doing Time in Jail*. New York: Oxford University Press.

Weber, Max. (1919) 1946. "Politics as a Vocation." In *From Max Weber: Essays in Sociology*, 77–128. New York: Oxford University Press.

Weheliye, Alexander G. 2014. *Habeas Viscus: Racializing Assemblages, Biopolitics, and Black Feminist Theories of the Human*. Durham, NC: Duke University Press.

Weiss, Robert. 1994. *Learning from Strangers: The Art and Method of Qualitative Interview Studies*. New York: Free Press.

Weller, Francis. 2015. *The Wild Edge of Sorrow: Rituals of Renewal and the Sacred Work of Grief*. Berkeley, CA: North Atlantic Books.

Wessler, S. F. 2016. "This Man Will Almost Certainly Die." *Nation*. www.thenation.com /article/privatized-immigrant-prison-deaths/.

Western, Bruce. 2018. *Homeward: Life in the Year after Prison*. New York: Russell Sage.

Winfield, Taylor Paige. 2022. "Vulnerable Research: Competencies for Trauma and Justice-Informed Ethnography." *Journal of Contemporary Ethnography* 51 (2): 135–70.

Wolf, Sonja. 2010. "Maras Transnacionales: Origins and Transformations of Central American Street Gangs." *Latin American Research Review* 45 (1): 256–65.

———. 2021. "The Making of Central America's Street Gangs." In *International Handbook of Critical Gang Studies*, edited by David C. Brotherton and Rafael Gude, 426–38. New York: Routledge.

Wolpe, Harold. 1972. "Capitalism and Cheap Labour-Power in South Africa: From Segregation to Apartheid." *Economy and Society* 1 (4): 425–55.

Wong, Tom, Sebastian Bonilla, and Anna Coleman. 2019. *Seeking Asylum: Part 1*. Report, U.S. Immigration Policy Center. https://usipc.ucsd.edu/publications/usipc-seeking-asylum -part-1-final.pdf.

Woodfox, Albert. 2019. *Solitary: Unbroken by Four Decades in Solitary Confinement. My Story of Transformation and Hope*. New York: Grove Press.

Ybarra, Megan, and Isaura L. Peña. 2017. "'We Don't Need Money, We Need to Be Together': Forced Transnationality in Deportation's Afterlives." *Geopolitics* 22 (1): 34–50.

Zarrugh, Amina. 2018. "'You Exile Them in Their Own Countries': The Everyday Politics of Reclaiming the Disappeared in Libya." *Middle East Critique* 27 (3): 247–59.

———. 2020. "The Development of US Regimes of Disappearance: The War on Terror, Mass Incarceration, and Immigrant Deportation." *Critical Sociology* 46 (2): 257–71.

Zilberg, Elana. 2011. *Space of Detention: The Making of a Transnational Gang Crisis between Los Angeles and San Salvador*. Durham, NC: Duke University Press.

Founded in 1893,
UNIVERSITY OF CALIFORNIA PRESS
publishes bold, progressive books and journals
on topics in the arts, humanities, social sciences,
and natural sciences—with a focus on social
justice issues—that inspire thought and action
among readers worldwide.

The UC PRESS FOUNDATION
raises funds to uphold the press's vital role
as an independent, nonprofit publisher, and
receives philanthropic support from a wide
range of individuals and institutions—and from
committed readers like you. To learn more, visit
ucpress.edu/supportus.